WEAVING A
TAPESTRY

Other books by Laya Brostoff:

Professional Handweaving on the Fly Shuttle Loom. Van Nostrand Reinhold, 1978.

Double Weave: Theory and Practice. Interweave Press, Inc., 1979.

WEAVING A
TAPESTRY

by Laya Brostoff

PREFACE and ACKNOWLEDGEMENTS

As I look at the redwoods outside my window, I realize that most of the writing for this manuscript is now behind me and what at first appeared as an insurmountable task is almost completed.

The chapters are arranged in the order in which most tapestry weavers' needs are likely to be met. While any arrangement is arbitrary because so many processes must be dealt with simultaneously, I have tried to disentangle the threads to make each chapter complete in itself. Each chapter is designed to present new material as well as to remind you of some you may have intuited and needed a nudge to try. The act of weaving a tapestry takes place on many levels of energy at once and is, at the same time, a simple, logical process, and nobody knows all the answers.

I have been compelled to leave out some sections to prevent this book from growing larger than it already is, and to include some material that may make you exclaim "Oh no, not again." There was no getting around the fact that some things must be included to lay a groundwork for what follows.

Among those things that must be included are my profound thanks to all who helped. I am blessed and boastful to count among my friends each of the following.

My husband, Gene Mailes, stoked the fire in the pot-belly stove, kept hot tea at my elbow and an all-pervasive atmosphere of love and encouragement. My good friend Dorothy DeLacy read and reread, cut, arranged and rearranged. My apprentices Jacqueline Baldwin and Cynthia Handel wove many of the samples. Jude Lamare read and asked questions in the chapters on color and design as did Gerald Citrin. Joan Hodgson ferreted out obscure library references. Ann Scott is accountable for the better line drawings, and I take responsibility for the rest, black and white illustrations as well as color photographs. David Hilberman cheerfully gave excellent advice on technical, photographic problems. Last, but certainly not least, Linda Ligon, my editor, has the insight and courage to publish in these times.

Laya Brostoff

First Printing
©1982, Laya Brostoff.
5M:882:JLP/VC
3M:886:JLP
Library of Congress Card #82-082243
ISBN 0-934026-10-6

INTERWEAVE PRESS, INC.
306 N. Washington Avenue
Loveland, Colorado 80537

CONTENTS

I
THE TAPESTRY WEAVER AS ARTIST

Motivation; Comparing Painting and Weaving; Seeing vs. Looking; Subjects of Tapestries; Tapestry History; Ways of Weaving Tapestries; Obligation to Study; Imitation and Influence; Dedication to Weaving; Exhibiting.

Motivation

What motiviates us to weave a tapestry? Certainly not merely monetary return, in today's economy. It must, therefore, be a combination of the need to see how the weaving will look when completed and the pleasure we find in the constant solving of problems as the work grows under our hands. We are rarely totally satisfied with the finished product and often see later what we should have seen earlier. Self-set standards constantly raised are essential to our growth as weavers and must not be lowered for expediency. When the finished work does not live up to what we had envisaged, it is at least evidence of the courage to undertake it in the first place.

Individuals who choose weaving as their form of expression have a need to be physically involved in their work. They need to touch and shape with their own hands. Sculptors have the same need, but their choice is a medium in which they can cut, chip away, or add to with solid materials, whereas weavers choose a soft, pliant medium.

Like any other art form, the designing of a tapestry must take into consideration all of the components involved. It helps if we are able to rid ourselves of previously learned prejudices and biases. We are then free to take whatever course suggests itself and turn it in whichever direction our imagination takes us.

Some of the purposes of this book are:
• To discourage outworn conventions which not only do not contribute to contemporary tapestry weaving, but delay the progress of the medium.
• To organize the necessary basic techniques into logical and useful sequences, thereby clarifying their relationships and interdependence.
• To divest the difficulties of both basic and advanced techniques of any misleading mystery.
• To organize design and color theories that relate directly to fiber, and indicate their relationships to other media.

It *is not* necessary for today's weaver to be attached to or remain faithful to one school of weaving technique or art style. *It is* necessary, however, to become familiar with different forms of expression in order to make knowledgeable choices. The twentieth century offers the weaver an unlimited range of choices and a multiplicity of styles. If we mix techniques and styles, we should do so out of choice, not happenstance. Our greatest limitations on our imagination and creative ability are self-imposed. Understanding and experience with fiber interlacement and construction are not enough. Weavers should not be left to flounder without equal familiarity in the organization and use of the materials which constitute their medium, primarily fiber, ideas, color and design.

Terms and definitions are a problem. I find them frequently contradictory and vague, particularly in their adaption to the fiber medium. The terms and definitions we use rarely define exactly what we mean, and should always be thought of as open-ended. After all, if our ideas could be expressed better in words or paint than in fiber, they should be developed in those media rather than be hand woven. If part of the design is decorative, it should be essential to the idea from its inception. The difference may also be seen in another sense between those architects who plan *with* the artist-weaver for tapestries to cover large cold walls in contrast to those who add the tapestry to the wall as an afterthought.

Today's textile artist initiates the idea and participates in the work to its final realization, whether performing all the work or delegating some of it to trained assistants.

A cartoon drawn by an artist who knows little or nothing about weaving is frequently unweavable. If non-weaving artists had to manipulate fibers from the cartoon, their focus would change to structural and textural approaches (those elements inherent in fiber); they would quickly abandon trying to impose painterly disciplines on the weaver.

What sharply distinguishes design for painting from design for handweaving tapestries are the limits that the handweaver knows exist in the fiber medium. Form and function as usually defined (the first following the second) are not of essential concern to the tapestry weaver. Tapestries do not have a function in the sense of a handle fitting the hand, or a construction stable enough to hold up a particular weight. The contemporary function of a tapestry, if it can be called that, is to please the weaver, or the observer, or both. Certainly the tapestry has to be compatible with the place in which it will be hung and the weaver must be concerned with durability regardless of whether it will be hung indoors or out. He or she must be concerned with direct or indirect light in terms of design, and with direct sunlight that may cause fading. The design itself, however, has no function other than to please, startle, prod for contemplation, or elicit some response.

One does not stand or sit in front of a loom and just start weaving. Long before that point is reached choices have already been made. We have been saying and thinking consciously or unconsciously, "I like this," "I do not like that," "I wish I could do that," or "I can do that better, I certainly would not do that that way", etc., etc.

Comparing painting and weaving

If we equate warp with canvas, then the weaver may be likened to the artist. A color, red, is woven or painted on a neutral warp or canvas in a given shape. A second color and shape is then chosen which relates, opposes or strengthens the red; to this may then be added a third color and/or shape and so on.

The painter has the choice of painting at the spot of inspiration. For the weaver this is rarely possible. In order to capture the image, we must make a sketch or photograph and translate it when we have returned to our studio. We rarely duplicate the entire sketch or picture and sometimes we use a design or picture produced by someone else.

A brushstroke made slowly is entirely different from one made quickly. A pick laid in slowly simply takes more time, but assuming that the technique used is adequate, looks no different than a pick entered quickly. The wetting technique that prepares paper or canvas before another color is applied does not exist in weaving. We do not have the advantage or challenge of other visual artists who confront a clean paper, canvas, sheet of metal, or block of wood. This energy or force is not present for the weaver. It is only when we start winding the warp on the loom that a limit to the space in which we will work begins to appear. It is only when we start interlacing another element, weft, that shape and color are defined. All of it is totally of our own making and is in some ways similar to the problems of the sculptor, who must build an armature (warp) to which clay (weft) is added. In both cases where previously there was nothing, a form emerges. Energy is expended and some form of expression results.

On paper and canvas there can be "soft edges" that glimmer and accidental drips and meandering color, translucid and fluid forms. There can be "scumbles" with oil and chalk for different effects and textures. In fiber, very little is accidental. Translucency and fluidity are possible, but are not inherent, in fiber. It is possible to soften colors or outlines by filmy additions, but there certainly cannot be any rubbing to achieve these effects. The closest we can come is to use a yarn such as mohair whose long protruding fibers can be brushed up to obscure outlines. We cannot scratch onto an already woven surface or build up layers of color as the painter can on a painted canvas or the sculptor on a shaped piece of clay; but we can play with texture as few painters can.

Paint is an obliging medium in that its fluid form yields to the demands of the artist. Stone, wood, and metal retain their original character, no matter how they are chipped away. Fiber in the form of yarn (and to some extent clay before it hardens), is soft and pliable to begin with. Fiber never changes its basic form no matter how it is manipulated.

If a woven area is brought to our attention by its color or shape, there must be a well thought-out, appropriate reason for its size, color, and placement. The absence of this planning will distract and detract from the whole. Each facet of the composition must add to what the weaver is trying to convey, not just fill in an empty space. No matter how well any individually woven design or color elements are presented, the general impression we receive is from their effect when perceived as a whole.

Since there is no "canvas" upon which the weaver works, the total concept takes final shape as the weaver works on it. The canvas plane on which the painter starts has a whiteness and flatness. The weaver must construct this surface as the work progresses.

In one sense all weaving is action painting. In another sense we cover comparatively small areas as compared to a painter who with one arm and body movement can cover many feet of space. It is possible to work in more than one style or approach at the same time. Leaving one piece of work where progress is not being made and pursuing another theme in a different style may open entirely new and ingenious routes. All ways of working are related in some aspects and the pursuit of one aids and abets the other.

As handweavers work with fiber, they begin to "see" with their hands as well as their eyes. As the fibers are handled and manipulated, a kinesthetic sense is developed. When fiber is manipulated by human hands, it is silent. Sounds such as those created by a hammer or chisel on metal or wood are not present. For those who weave on a vertical loom there is not even the clack of the shuttle or the thump of the beater. There is, however, a very satisfying physical body, arm, and hand rhythm as the butterfly, bobbin or shuttle is passed from one hand to the other through the open shed. Weaving is at once a strong rhythmic experience and a soft tactile one.

The term tapestry is used loosely to refer to various kinds of textiles which are hung rather than worn. A tapestry is constructed in the course of the weaving, and the tapestry itself does not have an existence or life until it is fabricated. Fiber works are slowly being accepted into the "fine arts" along with painting and sculpture and the number of major shows, museums, and galleries totally or partially devoted to fiber is steadily increasing.

Seeing vs looking

One is not necessarily born with the ability to visualize something and reproduce it in some form. We are, however, all born with some ability to learn how to express an idea, an ability that is extended in our early schooling through verbalization. Little attention is paid to developing our ability to see rather than to look. It takes explicit effort and deliberate visual training to acquire visual form experiences. The more fully our visual experience is developed, the greater is our understanding and pleasure.

The preponderance of prepared kits and patterns for fiber designs in which all that is required is to follow easy directions is evidence of the increasing desire by many people to express themselves through something they can create with their own hands. Those who choose weaving do so because of the pleasure of manipulating fiber into an organized form. There is a great chasm between learning how to weave and "creating" with fiber. The average person feels intimidated and settles for predigested instructions.

Neither originality nor technique alone will suffice to create a fine piece of work. Both must be combined for a determination of quality plus an objective appraisal, depending upon our level of understanding and emotional development. It may be a clarification or intensification or a new interpretation or some experience to which we respond with appreciation, sympathetic perception, passion, curiosity, thoughtfulness, uneasiness or solicitude.

Even the most original and isolated idea does not somehow come with sudden insight. It grows out of an objective network of thoughts which bind all artists, weavers, and people together.

Genuine creativity is sometimes difficult to achieve because the need or desire to please others interferes with our own honest expression. Pleasing others may result in a sale and is justified if one is trying to sell one's work, but it is more often than not a frustrating experience. One rarely pleases oneself and others at the same time. There is also the need to dominate others by "being the best in the show", which rarely results in genuine creativity.

When developed, our ability to "see" intensifies our intellectual grasp of reality and its relation to illusion. Increasing our ability to interpret the world around us by what we "see" sharpens our awareness of that world, heightens our sensibility and disciplines our vision. The creative act does not create something out of nothing. It uncovers, selects, reshuffles, combines or synthesizes already existing facets, ideas, faculties and skills.

It is an extension of our conscious horizons. That which we consider beautiful evokes a deeply satisfying awareness or feeling. That which we consider ugly evokes revulsion. If we wish to make a statement about war, then we choose those shapes and colors which we have learned to associate with war. For peace and serenity we utilize shapes and colors which we have learned to relate to these themes.

In our imagination or in short, quick sketches, we can look at a shape and see it from different points of view. We can regard a tree from the top downward, where branches join each other in ever thickening diameters into a common trunk. We can start at the roots, which are ordinarily not seen, and include the bottom of the trunk but leave the objectification at that point. We can choose a small section of the trunk, a single leaf or branch, as a symbol of the whole tree. We can imagine looking down on the tree from above as though into the depths of an ocean of green leaves. Or we can sit in a tree house and be surrounded by branches and leaves.

Part of seeing is finding new relationships and proportions for things that we have previously looked at only in their usual position and sizes. If you take a cloud out of context, isolate it, and juxtapose it with something seemingly unrelated, like a couch, it assumes a markedly different reference and could be thought to be a pillow. Some parts of the original shape may become less important and may be de-emphasized or totally eliminated. Other parts may be exaggerated or connected to unrelated parts. These connections may then become the center of interest and the original emphasis diminishes or disappears. We can extend, contract, distort, deviate, add, eliminate, isolate, emphasize, alter, or whatever. We can play with designs. If they don't work or satisfy us we can throw them out and start again with entirely different ideas. We quickly realize that most of what is a useful sketch for other art forms may not necessarily work for tapestry. The materials we use to realize our sketches or cartoons are not liquid or hard, but soft and malleable. It is not necessary or important that the finished product relate to or resemble its source of inspiration.

Just as science tells us nothing new is created in the world of matter, so in design. Each design springs from age-old classical motifs which in their turn were abstracted or copied from something else. Once we stop worrying about being original, we are free to experiment and build on what has already been done. Each initiator brings his or her own identity to the project, and it is this singularity which makes it unique and original. A woven tapestry is as much the result of the intellectual and intuitive processes of the weaver as it is of the sensitivity of observation and application of past experience.

Subjects of tapestries

If it is true that our art expressions symbolize personal, group and cultural values, then the importance of the subject and its relationship to the culture of which we are a part must be recognized. In this light, much contemporary work in fiber as a visual art form is questionable. Handweaving has the power to represent not only physical appearances, but has the responsibility also to concern itself with world values. These need not be represented realistically. They may be implicit or symbolized, but some aspect should be present.

Abstract symbols are just as evocative as representational ones to express personal or group values. Firm rectangular shapes may be just as compelling as "hills and valleys", depending on how they are designed and woven. In choosing one method of presentation over another, one must be willing to take a stand, make judgements, and accept consequences, else there is no individual artistic growth.

Any art expression gives us a kind of testing ground. All that can be lost is time in execution, some money for materials, or acceptance by the public. On the other hand the opportunity for learning and growth is immeasurable. Those who wish assurance that their first tapestry will sell immediately perhaps should look elsewhere for a way of life.

The first ideas for a subject may be triggered by any number of things: an idea from written words, spoken words, something seen or suggested or a combination of ideas which have been unconsciously generating for some time and have suddenly come together in one exciting mental image. In the course of the creative process, both before and during the weaving, the idea is refined, reorganized and often changed to emphasize that which now appears more important and to eliminate everything that isn't totally necessary to the expression of that idea.

Many subjects that appear to be unattractive, impolitic, inappropriate, unsuitable, emotional, ugly, banal, or stereotyped have been the inspiration for some of the greatest art known. Perhaps the grayness and lack of imagination of the subjects of many weavings result from their inception from the last technique to which the weaver was exposed, rather than an idea which the weaver felt impelled to express.

Something like this passes through our minds: "I have just seen an interesting demonstration of twining and I would like to try it," or "It is about time I wove something new for the next show," or "What were those colors to which the theme was limited?" or "Can I combine all of these and have it ready on time?" Instead of "I have been considering the different aspects of this idea for some time." or "What shapes and colors will best express it?" or "If I use these yarns will that technique be the best or should I consider the technique first and adapt the fibers to suit?" or "The clean, fresh shiny feeling of those tree leaves after the rain was really caught by that watercolor artist. How can I elicit a similar shimmering effect with fiber?"

One subject that tapestry weavers have tended to reject is concern with people and their daily activities. For some reason we find it much easier to deal with the shape of a tree that is reaching up or being buffeted about by a storm than to portray people who are striving or are embattled. The claim that we are not able to sketch such subjects is hardly sufficient reason for their absence. Most tapestry weavers learn to sketch sufficiently well to serve their own needs, especially when they symbolize rather than sketch realistically.

Protest as a subject for tapestries has been almost totally ignored, although many of the world's greatest artists found it a fitting means of expression against degrading conditions of work, life, and war. There is a long tradition of personal expression by artists such as Rouault, Picasso, Kollwitz, and Goya, whose work has inspired millions.

Playfulness as a subject has also, to a great extent, been neglected — playfulness as felt by a child but not woven in a childish technique. Nor should humor, personal or social, be ruled out as subject material for tapestries.

Years ago it was enough to reproduce a particular type of rolling hillside. Now with movies, television and photography, people have been exposed to more sophisticated representations. Although the act of choosing a particular hillside may be considered a personal artistic decision, it becomes more eloquent when we weave into it our awareness and reaction to the same hillside.

Weaving another landscape is like painting another landscape. There is no point to it unless it has something to say that adds to landscapes, or else the weaver needs to experience color understanding or design fundamentals or weaving techniques. This latter may make it a useful exercise, but not perforce one that should be shown or sold.

A landscape that has been copied exactly from a photograph remains a copy, although the medium has been changed. Something expressed well in one medium can rarely be translated adequately into another. If it has been truly absorbed and reworked in the weaving medium, then it emerges as a newly created concept and becomes our own.

In weaving, as in the rest of our lives, most of us learned very early not to take chances. We were taught first to take on the values of our parents and then of our teachers. It must be our own idea rather than one which we have been taught is a desirable one. The subject for a tapestry need not be related to any one particular thing; a shape or color may trigger an image, an emotion, or a sensation, which can be translated into a design for a tapestry.

In describing a piece of work terms such as "beautiful" or "ugly", "good" or "bad", no longer serve a useful purpose. Such expressions as "does it work?" meaning, is it an acceptable solution, or "does what the weaver intended to convey come through?" are more helpful and at the same time avoid judgmental comments which help neither the weaver nor the viewer.

A subject is not a prerequisite for an art composition. In literature we are more aware of a subject than we are in architecture where it is least recognizable. In music as in art, reference to a subject can be totally absent or present to various degrees.

Tapestry weaving reached a high degree of perfection during the Middle Ages. Many examples remain as valued museum possessions. Although traditional tapestry weaving methods are still practiced, American handweavers, as well as others throughout the world, have tried to free themselves from the major traditions using new approaches and techniques. They are more concerned with the integrity and feeling of the tapestry than with following some technique which does not necessarily suit the subject. The concern over whether we are really creating art disappears with the pleasure of the effort.

The simplest, and at the same time most difficult, solution is to stop worrying about whether it is art and to become involved with that aspect that is most appealing to use. If permitted, the uniqueness of each individual will find its own form of expression.

Each of us has a potential that is unique, individual, and remarkable. When we have realized the essentials of our medium, the thought and energy we expend will create something which will result in a moment of exhiliration and satisfaction that is uniquely our own.

At the outset we must accept the limits of the medium, including the type of materials used to construct our work. They are fiber-like whether we choose wool, cotton, linen, silk, wire, or rope. Unlike paint or clay, their manipulation does not change their intrinsic original form. If we change our ideas and want to take out what has been woven in, the material will still be fiber-like in form. If we use the fiber before it is spun, as in felting, we are engaged in another type of construction.

Those tapestry weaving traditions which continue to serve our purposes need to be retained, of course. Those that place an unnecessary hobble on our work should be discarded. Our major concerns today are more with the integrity and feeling of the work than with adhering to some technique that may be traditional but is not suitable.

Some weavers work in series, i.e., they pursue all of the possibilities of one idea until it is exhausted. Others work at several tapestries at the same time, each with a different theme and technique. Sometimes we may return to a subject or way of solving a weaving problem with a fresh idea or solution years after the theme was originally pursued. When first conceived or woven, most ideas are not exploited to their fullest potential. There is no correct or incorrect order in which tapestries may be woven.

Tapestry history

Ateliers or workshops where individuals or groups of weavers produce contemporary woven wall hangings are proliferating in a tapestry renaissance. Beginning about 1930, after a long quiescent period, many artists and weavers found their inspiration in two major sources, medieval tapestries and French paintings. In its early forms, the traditional techniques of Aubusson and Gobelin were strictly followed, but as modern art set forth in different directions, so, too, weavers searched for greater freedom of expression in the use of fiber.

Apprentices and journeymen are part of the tradition of weavers and the guild system which they developed. The purpose for this development was twofold. The apprentice took over some of the time-consuming manual labor, leaving the artist free to think about and start new projects. The apprentice was given the opportunity to work and be exposed to a producing environment rather than learn a series of disparate techniques in an academic setting with the hope of using them later on.

The historical aspect of the term "tapestry" combines both the image of the affluent who could cloth their walls with the labor of the 12-hour-day weaver, and the art of the various cultures. At one time the tapestry maker was differentiated from the weaver. The former worked with separate small bobbins over small areas whose outlines rose one position vertically and laterally, with the adjoining areas relating to this movement vertically but moving in opposition laterally. The weaver was thought of as inserting the weft on larger bobbins in shuttles, from selvage to selvage, using the whole width of the cloth.

Originally the two styles of interlacement were kept separate with forms of the word *Tapissies* from the French leading to the term *Tapis*, which meant "that which was hung on a wall." The word "weaving" referred to all other cloths. Today almost anything that is hung on a wall is called a tapestry, including many that are in no way related to yarn interlacement.

The chief purpose of tapestries has always been, and continues to be, to provide an embellishment on the walls in keeping with the atmosphere in which they are hung. Tapestry sizes varied, depending on whether they were to be hung on stone walls in large halls, or smaller rooms. Sometimes several tapestries and panels were combined when they were not large enough to cover. When the tapestries were too large they were hung as a continuation from one wall to the other by covering the corner between the two walls. Smaller tapestries were also used to cover doors and were cut if they did not fit exactly. A secondary purpose was to protect the residents from the cold. Today we cover the walls with tapestries not so much for actual warmth as for aesthetic warmth.

In the fourteenth and fifteenth centuries, the subjects for tapestries were mainly historical exploits of kings, mythology, the Crusades, allegories and religious themes. The sixteenth century added scenes involving various forms of hunting.

The designer and weaver worked closely together, each being responsible for the total work. In the seventeenth century, as appreciation for tapestries increased, weavers started to specialize. Some stressed pastoral scenes, some wove only animals, others people, and still others mainly trees and flowers.

Contemporary weavers in this country generally combine all functions and bring the designs to fruition through their own labor. We must, then, become capable and comfortable in both areas. Techniques for conceiving, designing, sketching, and coloring must be learned along with weaving skills. In those situations in which one person's ideas are woven by someone else, the designer must know which ideas and design elements best lend themselves to weaving and be able to utilize those techniques which will best express them.

Gothic tapestry techniques are said to stem from the Copts, Christian Egyptians who lived between the third and seventh centuries. Gothic art flourished from 1350 until the mid-sixteenth century. The tapestries woven during that period appear to have two directions. One was concerned with isolated figures which were outlined like stained glass windows that ignored perspective. The second used many figures and botanical details and patterned itself after the oil paintings of the time.

It was difficult to copy a cartoon exactly on a horizontal loom because the tapestries were woven face down. The high warp looms, although slower, were used for more exact reproduction and larger scale work. The average number of ends per inch (e.p.i.) in these early tapestries was 13 to 15. To make a weft-faced tapestry, the weft had to be very fine.

As Italian Renaissance painting started to dominate the art world, tapestry weaving diminished as an art form and became imitative. Gothic weavers were freer to use cartoons as suggestions and colors without restraint as inspiration moved them. Renaissance tapestry weavers, on the other hand, prided themselves on their ability to copy faithfully the cartoons which came more and more to resemble paintings.

This is not the place to track the circuitous phases through which tapestry weaving passed until it reached its contemporary character. From what can be called an imitative reduced state for nearly two centuries, tapestry weaving reemerged with its special qualities which are so completely in harmony with contemporary life.

Ways of weaving tapestries

Today's tapestries are not copies of paintings, but are art forms in their own right. Contemporary approach to tapestry weaving may be said to have started around 1940 when Lurcat and several other artists were commissioned by the French government to settle in Aubusson to initiate and supervise the execution of a group of new tapestries. Although we are most familiar with the names of Gobelin and Aubusson, there were many other tapestry centers in Europe and the rest of the world deriving their names from their place of origin.

The Gobelin tradition, which continues in practice to this day, now uses both the *haute lisse* (high warp) vertical looms and the *basse-lisse* (low warp) horizontal looms.

On the vertical high warp loom the cartoon may

be hung behind the warp, leaving enough space between it and the warp so that the fingers have room to create a shed and enter the weft. With this method the tapestry face is toward the weaver and its progress can be closely scrutinized.

If the tapestry is worked with the face away from the weaver, mirrors may be used to check on the correct weft entry and design.

Frequently the design is also traced onto the tensioned warp. In either instance, whether the face or back of the tapestry is toward the weaver, the traditional process is a slow one with the weavers averaging one to two square yards per month. This necessarily requires more than one weaver working on a tapestry to complete an average size piece within a reasonable time.

One person has the total responsibility for the work in progress and completion, while the other weavers are workers. The warp is beamed on rollers on which it progresses as the work proceeds. The weaver remains seated on a small stool and always works at the same level. Many weavers spend their whole lives working at the same factory with arrangement for their children to take their place at the looms when the are ready to retire.

In traditional European apprenticeship programs, weavers spend at least three years learning and practicing various weaving skills and then several more years under strict supervision before they are considered sufficiently competent to transcribe cartoons to tapestries exactly as required by their master teachers. The artist who conceives the idea and draws the cartoon and the weaver who transforms it into a woven reality rarely exchange roles. The contemporary weaver, though, frequently combines these two functions; but unless the combination results from training and experience in both color, design, and tapestry weaving techniques, the result is usually one-sided — either fine design badly woven or poor design well woven.

Obligation to study

No set of rules can create a work of art, but the rules can serve as a starting point or as a check point.

When we wish to understand and learn a new language and the culture in which it is used, we are prepared to study that language and culture. If we wish to become tapestry weavers we must be prepared to study *its* language, history, techniques and contemporary expression just as diligently.

With fewer traditional constraints and limits, the artist-weaver feels freer to use weaving styles, techniques, colors, yarns or textures that best serve the purpose of the desired result. We need not limit

ourselves to narrow definitions of a tapestry:
• That it must be reversible.
• That the weft completely cover the warp.
• That it is woven completely in plain weave.
• That it must have a cotton warp and a wool weft or both must be wool or the warp must be linen.
• That only one type of fiber is used for the entire warp and weft.
• That it may serve only as a mural type of decoration.
• That the weft and warp are so organized that warp ribs result.

Without entering into a controversy between tapestries and wall hangings, it may reasonably be stated that if it is constructed of fiber, interlaced and hung on a wall it may be called a tapestry, regardless of the techniques or yarns used.

As a teacher I may ask, "Why do you wish to learn this particular technique?" Usually the answers are some version of "I want to make . . .", rather than "I think this technique will help me express an idea I have for . . ." The exploration for expressions must be open-ended or they become sterile. Repeating the exact steps that someone has already investigated without adding something of your own or changing it may be a helpful exercise, but it should be one that is filed away along with other learning experiences. It is rarely a creative experience that warrants showing.

We close our eyes to those aspects that challenge, stimulate or disturb us and settle for passing casual pleasantness or mild interest. We tend not to look at most of the objects with which we are surrounded. It is usually when something is created to be looked at that we truly look at it. Our sensitivity and understanding continually increases as we move back and forth between that which surrounds us and that which is within us.

It is out of these and many other attempts that an exciting and moving piece of work may be born. As we fulfill our own potential, the basic techniques we struggled for hours to learn will spring to hand as needed.

Observer acceptance

Whether a tapestry is accepted by the observer depends to a great degree on the success the weaver has attained in expressing ideas and/or emotions in visual form. The extent to which the observer takes part is determined by a willingness to become involved. It is part of the art of the weaver to be able to elicit some involvement from the observer; otherwise the work remains "looked at" but "unseen".

Most viewers or purchasers of tapestries have little concern with the technique that was used. They are more interested in the appearance and feeling conveyed by what they see. But weavers are by definition concerned with technique, and use those which best give expression to their idea. There is no right or wrong technique — only that one which furthers the desired expression. There must be, however, a self-imposed standard of honesty that whatever technique is used, it will be executed in such a way that the work is well constructed and will hold up for a reasonable length of time.

Average untrained observers frequently cannot make much sense out of what they are seeing because they have not had much experience in selecting out that which is important and disregarding that which is irrelevant. They may increase their perception of everyday objects but when they are confronted with different designs, shapes and colors that appear at first to be chaotic and unreadable, they tend to reject them. No value system has yet been devised that has proven adequate to help them separate "good" from "mediocre", "poor" or "bad".

There is also the difficulty that rules which work for one period of art history are successfully defied in another. We must depend on our own individual ability to achieve aesthetic experiences aided by those whose lives have been devoted to learning, judging, and reacting to all art forms, whether in the spoken word, the written word, body movement, or visual arts.

Tapestries are products of skilled control of human effort which has been organized to communicate experience. The contemporary art viewer can no longer use the photographic reproduction as a standard and must be prepared to set aside previous conceptions and react freely to what the artist has tried to communicate.

Imitation and influence

There exists an infrequently admitted feeling amongst tapestry weavers that it is somehow not professional to admit being influenced by other weavers or artists. It is practically impossible not to be influenced, but there is a distinct different between influence and imitation. Even when something is copied, the point of view in relationship to the entire composition is already a choice that affects and changes the original source.

It is not always necessary to decide in advance what the total weaving experience of one piece of work will be. The weaving of the work, the total body and mind involvement, become the experience. When starting to design for a tapestry, a sort of inner dialogue takes place as the pencil moves across the paper. "This space needs breaking up . . . no, not quite so far . . . now change the direction but thicken it . . . . I should have started lower; yes,

but that upsets this relationship here . . . . I had better . . ." and so on and so on.

If here and there parts of an abstract design resemble something that is recognizable, we should not be disturbed or influenced to change it solely because of its resemblance. The need to relate shapes to known objects is very strong. At the same time we should not feel compelled to follow or stay with the original concept. As the work progresses, the idea itself may develop further or the type of yarn or technique being used may be allowed to distort the original design.

It is here that the joy and pleasure in weaving occurs. The yarn seems to come alive in our hands and hours later when we stand back and look at the result of our work, we often find that we have not woven so much what we thought we would weave, as what we felt.

Weaving a tapestry involves exploration and control. The first calls for courage and the second for experience and knowledge. Most solutions are not found in books, although the original impetus to explore may have come from them. Fear and self-consciousness are among the greatest hindrances that blanket and smother creative ability.

Notebooks are of infinite importance to the handweaver. They should be subdivided into whatever categories are most logical for each person. A collection of cuttings from old magazines and newspapers with personal comments made at the time of entry into the notebook become an invaluable source for ideas. Such a helter-skelter collection of notes from travels and travel literature, gallery exhibitions and catalogues, lists of color combinations, old art magazines and newspapers have meaning only to the one who made the notes. My notes may read "lighter than medium chocolate, leading to a pinkish yellow orange and fade out."

One part of the notebook may contain ideas for color combinations; some colors that have been tried and require further exploration, some that have been tried and rejected, some that have never been tried for lack of the right yarns or looms or for whatever reason. These ideas might be supported by yarn swatches, written notes, colors torn out of magazines, or sketches in ink, paint, or pastel.

Other subdivisions might include design ideas further divided into types of design such as circles and holes, drips, people, sculptured shapes, hills and valleys, etc.

Such a notebook acts as an inspiring springboard for endless sources of ideas and variations. It also acts as a reminder of what to avoid in future work, if notes on reactions to already woven work are kept. Evaluation of current work and ideas for future work goes on constantly. Most weavers never weave all the ideas that occur to them as they work on one project. This means of keeping a constant reminder of ideas, suggestion, rejection of ideas, etc., keeps ideas vital and alive so that we are less likely to fall into a trap of interminable repeat of one idea or already rejected ones.

As long as the sketch or doodle is understandable to you, that is sufficient. The very act of putting a fleeting thought down, even if you never look at that note or sketch again, seems to retain the thought far back in your mind until such a time as it is needed. Then in a peculiar combination with many other supposedly forgotten ideas and memories, it all somehow jells into a solution to some problem in the project at hand.

Dedication to weaving

Tapestry weavers do not lack for examples to emulate. There is evidence in tapestries and reproductions that Lenore Tawney, Magdalena Abakanowitz, Sheila Hicks, Claire Zeisler, and many others, are turning to subject that relate to feelings and concerns regardless of what style their expression takes.

Weavers have to learn to work constructively with each other to raise their level of understanding of the materials and tools with which they work. We also need to look critically at each other's work with an unprejudiced and disciplined study and honest evaluation. We must be willing to risk ourselves creatively. This does not necessarily imply a commitment of our whole life to develop creative effort, although it will inevitably change our life in terms of priorities.

We become perpetual questioners rather than perpetual accepters. We learn to trust our own natural ability more, and, having absorbed some basic techniques, start applying them in ongoing experimentation. Our major growth is through the process rather than the end product. In this process, being dissatisfied with the result of our work and understanding the reason for our dissatisfaction is as important, or sometimes more important, than weaving a so-called successful piece.

Handweavers have tended to build up a halo around each piece produced, as though each composition is "a work of art". In part this stems from the myth that if it takes a long time to complete, it automatically falls into that category. When we have spent many hours planning, finding correct materials, colors, buying or dyeing the yarns, preparing the loom, warping, etc., to say nothing of the long hours of actual weaving, it is understandable that we may be reluctant to face the fact that the finished product does not live up to our expectations.

Perhaps the concept was not carefully thought through. Perhaps we compromised for colors which were readily available, but were not those we had envisioned. Perhaps the techniques used to weave the piece were not suitable for the realization. Sometimes we start a piece and persist in finishing it as originally planned even though, as it progresses, another solution is obviously called for. Other times, having carefully planned a project, we permit ourselves to be tempted during its weaving by other solutions with diluted or disastrous results.

At best, when all goes well and the work is completed and hung and we stand back and look at it, we find something that could have been left out or added, or that could have been better explored. As the days go by and the tapestry becomes part of our environment, we see the minor flaws less and accept the overall response it produces in us. It is a good practice to let each new piece hang, at least for a while, where we can see it daily.

If we continue to be unhappy with the finished piece, the best solution then is to put it away out of sight. If after considerable time has passed we still don't like it, those materials that can be salvaged should be kept and the rest of the piece destroyed and thrown out. If we have signed a piece, it is a sign of our acceptance of it. Giving the work to a friend or selling it, although we really do not like it, diminishes our objectivity and self-esteem. Without self-criticism we will not grow, and without constructive criticism from our colleagues it will take us much longer to recognize those areas in which growth is possible or necessary.

The majority of tapestry weavers are more interested in the creative process than in selling their work. It is inevitable, however, that after a period of time acceptance of their work by the public, beyond immediate relatives and friends, starts becoming important.

Actually, failures and mistakes that are thoroughly examined are a useful learning tool, as compared to being told that your piece "is interesting". We must learn to set aside defensive mechanisms which arise at the slightest hint of criticism. Perhaps some form of "critic-in" should become part of the weaving system for weavers who respect each others opinions.

There are many steps during the weaving and at the completion that, if shared, could be more useful than "being hung". A resumé that lists participation in group or one-woman shows over a peiod of years is a questionable reward for years of weaving. We don't weave with a long resumé in mind. We weave because we love to handle and manipulate the materials of our craft into some form of expression. The actual touching and fingering of fiber is as enjoyable — and in many cases more pleasureable — than the net result.

It is in this intermediate step that weavers can share and develop. Basic techniques may be learned in a group or alone, but it is in the sharing of technique exploration and limit-pushing that we can extend and expand. Weaving, by its nature, is a somewhat lonely activity. The secreting and not sharing any "better", "quicker" or "more interesting way", is self-defeating and wasteful.

The very thought of communicating and exchanging feelings about our own colleagues' work while it is in progress, or after it is completed, is a little threatening. It is like exposing one's self at an intimate moment. And yet, with whom else can we talk, exchange ideas, and solve problems? There are always a few individuals for whom any sharing is frightening. Theirs is a lonely struggle. When we start identifying and empathizing rather than competing and envying, then the energy that was wasted rivalry can be channeled into constructive, productive work.

Exhibiting

Much critical examination of our work has been left to so-called juries who, for reasons of personal, predetermined taste or dogmatic attitude, limited space, slant of the show, or desire to tickle the current public palate, accept or reject a piece. Their acceptance or rejection may have little to do with the true value of the piece. More important, the weaver who submitted it is not helped or served either by the acceptance or the rejection. Approval may mean it fits into a preconceived mold and exclusion may merely mean that the colors used are not those with which the jury is comfortable or it may not work well with the other pieces that have been accepted. Just as there cannot be a totally objective,

unbiased opinion, so no juror can help but react most favorably to those woven pieces that are closest to his or her own style of working.

As we start to consider a juried project we ask ourselves, "What form will our idea take?" "What do we wish the finished work to say?" What techniques, designs, size, and colors will best express our concept?" Despite ourselves, we take into consideration to some degree who will be on the jury and what they will be looking for. "Does our work fit into the current trend?" "What are the 'going' colors this year?" "What will I do with the piece if the jury doesn't accept it since I never would have bothered with it if it had not been for this particular show?" We rarely verbalize these thoughts, but if pressed, will admit to entertaining them. We have also, of course, thought, "I don't care what they say or want, this is what I want to weave now."

Juries rarely accompany their reply with an evaluation that assist weavers in a better understanding of their submitted work. Acceptance means the work has passed a gauge with an unknown criterion. The piece hangs in a show for a time, is seen by an unknown number of viewers and may receive some formal recognition by having a ribbon pinned on it. It is then returned to the weaver who has no more understanding of its merit or lack of merit than when it was sent out.

Perhaps it is time to take a long look at this self-perpetuating system and approach our work from a different point of view, that of being "self and colleague" jurors. Consciousness raising has become a somewhat derisive term, but what about "standards raising" or "competence level raising"? Perhaps the time has come in our country that the search for closer interpersonal relationships may be extended to the realm of handweaving.

II
TAPESTRY DESIGN

Art Movements; Subject Material for Tapestries; Abstraction vs. Representation; Harmonious Design; Doodling and Scribbling; Designing; Design Classification; Frame.

Art movements

The twentieth century offers the weaver an unlimited range of choices and multiplicity of styles and has produced more than its share of art "isms". Although it is not necessary to confine our weaving to one or another school of expression, it is important constantly to be sensitive to stimulating ideas and expressions in any medium.

The material presented in this chapter is offered as a basis for conceiving, designing and weaving tapestries. It is beyond the scope of this discussion to delve deeply into the "physiological and psychological phenomenon" of art, or to detail the various art movements and artists who have explored them.

If our claim for tapestry weaving as an art form is justified, we have an obligation to think and work as artists rather than to contribute a decoration to fill an empty space on a wall. Whatever the result, a tightly planned design organization or an accidental happy choice, pleasing a potential audience is not the only aim of tapestry weaving. We are also concerned with disturbing, delighting, moving, agitating, surprising, soothing and exciting the eye, mind and heart.

Weaving, as any other art form, serves one of two functions or combines them in various proportions. It can reproduce and recreate familiar ideas or scenes in approved and acceptable forms, wherein the spectator is comfortable and not challenged. The second function expresses a sensitivity to something requiring a new form of expression or altering an already existing one. The expression dictates the form. Diminishing the number of components in any particular work helps pinpoint the most functional, utilitarian approach to the techniques necessary to achieve the desired end. This is particularly important in weaving, which is at best a slow and laborious process.

Appreciation of modern art cannot be taught, but once the direction is indicated it can be an on-going experience. Someone may conceive a work of art, someone else may create it, but for it to be meaningful, each of us must work while looking at it. Every art experience is personal and individual and unique. A receptive attitude and constant exposure are the main channels to understanding, acceptance and enjoyment.

If we are not comfortable when confronted with an unfamiliar art style, we might remember that most new art "isms" eventually overcame their initial rejection and eventually became acceptable and admired. The initial rejection of Abstract Expressionism and Cubism has long ago given way to adoption and reward for those insightful enough to acquire some of these styles.

Subject material for tapestries

The subject material of tapestries has generally fallen into three main categories: early tapestries that glorified individuals and their way of life, scenes copied from nature, and purely abstract approaches that involve design and color and rarely relate to an identifiable subject.

There is a long path from the concept starting in the mind, passing through the arms and fingers that in turn manipulate the fibers. Sometimes it seems that an idea comes in a momentary flash of inspiration. Actually that flash is a combination of what we are at birth and what we have absorbed from our environment and individual experiences, from the conditioning of parents and teachers, interaction with our friends and family, reading and traveling. It is a distillation of our entire existence up to that moment of inspiration. This is not peculiar to weaving but is equally true of all creative activity.

Sometimes words are inadequate to describe and define feelings, and may even help destroy the very feelings they are trying to describe. Fortunately for us we have textures, colors and shapes that combine into structures to take the place of words. It is the way in which the weaver delineates the content that transmits its meaning to the observer.

If it is true, and I believe it is, that all periods of art are a reflection of the social order and economic condition of their time, then we must seriously question what we are weaving about today. Part of the weaver-artist's concern must be to search out forms of expression that are symbolic of life today. This requires a sensitivity and ability for uninhibited and objective viewing. It also requires understanding of other contemporary art forms and their representation.

Art serves a greater purpose than mere reproduction, whether abstracted or representational. Art helps us understand ourselves and our place in the world. Each of us experiences our own reality in a unique way and thus our realization of it in a tangible form will also differ. No one weaving style is right for everyone, and new styles and their variations and mixtures with old ones will continue to act as avenues for expression. To all of this one must add the sheer pleasure we derive from handling fiber, and the challenge of its possibilities and limitations.

Perhaps one of the reasons we have learned not to really "see" when we look is the bombardment of all of the things around us that demand to be seen and attended to. We insulate and protect ourselves by screening out that which disturbs us. Tapestry designers learn to pick and choose to "see" that which is essential for immediate use. That which cannot be used immediately is stored away for future use and translation into tangible forms. That which cannot be used at all is rejected and ignored.

Not "seeing" is like having a muscle that has never been used or one that was used and permitted to weaken. It needs to be exercised, reinvigorated, to be fully functional again. A certain maturity in our work is reached when the creator and the critic in each of us can move easily from one role to the other without exaggerating either.

We are all surrounded by a multitude of objects and ideas that can become the basis for subjects for tapestries. Each of us has had years of "seeing" that can be organized and converted into our visual woven expression.

Content, i.e., the subject of a tapestry, may contain elements beyond the obvious. The subject may be obvious because its representation is easily recognized. It may be less obvious and its recognition result from clues which the weaver has left for the observer. Or the subject may not be discernible from the work, and the observer is left to reach conclusions that are based on his or her imagination and/or experience. Although good techniques increase our appreciation by enhancing the work, the subject of a tapestry is not necessarily related to the quality of the weaving. We cannot content ourselves with adequate

techniques that merely render banal subjects.

Much contemporary art appears to have neither an obvious nor a hidden theme, leaving the observer without any external reference. We have learned to accept this more readily in music because it is a non-objective, non-visual medium. In non-objective art, understanding is derived from shapes, colors and organization, since there is no obvious objective content.

If there is a subject that interests us, we are more likely to weave it in a singular form than in a plural one. We are more apt to weave about one leaf, one pebble, one star, one flower, one person or one raindrop. Nor are we likely to weave a design which requires an exact small repeat pattern unless that pattern is threaded through the harnesses so that they are woven automatically. We are also less likely to want to weave the details found in thousands of leaves, a pebbled beach, a starry sky, a field of flowers, a crowd of people or a shower of raindrops.

Most of us have been educated in a system where the greatest emphasis is on memorizing factual information. Temporary memorization has been stressed at the cost of creativity. To discover, to search for new ways instead of passively waiting for directions and answers has been discouraged.

The creative experience is a constant process of absorption and association, using all the senses to encompass the vast amount of information and sensation, assimilating and expressing them in new forms. An interaction occurs between the self and the environment that results in a creative act.

The first ideas for designing a tapestry may be triggered by any number of things, perhaps written words or something seen or suggested or anything to which we are momentarily exposed or were exposed to a long time ago. In the course of the creative process the work is refined, leaving and emphasizing that which is important and eliminating the extraneous.

Any source of inspiration may be used for tapestry design. However, it is important to remember that weaving has its own limitations. Weaving has a mathematical base, an interlacement of over and under in different proportions. The most rounded handwoven shape is made up of minute geometric squares. Underlying every curve is a straight line relationship.

There is more to weave about than we perceive with our five senses. There is more than one kind of landscape. There are inner landscapes whose limitless boundaries are imposed by the self. They can touch all human emotions and conditions, transcending "hills and valleys". There are also innerscapes evolving from dreams, feelings, values and relationships to people as well as objects.

For some people landscapes are cityscapes with ribbons of roads travelling in different directions, billboards, neon lights, cars and noise. There are seascapes where land, sea and sky meet in quiet salutation or angry clash. In one sense we cannot weave about any "scape" without internalizing it first. Generally, only the most obvious scape has been the subject for tapestries.

Science-scape is a relatively new field in which magnification of scientific data shows design never before seen or imagined. Highly enlarged cells are a rich and as yet little touched source of subject material, as well as structures now made visible by x-ray, laser beams, etc. Our lives, so intricately bound up with science, must be mirrored in our work, else the work becomes a titillating ornament rather than a human expression.

There is considerable disagreement over what is and what is not original. Originality is a concept that has been debated by every artist or craftsperson who has tried to produce an "original". The only way a design or concept could be completely original is if someone were totally isolated from the moment of birth and never exposed to anything that could be seen, heard, smelled, tasted, or touched. Such a person with no memory of any previous exposure, would produce an "original". Other than such a set of impossible circumstances, we are all influenced by what we have seen, heard and been taught.

We copy, consciously or unconsciously, but we all copy. Only when we accept this premise do we stop being self-conscious about our creative ability. Exact copying is dull and uninteresting and is usually rejected after a few attempts. We also soon realize that the copy is rarely as good as the original. If the adaptation is an improvement on the original, then it is no longer a copy. Each weaver's use of even a standard accepted color or design scheme will usually turn out to look highly individual. The manner in whch we use it, the proportions we choose, the colors we juxtapose, make it our own.

It is not mere copying as long as something happens between what you see and what you do with it. If nothing happens, you are depriving yourself of a creative experience. Throughout history artists and designers have learned by copying, but we have been taught to feel guilty when we duplicate, no matter what we bring to that copy.

Imitating what has already been done is part of learning but cannot be an end in itself. It may improve our technical ability but could stunt our creative ability. There is a danger that we may become so aware of our own inadequacies that we develop a lack of confidence to do as well as our models. Imitation relies on the thoughts and expressions of others. It can become a form of dependent thinking, leading to inhibition and frustration. Adults who never enjoyed or learned to draw find it

difficult to simply start sketching an idea. Children who have been encouraged to draw freely do not have the problems of those who grew up using a pencil only for letters, numbers, or coloring books.

Abstraction vs. representation

Today's tapestry designer is concerned not so much with whether the design is abstract or representational as which of these broad categories will best serve the idea.

Art long ago rejected the "art as imitation" principle, but it is not necessary to abandon all imitation. Representation is still one of the essential forms of expression. Each choice of subject matter is a value judgement to some degree, since our choice immediately declares its importance to us. As long as there is some residual resemblance to the recognizable, deviation from or exaggeration of nature is more acceptable to the conformist. The modern abstractionist hurdles the obstacles of recognizability by making it adaptable to his or her purposes rather than an end in itself.

The visual artist does not present art in a momentary appearance like the pianist or the actor. The weaver, like the painter, must offer a representation, whether it is recognizable or not. Recognizability or the lack of it are not at two opposite poles, as we may have been led to believe. True representation is almost impossible even in a photograph, so abstraction becomes a matter of degree. Although contemporary art is widely thought to be synonymous with abstraction, this is not necessarily true.

As did other fields, art experienced wide diversification during the nineteenth century. Although there were individual exceptions, the general trend was away from representational portrayal, passing through gradations of subjectivity, eventually arriving toward a product that was the result of the artist's sheer physical urge to paint. Modern art paralleled the movement from scientific invention to investigations into the subconscious and dream world. Concurrent with this movement, the observation of nature changed from a camera-like registering apparatus to the combined use of the eye, mind and emotions.

Goya, a predecessor of this twentieth century art movement, opened the door to this approach when he said, "My brush has no right to see better than I." He epitomized the change in thinking about volume (shape) when he said, "Color does not exist in nature any more than line . . . only advancing and receding planes exist." Corot was the first painter to use the term Impressionism, meaning the emotional impression that is received when viewing scenes from nature.

Seurat painted with pure colors of the spectrum which, viewed from the proper distance, blended automatically in the eye. The law of simultaneous contrast formulated by Chevreul in *Principles of Harmony and Contrast of Colors* expressed the concept that when two shapes of different colors are next to each other, a new color, influenced by both, appears. Because this illusive new color is an optical mixture rather than pigment, it is far more intense. It was a logical step from Seurat's optical color mixtures to Van Gogh's use of color as an emotional experience. Seurat's technique, called Pointillism, is of particular interest to the fiber artist because of its direct relationship to the way in which color is used in tapestry weaving.

At the turn of the twentieth century, painting was further liberated from representation by the use of color alone to express meaning. Matisse recreated his subjects, building up shapes simply by combining various colors. Early Cubism stressed geometric precision. Actually it created a new kind of perspective, which showed all views of an object simultaneously as seen from different angles, depicting the ideas we have of them rather than the way they actually are.

Picasso, whose work spanned several periods, underwent many changes and his influence on shapes left a permanent imprint on all art media including tapestry design.

Harmonious design

There is great disagreement about the role that harmony plays in a design. What may be harmonious and pleasing to some is discordant and unpleasant to others. Taste and standards of what is or is not harmonious keep changing and continue to be hotly debated. We constantly make choices based on our attitudes and taste. Most of the time we do not have to justify our preferences, but when we start selecting design and color, we may be more pressed to defend our personal bias. Aesthetic standards have been disputed for centuries and many people, distrusting their own judgement, assume the protective robe of current fashion. Good taste presupposes an authority for aesthetic discernment and bad taste, a lack of discrimination. However, there is no infallible rule for good or bad taste.

Whatever our source of inspiration, it is important that we recognize and accept the fact that we are influenced, consciously or not. When an artist finds a scene or theme or shape or color that presents a likely idea, he or she becomes more than a human camera. Choice of subject is just the beginning of many choices. What to retain, what to reject, what to eliminate, what to change, and what to enlarge or diminish, are among the options in creating a new artistic image.

"Abstraction" is a concept which has been practiced in various forms since the cave paintings. Representational art takes specifically seen or felt images and reproduces them in recognizable forms; in abstract art, we form these images so that their content depends solely on their intrinsic shape.

Abstractionism is one of the least understood and most abused words to explain a concept for which no other words have been found. It is an imprecise term whose meaning has changed as art expression has changed. In the eighteenth and nineteenth centuries the concept of abstraction was championed as a search for the highest art form, while its detractors condemned it for being too far removed from the so-called natural truths and being too easy. Over the years the term has been broadened to include a skillful freedom to manipulate natural forms by stretching, blurring and distorting distinctions between objects and shapes in space. Twentieth century dictionaries define it as "to pull away from or out of", "to simplify", "to clarify".

Abstraction is another way of presenting a subject. It may be the artist's idea of the subject or a feeling about it. Abstract artists may use a subject which is totally unrecognizable, partially changed, or has a remote object relationship. "Non-objective" is used, sometimes as a synonym.

There appears to be no one reason for a movement away from or back towards realistic representation. Perhaps it is an increasing concern with the personal inner world of each individual as well as an increasing interest in the exploration of the components of each art idiom as a satisfying aesthetic experience without the frustration and dependence on ability for exact image reproduction.

If we think of abstraction as a simplification, then we may stop avoiding the term and realize that in actual fact, we all use this method to make our daily existence possible. From the complications with which we are all beset, we extract or abstract that which is essential or appears most important, setting aside or ignoring that which confuses and obscures.

Representational art does not necessarily mean a literal resemblance to the original so much as evoking the feeling of the original. It is not an imitation but rather a representation of some particular thing, an embodiment that takes on artistic significance. Unless exact reproduction is required, the designers of realistic art rarely hesitate to make peremptory changes as the work progresses. Slavish imitation is not necessarily a creative act, no matter how difficult it is.

Abstract expressionists and color field painters, much in vogue in the mid-fifties, were then and still are more concerned with the act of painting and the resulting color sensation than with space.

Pop artists such as Warhol derive their source of material from contemporary objects not usually considered artistic, e.g., Campbell's soup cans. Op artists such as Vasserelly create illusions through spatial movement of color and geometric shapes.

The term "absolute" is understood to cover the area of artistic form which is neither representational nor abstract, whose source is the medium itself. It is neutral in its derivation and in its expression, having no symbolic reference of any kind.

One of the art movements least explored and least incorporated into tapestry art has been Surrealism. Perhaps the traditions in which tapestry weaving have been steeped have kept this art form from being translated into the fiber medium, but as weavers move away from the deceptive separation of fine arts and crafts, the inclusion of symbols of the unconscious will broaden our choice of subjects.

Surrealist art uses symbols as a kind of shorthand to clue the observer as to where to find the subject of the work and how to react to it. Dali and Chirico popularized such referential subconscious dream signs as soft clocks and burned out trees.

Expressionism and Constructivism are two currently recognizable trends. The first stems from a subjective point of view that incorporates emotional preoccupation. The second has a more objective approach, implying rational and logical judgements. These movements are not mutually exclusive, some artists developing in one direction and then another.

Impressionists, Cubists, Futurists, Surrealists and Pop artists all have used photographs as a direct or indirect source for design ideas. Some have used them openly and others surreptitiously. The relationship between photography, painting and weaving reached its greatest prominence in the photorealist movement of the early nineteen-seventies.

Photorealism has been adapted by some tapestry weavers. Although a photograph or blueprint cartoon may be copied exactly, its reproduction in fiber adds another dimension contributing yet another form to the medium. The result is more than mere representation. It is a choosing and editing of the seen world, rather than an attempt to create a new one. The expanding use of photography has enhanced the relationship between it and other art forms. Photography as a source of cartoon shifts the creative process from reproduction to editing, with imagination aiding and abetting the choices and changes.

Tapestry construction is sometimes loosely compared to the Constructivist approach in which shapes are built rather than cast or carved. The emphasis is on feeling, that of the artist and that of the observer, which may be both liberating and threatening as there is nothing to rely on but the self. Artists pull out of themselves that which demands release in the spirit of their times.

Because Constructivism is not related to any image, it usually appears as a clean and quiet construction in shapes that may be borrowed from the environment but are not directly related to it. Equilibrium is not achieved by symmetry but rather through proportional relationships. The total concept aims at the development of a new, contemporary visual idiom. Planes and lines emphasize space. In this sense, contemporary tapestry designers see their constructions as part of a continuing search and discovery, tempered by the acknowledgement that experimentation and newness do not necessarily result in art.

The terms "absolute", "representational", and "abstract" are essentially working terms which are used by themselves or in mixtures which help us understand and communicate with each other.

It is a matter of personal choice whether a weaver wishes to design in abstract shapes and colors, wishes to represent a recognizable object or wishes to move in the broad area between.

As weavers search beyond surface appearances, other aspects of reality become evident. Weavers become aware of shapes in space; and when these are transposed and become visual, they take on non-representational or abstract forms, becoming designs in their own right. The weaver is then free to invent new shapes without reference to the original stimulus.

Creative imagination is stimulated by images which in turn suggest other images. These may be imagined or real, i.e., something actually seen or experienced, or they may provoke further image fantasies and investigations. Sometimes the memory of an object or emotion is sharper and clearer than when originally observed or felt because the recollection is free of non-essential details and distracting associations.

Doodling and scribbling

Doodling or scribbling should be encouraged rather than discouraged or derided. They engender a feeling of freedom with a drawing tool held by the fingers which may lead to images that can be developed without recognizing or remembering their source. Not being able to draw well or in exact detail can be an asset rather than a handicap for the hand-weaver. Details are left out and exaggeration of other parts sometimes helps the design.

There is nothing magical about developing an ability to create designs for tapestries. As in everything else, this skill increases with experience. Each of us, on our own level, designs every day. We arrange furniture, gardens, book shelves and so on, but do not think of these activities as designing. Organizing our lives is a form of designing.

Our designs can be either structured or eccentric. They can be part of the current fiber fashion or move against the general trend. What is most important is that we weave as we wish, keep on weaving and become better weavers. Our work may gain little acceptance by the public, but we will have had the exhilarating experience of doing what we want to do. Then there are those rare occasions when we have the satisfaction of doing what we want and having it accepted.

The beginning of this century saw changes in the visual and plastic arts which have permanently affected our lives. We are starting to reject convention in favor of experience as a valid design source. The physical nature of our materials has assumed equal importance with our source and execution of ideas. We are developing a personal inquiry, rather than solely theory, for individual solutions. But the emphasis on intuition and analytical approach must not be made at the cost of high standards of technique.

Even when a design is clearly organized, the net results can, with the best intentions, be a disaster. It is the individual vitality which each weaver brings to the work which, even if all design principles are ignored, breathes life into each piece. I have come to believe that chance is not all that accidental but comes about as a result of years of trial and error.

There are many design elements particularly pertinent to tapestry design which are present all around us. Effective weaving design converts an inert fiber into a dynamic vital creation. The personal involvement of the weaver generates this alive feeling, but the final result depends on individual choice and use of design elements.

It has often been said that any good design is, first of all, a plan for order. One shape has to be separated from another shape so that certain ideas can be included in one and other ideas in the other. Second, any design must be an expression of the material in which it is executed. If the design does not fulfill this purpose, it has failed, no matter how decorative it appears and decoration or embellishment should relate to the original purpose of the design.

There are basically two approaches to designing. Some take the first path of solving design problems, i.e., choosing one or more elements or principles and exploring their possibilities.

In the second approach the weaver chooses a subject or a recognizable shape and reproduces it in an individual way. The two methods combined result in a specific subject organized in such a way that the challenge lies in the interwoven expression of the chosen design elements and the particular subject.

Unlike the artist, handweavers cannot freely scribble or superimpose torn papers or arrange found objects, use preformed shapes, spray guns,

etc. The doodle that takes a few minutes with a pencil on paper requires many hours of painstaking labor to reproduce in fiber form. This is one of the most discouraging factors for a beginning weaver, because inevitably, after many hours of weaving the feeling arises that there should be something more to show for so much concentration and effort. Each art form has some proscriptions and limitations, and pick by pick interlacement is both the limitation and the challenge that tapestry weaving offers.

For most weavers, many more designs are conceived and sketched than are ever executed. It is much easier and quicker to visualize or draw a cartoon of a design than to weave it. It is much easier to reject a cartoon that does not meet our standards than to destroy a finished woven product.

When the weaving is the initial process, without a cartoon, improvised as the work progresses, we must be prepared for unexpected results. A delicate balance exists between preformed concepts and intuition that may result in a tapestry design never imagined when the work was begun.

When handweavers start thinking about design, they begin to see with their hands as well as their eyes. A kinesthetic sense develops as the fiber is handled and manipulated. They start collecting different colored and textured yarns without necessarily having an immediate use for them but recognizing in them interesting possibilities either for future use or for just pleasurable contemplation.

Designing

Some weavers are able to see the entire design before they start, others let colors and textures dictate the shapes and let their interactions determine the growth of the piece. Some use a combination of the above, starting with a preconceived approach and then letting the movement and mood and materials suggest the next steps. There is no right or wrong here. As we gain in experience we combine the known and unknown and learn to trust our choices.

Design elements and fundamentals have been organized by different designers and teachers of design into various groupings, all overlapping, which, by contemporary standards are quite arbitrary. In the following section, I have included those which particularly apply to tapestry weaving, stressing those I have found to be most useful.

Design classification

Design is an expression of an individual's feelings, experiences and reactions. It is usually defined as "order" and an honest expression of the materials that are being "ordered". The basic components of design are the same whether applied to paint, metal, clay or fiber, but their importance, emphasis, and use varies with each form. Design may be subdivided into various categories depending on the point of view of the designer, the author or the art or craft which a particular design is to serve.

Decorative design involves ornamentation or embellishment and is usually added to an already existing object like a pot on which the potter scribes, or embroidery added to an already existing textile.

Design in handweaving is usually not considered decorative unless it is some form of braid, brocade or band added later. Handwoven design is usually intrinsic to the whole, with the weaving itself creating the design. It can be an overall repeat, as in traditional patterns, or some other arrangement of shapes.

Much of decorative designing has been relegated to such forms as screen-printing and block-printing. Enlargements and extensions of these ideas have been rarely considered as design possibilities for tapestries. There has been some use of traditional patterns associated with fabric yardage, usually a form of expanded threading with the individual elements of the repeat stressed through exaggeration and distortion. Combinations of this type of designing as a background, with other shapes in the foreground, are less common but offer another design approach.

Geometric designs are based on pure forms, the dot, line, square, stripe, triangle, circle, which may stand alone or cross each other and assume shapes that resemble something from nature or are purely geometric. Because warp ends and weft picks usually cross each other at right angles, geometric construction is inherent in the weaving process. Since so many of the shapes that surround us are geometric in concept and appearance and construction, such designs are among the easiest for the beginning weaver.

Design from nature has always been a source of inspiration, whether representational or stylized or abstracted. One premise for the source of design holds that the organic processes of nature are the basis for our artistic expression. Being a part of nature, our efforts are a continuous expression of its procedures.

Design is part of the human experience. Unconsciously we think of direction in terms of our own body. We sleep horizontally and relate this direction to repose. We run leaning forward, thus relating diagonals to movement.

Structural design is inherent in handweaving and is basically the type of design with which we will be concerned in the following condensation of principles.

Structural design may supply a skeleton. On the whole, in its simplest form, it is least useful to handweavers because it implies a framework which in turn suggests lines. We are more likely to weave costumed figures in dance movements or athletic confrontation than skeletal symbols in the same activity. We are more likely to use full leaf shapes in various relationships than suggest foliage through veined lines.

The boundary or outline of a shape is entirely dependent on its skeleton, but weavers are more often concerned with the outer shape than with the inner structure. The best way to understand animal or human figures and how they move is to realize the full significance of the relationships between bone and muscle and what happens to them when bodies assume different positions. This understanding is also necessary to the handweaver if what is woven involves human or animal movement or bird flight.

We are all familiar with tapestries, both traditional and contemporary, in which we get lost looking for something to which we can relate. Innumerable embellishments and detail may be admired but cause the observer to lose interest. Today we are disposed to prefer spareness and to say what has to be said with less.

Free form design may be accidental and non-representational, but the observer almost always seeks to relate to some recognizable feature. A simple circle suggests the moon; if the circle is slightly distorted, it could be a rock; if the line is opened up, it could be a horizon of hills.

Free form or biomorphic curves have always been one of the most obvious sources of inspiration, since we ourselves and most of our natural surroundings fall into this category.

Frame

The frame, whether actual or existing as an edge, is the framework within which the total area of the work appears. The choice of subject determines the outside dimensions of the work. The lines of the enclosure (outside dimensions) are part of the tapestry and must be taken into consideration. For this reason, a square shape is more difficult to handle than some others. There is equal tension from all four corners to the center. Geometric designs are aided by the vertical and horizontal enclosure, but in a design that has curves, such as hills and valleys of a landscape, the corners of the frame, or edges of the tapestry must be considered or they will not be consistent with the rest of the design.

Rectangles placed vertically or horizontally are easier to incorporate into a design. When placed vertically, the rectangle shares the qualities of vertical lines. When placed horizontally, the softer and more tranquil designs seem appropriate. Irregular shapes usually fall within the square or rectangle formats and may be dealt with accordingly. The circle is a difficult outline to fill since the eye is not given a resting place and continues to circle around unless the design within the circle has a stopping place.

The boundaries of a tapestry, similar to those of a painting, establish a visual frame which may be rectangular or round or curved, but which surrounds the flat surface. A plane is characterized by this two-dimensional surface. The flat area is called a picture plane or field or ground, and a relationship must exist between the frame or border and the shape and ground.

The position of a design unit or shape on a plane must be oriented to the center, to one or another side, or touch the edge of the plane. A large shape with very little ground around it, contained within a small frame, will appear to want to explode out of its boundaries; and a small shape may get lost on a large ground. If explosion or loss are the desired themes, then such arrangements help further the idea. If not, then the resolution between shape, ground and contours which confine them was incorrect.

III
DESIGN ORGANIZATION
IN SPACE

Part 1: Design Elements in Tapestry Composision; *Dots; Lines — Vertical and Horizontal; Squares; Stripes and Bands; Diagonal Lines; Triangles; Curved Lines; Circles.* Part 2: Design Fundamentals in Tapestry Construction; *Contrast; Balance; Symmetrical; Assymmetrical; Radial; Direction; Weight; Tension; Emphasis; Dominance; Movement; Repetition; Rhythm; Proportion; Shapes; Space; Positive and Negative Space; Size.*

Part 1: Design Elements in Tapestry Construction

Dots

The dot is the smallest and simplest element. The next element, the line, may be made of a string of dots. Studies using dots are one good starting point for students of design as their manipulation in size and placement offers a wide area of interplay not diluted by other design elements. However dots, unless they are part of an all-over pattern, are not often used by tapestry weavers.

When there is more than one dot, they establish relationships among themselves, creating tensions in the space between. An enlarged dot becomes a spot or a circle and when one is enclosed within another a tension is set up between them.

When the dot is extended by distortion, enlargement or abstraction, it takes on a different design im-portance. When expanded, the dot becomes a less contained shape. In its smallest aspect it takes up very little space. It can expand to take up all the space or can be punched in or pulled out like a lump of dough, at which point it becomes a design. When several lumps are superimposed on each other a third dimension is suggested. Sometimes, without deliberate intent on our part, the shapes may become directional and also take on emotional connotations.

The Pointillists' use of dots resembles a plain weave with color changes forming the shapes and content.

The dot may be a point of focus in a design, comparable to a pause in the flow of spoken or written words. It is irreducible and basic. It is brief, static and unmoving, unless representing a symbol such as a raindrop. We usually think of a dot as small and circular, but it is not limited to that shape. By itself, its inner tension is not great but as soon as another dot or element is added an immediate tension is

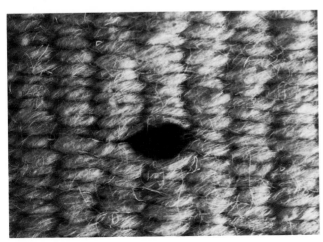

Fig. 1. *One dot.*

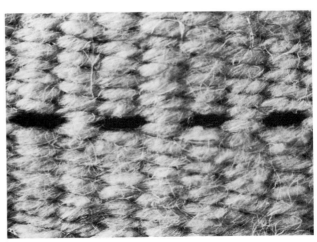

Fig. 2. *A string of dots.*

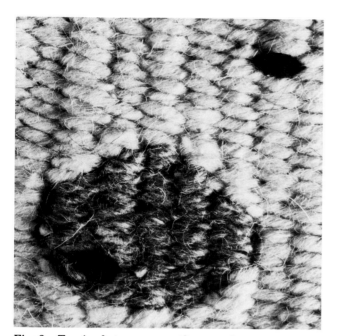

Fig. 3. *Tension between more than one dot.*

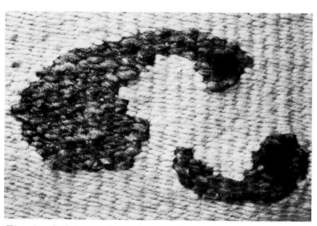

Fig. 4. *A dot can expand or contract.*

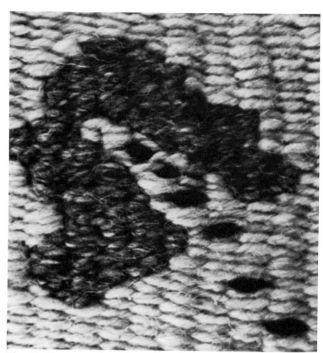

Fig. 5. *Dots on the edge of and penetrating a shape.*

Fig. 6. *The same size shape looks smaller in a larger area and larger in a smaller area.*

established between the two. The more dots and other design elements added, the more interaction and tension results.

Even the smallest unit by itself in a design creates immediate relationships with the edges of the total surface and becomes a center of focus, no matter where it is placed in relationship to the edges. Two such units relate or pull towards each other, as well as each relating to the edges. As the number of units increases, the interrelationships and pulls grow more complex.

If the two units are similar in shape there is also the attraction of similarity. Those design units placed near each other in space seem to set up a familial relationship or competition.

Every design has an implied content. If we accept the premise that all art, in whatever form, has content, then we can take the next step of trying to

separate out recognizable principles upon which we can agree. The moment we place a dot on a blank surface, several such principles are involved.

A dot interrupts the smooth surface and sets up a tension between it and the boundary lines and that tension varies as the position of the dot changes. When it is equidistant from the sides, the forces press in equally, but if it is moved into the neck of a shape, the areas around it are decreased and the large open space starts exerting greater pressure on the smaller neck area.

A dot, spot or point is the result of a collision between a tool and a plane, or a brush and a canvas. No such collision occurs in weaving. We may see it as a small speck on a white ground that is lost or searching or growing or whatever interpretation we wish to attribute to it. It is the surrounding area, whether empty or filled with similar or other design elements, that determines its definition.

On a 6'x 6' woven area a ¼" dot will appear very small, whereas on a 1' square area the same shape demands considerably more attention.

Lines

In its simplest form, a line is a point or dot moving through successive positions. We walk from one point to another in a line whether straight, broken or curved. The frames, doors and windows of our dwellings are in lines. Rugs are aligned with walls which rise in a line to meet the horizontal ceiling line. Nonetheless a line by itself does not show color unless it itself is colored.

Lines — may be straight, broken or curved
— may move actively or passively
— may outline, enclose, pierce or divide
— may have expression or content without being descriptive of any particular idea
— may act as a boundary between shapes, having no real existence (Thin lines are used less frequently in weaving because it takes two warp ends upon which to weave them. Unless the warp ends are very fine and closely set, the line becomes a stripe, which may not be a desirable part of the design.)
— may divide or cut through shapes (Shapes may border each other without a dividing line, the division being inferred.)
— may be described as a series of connected dots or as a moving point suggesting motion
— may become an outline enclosing a space and forming a shape
— may suggest speed, rhythm, length, or directional change
— may convey a sense of depth by changing placement, direction or width
— may dissect space in a cold, rigid way or in a squiggle
— may exist by themselves or meet or cross or be met or crossed by other lines

It is quite possible to weave a rendition of a forest with its many trees, hundreds of branches, thousands of twigs and millions of leaves, using skeletal lines as the main design element, but it would take a lifetime of laborious weaving. Weavers are more likely to use lines as outlines of mountain shapes and valleys arranged in their relative positions or use a tree with a few branches outlined to suggest its size and the shape of the foliage. When a weaving does not suggest something which we recognize, then line as a design element takes on different purposes.

Regardless of their direction, lines by themselves or as imagined division between two shapes are probably the easiest design element for the handweaver. Lines may be drawn with a straight edge tool and be geometric and strong, or be drawn freely with all the human emotions of personal expression.

A line is the most primitive and universal means for creating a visual image. It is in the translation from the cartoon drawn with lines to the tapestry woven in horizontal picks to make shapes, that communication often breaks down. When drawing cartoons it is preferable to think of lines as contours of shapes since objects such as trees, hills, tables, or people have no actual line to delineate their shapes.

A line changes its quality when it is widened, shaped or squared. A shape with parallel lines is a stripe or band. It may retain its direction and remain straight, or change its direction or curve and thereby change its total nature. Although we usually think of lines as defining shapes, they must also be considered in their relationships to the sizes and edges of tapestries. There exists, too, a distinct although perhaps more subtle affinity to the content and energy of the piece.

A straight line is rare in nature and is more often the result of manufactured surroundings such as telephone poles and buildings. Straight lines are

Fig. 7. *Quality changes in a line.*

Fig. 8. *A single pick and two picks.*

rigid and stiff, and where nature uses them they are usually combined and softened.

In tapestry design, lines function primarily when they are broadened enough to become stripes or bands. A single pick, when beaten in, does not make a line because the weft that passes under a warp end does not show on the face. When a single pick of another weft color is beaten in, it looks like a series of small dashes. It takes two picks to make a line. The second pick shows on the face where the first one is covered.

A line can be expressive whether it is a vertical slit, an imagined but non-existing line that divides two areas, the edge (selvage) of a tapestry, the outline of an open area within a tapestry, or an actual woven line.

Strangely enough, fiber is by its nature line-like, a quality that must be considered since we weave with straight picks; but the final product rarely shows the fiber as a design element. When a line is drawn, a path is provided for the eye to follow. Our responses to lines are influenced by remembered past responses to similar stimulations whose association is renewed.

Visual shapes are defined by their contours or edges. Contrasts become visible when shapes are separated or at their point of contact. In neither case need there be an actual line. Weavers may use lines for design but their use is limited as compared to other art media.

A stripe, one form of a line, can be bold and direct or timid and wavering. It can be discontinuous and pass behind, around or in front of other

Fig. 11. *An imagined line between the selvage and the area next to it.*

Fig. 9. *A vertical slit line.*

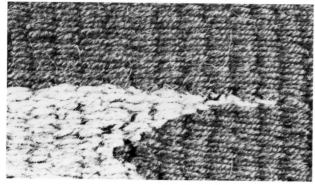

Fig. 10. *An imaginary line dividing two colors or shapes.*

Fig. 12. *An imaginary line outlines the unwoven area.*

shapes. It can be a continuous strong line that connects other shapes or pierces them. A line can narrow or broaden and split and then come together again, or remain branched.

When a small line is introduced into an empty two-dimensional space, many things take place, including breaking up the space, setting up tensions, or suggesting meanings. Just as certain colors are said to advance and recede, so thick lines seem to come forward and thin lines appear to recede.

Straight lines do not change direction. Broken lines change direction with each successive segment. Branching lines suggest unfolding and opening or infolding or enveloping. Zigzag lines hint at excitement, irritability or defiance. Vertical lines are stable and dependable. They connote poise, balance, force, dynamism and dignity. A strong, broad vertical line or stripe can symbolize a standing figure, a tall tree or a building. Vertical lines may be strengthened by placing them in opposition to lines in other directions. Horizontal lines suggest relaxation, contemplation, extension, stability and peace.

A straight line about the width of one warp end cannot be woven. It can only be wrapped. It takes at

Fig. 14. *Some possible stripe changes.*

Fig. 13. *A woven line passing beneath and above other shapes.*

Fig. 15. *The diagonal and horizontal lines strengthen the vertical line of the burned out tree.*

Fig. 16. *Horizontal lines.*

least two warp ends to interlace a weft in a figure eight fashion. Therefore, if straight thin lines are required in a tapestry design, the cartoon must be turned 90° so that the lines can be entered in the weft.

The other way to weave a line is by using a soumak technique, eliminating the flat line look by the wrapping effect which adds an extra dimension. As soon as the line departs from the exact vertical and assumes even a small diagonal direction, a jog appears. Successive steps like this may appear to be a straight diagonal line from a distance, but are distinctly step-like up close.

Squares

A square is a combination of vertical and horizontal lines that conveys a feeling of weight and gravity. It has a built-in, controlled balance that implies containment rather than an empty void. Unlike a circle, which suggests a wheel or the sun, it is a simple, self-contained shape with no strong reference to any object beyond its own design. It is stable and does not roll like a circle or point like a triangle.

The square is balanced and quieting because of its verticals and horizontals. The diamond, the same shape as a square, turned 45°, is much less stable, standing on its point. Its diagonal lines give it more animation.

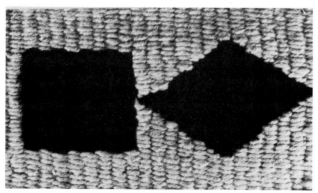

Fig. 17. *A stable square and an unstable diamond.*

Stripes and bands

When stripes or bands are used in groups, they tend to behave as a single unit rather than individually. The designer must, therefore, be aware that a wide stripe or band next to several narrower ones that add up to the same width as the wide one, will appear equally wide. Stripes and bands call attention to themselves whether used as a main motif or as background. Stripes are, in fact, widened lines in their most energetic form.

Stripes were used very early, sometimes as two lines filled in or many lines closely arranged so that they appeared to be almost touching each other as one unit. Woven stripes can vary in their thickness, in their continuity or discontinuity, or in their direction. They are an intrinsic part of tapestry design tradition.

Fig. 18. *The lower stripes behave as a unit.*

Vertical stripes have an up and down pull compared with horizontal bands which, like the horizon, tend to divide space. Stripes can create an interest in their own right or act as dividers between spaces.

Broad and narrow stripes of different or contrasting colors are among the simplest of all weaving design effects. They need not remain parallel, but may wander as a supplementary warp or weft, intertwine and travel to a different place from where they started or return to the ground weave or their source.

If the stripes are vertical in the warp, the addition of horizontal bands in the weft create a checkerboard effect; and to add interest, shapes may be placed inside the check.

Diagonal lines

Diagonal lines are equated with tension and dynamic movement. They are neither vertical nor horizontal and the tension results from the position between these two directions. Deviations from a stable position give them a latent energy, creating a dramatic impact. Diagonal lines may suggest movement and transitional action. The greater the diagonal angle from the horizon, the greater the implication of action or falling over. Sloped lines that meet suggest strength underneath their meeting place, but when they cross or appear in opposition to each other they give the impression of conflict.

If chevron type designs are necessary to the composition, they will weave more quickly if the work is turned 90°. Generally such motifs are smaller and are used in borders or backgrounds. They are very time consuming because of the many wefts that are in use at the same time.

Six-sided hexagonal patterns, of which snow crystals are an example, are similar to chevron-like patterns and are better solved in warp threading to a pattern than in free-form weaving.

Fig. 19. *Three diagonal lines.*

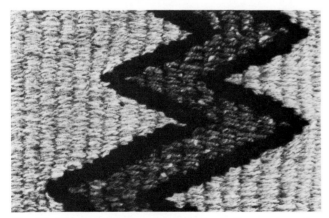

Fig. 20. *The same design woven horizontally requires nine wefts in the same pick in the center area. This one took only five wefts.*

Triangles

A triangle may appear as an individual unit or as a divided diamond or rectangle. Alone, in its most basic form, it has its own strength and discipline. Presented in a less strict form it may take on different connotations.

The triangle can suggest two opposing feelings. When the sides are shorter than the base, it produces a squat, heavy, stable effect. When the sides are longer than the base it becomes a slender, pointing form. Unlike the rectangle, the triangle can be inverted when it becomes unstable and threatening.

A cone has a stabbing effect. Depending on the relationship between its height and the size of its base, it can look tall with an upward movement or low and squat with a sideward or static feeling. A tall, spire-like shape is obviously more exhilirating than a wide-based, angled roof that hugs the earth.

Wavy lines present the same problems as connected, diagonal lines or chevrons.

Fig. 21. *Three triangles. One is stable, one is not and the third is slender and pointing.*

Curved lines

A curved line is a series of straight lines which meet each other at such an angle that their continuation gives the impression of a curve. It has constant changes of direction, depending on the angle of its curve. It suggests activity, whether in a short, lively curve or a long, slow, graceful one.

We may think of a curved line as a straight line whose direction has been changed by pressures from the outside. Different pressures from different directions will create different curves.

There is another kind of line which the eye follows but which is not explicit. It is the way in which the artist has arranged the shapes, whether literal or abstract, that causes the eye to follow or flow from one to the next or back and forth as the artist has planned.

Fig. 22. *A curved line is a series of straight lines.*

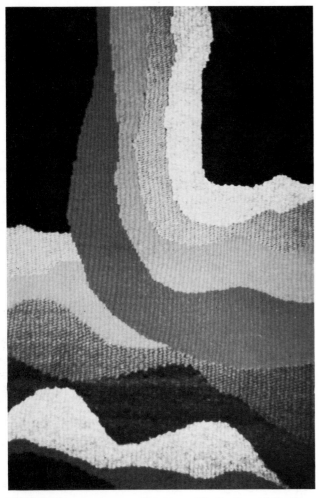

Fig. 23. *The eye changes direction with the flow of the line.*

Circles

A circle is a continuous line which curves at an equal distance from a central fixed point. It is the next logical design element that follows after the curve. A circle may be described as a continuous curve of a sphere without flat surfaces. It may serve as a symbol for the sun or the moon. A circular shape may gather to itself and hold something, or be empty and hold nothing. Circles have taken on talismanic significance as targets and religious connotations as halos.

Circles or enlarged dots are among the more difficult shapes to weave in view of their vertical and horizontal interlacement of warp and weft. If a circular cardboard shape is placed on the warp, it may readily be seen that the sides rise vertically without curving for several picks. Without a guide, the eye is misled, and as the shape grows the sides will tend to broaden rather than hold their shape, and the circle will become a horizontal oval. The number of vertical picks forming the sides of the circle are determined by its size and the number of e.p.i., and p.p.i..

A simple circle has no direction of its own, but if one side is extended it assumes a pull or direction in accordance with the extension. If two overlapping shapes are pulled in different directions, several things can happen, depending on how they are

Fig. 24. *Overlapping circles.*

designed. There can be a concentration of strength in the overlapping area if depth is added, or a feeling of tension in the shapes as they pull away from each other. If other small shapes are close by, they can appear to be strongly attracted to the larger shape and want to be drawn to it, or they can be repelled by it.

The spiral is also not a practical design for the tapestry weaver, as it involves many wefts that travel for short distances and must be handled at the same time within one pick.

Combinations of wavy lines, straight lines, diagonals, squares, triangles and circles are the most involved and time consuming designs for tapestries. Although their designs are not always thought of in terms of these basic design elements, they and their variations are always found in some form when unrelated or irrelevant material is blocked out.

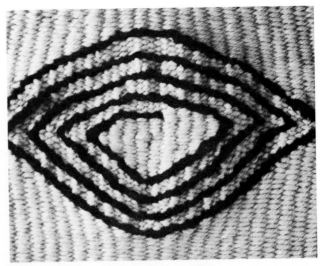

Fig. 25. *A spiral. At its widest point it required 17 individual wefts in the same pick.*

Part 2: Design Fundamentals in Tapestry Composition

The following principles of design are discussed in terms of their particular application and use in tapestries.

Contrast

Contrast, whether in color or shape, is the most important principle in tapestry design. It is in opposition that the dynamic significance of a composition appears occuring almost without deliberate planning.

Fig. 26. *A black shape on a white ground and the same shape, white on white.*

The eye tends to search out and recognize similarity in shapes. Size and shape are seen in relation to their position. Contrasts can be defined only by comparison. For instance, a design unit may appear small when grouped with a larger unit, but appears larger if placed among smaller ones. Contrasts between large and small, high and low, long and short, light and dark, close and far, are all relative. There are extreme contrasts between black and white and there are all the subtle gradations of grays between them. These subtleties are more easily recognized in shapes than in contours, e.g., a black shape on a white ground rather than a black line moving through a white space.

Balance

Although many disagree, it is generally maintained that some state of balance should exist in all design. The eye is said to have an intuitive sense of balance and is more comfortable when shapes within a boundary are arranged in such a way that they balance each other.

In sculpture the composition of necessity establishes its own support in which the balance is visible as well as felt. Even when the representation is static, it can convey a sense of movement and life. An unbalanced composition is unstable and unsettling, but it does not follow that there must be an equal distribution of design parts. It is just that their ine-

A study in complementary color contrast. The small cartoon from which this was woven was totally abstract. Its expansion into the tapestry produced an unexpected landscape effect. 35" x 57"

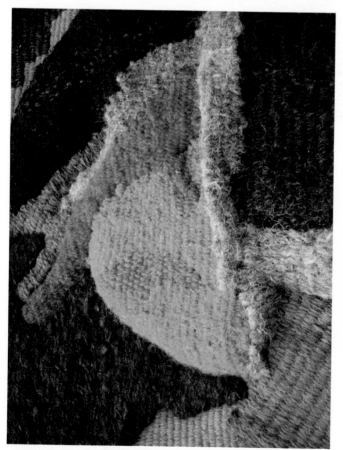

An enlargement of the central section of a bas-relief with six supplementary warps. 46" x 58" x 6"

ALL PIECES SHOWN IN THE COLOR PLATES WERE WOVEN BY THE AUTHOR.

A framed tapestry with three central shapes woven in soumak to raise them from the surface and draw attention to their vertical strength. 41" x 45"

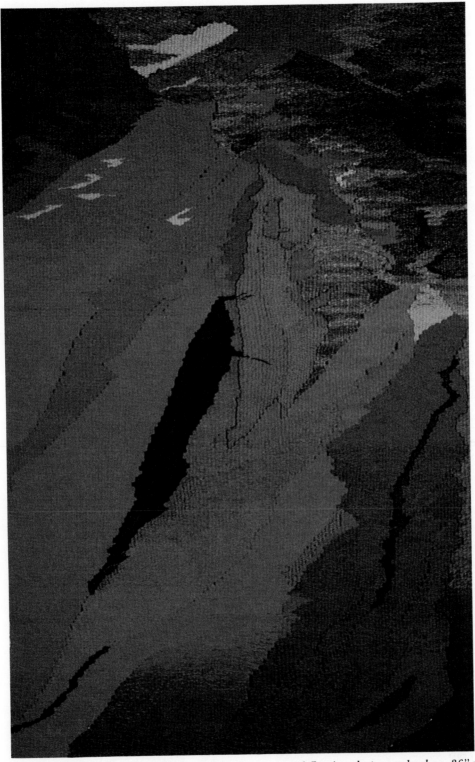

Magnification of a small crystal resulted in rising and flowing shapes and colors. 36" x 53"

quality must have compensating components.

Textures, sizes and shapes may all be used in or out of balance. Balance does not have to be a mirror image, but may be achieved by juxtaposing shapes within the design.

The visual elements, balance and rhythm, are fundamental to the design process. Balance is an accommodation in which opposing forces are held.

Balance is an interacting of forces which compensate for one another in such a way that no further change or addition seems necessary. Perfect balance is rarely found in people or in nature, nor is it necessarily best for tapestry design. The balance principle is much more subtle than assigning a shape in one part of a design and balancing it with one of fairly equal size and weight in another. However,

Fig. 27. *Balance with a mirror image.*

Fig. 29. *Balance affected by direction of movement.*

Fig. 28. *An asymmetrically balanced shape leads the eye to an internal balance.*

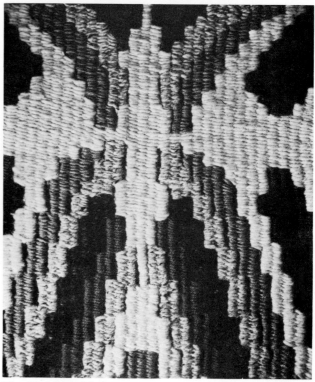

Fig. 30. *Radial balance.*

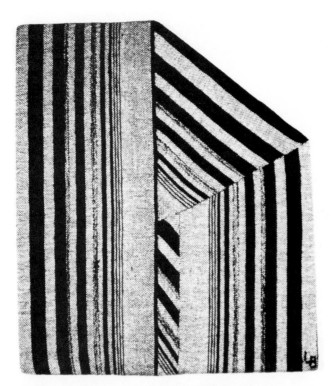

Fig. 31. *Centering interest in radial balance.*

Fig. 33. *A shape that is heavier at the bottom.*

Fig. 32. *The design includes both anchored and floating shapes.*

Fig. 34. *A heavier shape in the upper part of the design.*

Bands of supplementary warp add rhythm and movement to a tapestry that was woven on the fly-shuttle loom and then stretched and hung on a vertical loom. 57" x 32½"

Hatching in the upper section and lazy lines in the central, gray area counterpose each other to create a dramatic effect. 45" x 41"

The black tracery in the upper section relates to, but does not counter, the hatched larger and darker shapes below. 58" x 68"

deliberately balancing unequals can result in a design that is stale and lifeless.

Balance implies an equal division into two parts, one on each side of the center. This mirror image is a safe, unthreatening, and not very exciting approach. Such equilibrium is used less and less in contemporary art and may more readily be seen in architecture. The eye tends to relax and lose interest in equal divisions that offer no relief. However, the visual strength and purity of bilateral symmetry must be acknowledged.

A sense of balance may come from opposition of two shapes as well as from their symmetrical likeness, and may be more easily understood if thought of as equality of opposition. Assymetrical balance is less formal, with shapes and unequal spaces leading the eye to become involved in internal balancing. Asymmetrical balance can suggest an implied symmetry rather than an obvious one.

Balance is also affected by the direction of movement of a shape with counterdirections adding tension. Direction can be incorporated within the shape itself or balanced by several shapes

Radial balance is a movement in and out from a central focus, and can be either symmetrical or asymmetrical. It is used less frequently in tapestry design because of the problems of perfect duplications of such shapes as flower petals, wheel spokes or snow crystals. Power or dobby woven designs can use this principle more easily than tapestry weavers.

Radial balance can lack an actual center, and may thereby highlight the relationship of the other shapes in the design in a "felt" rather than actual equal pull around a center. Conversely, radial balance can be used as a basis for centering interest which focuses on the coming together of the various shapes as opposed to their spreading out.

Balance direction is affected by weight. A large shape and a smaller shape may appear in balance if their location is such that their weight is equated. If one part of the design is anchored, the eye tends to travel in the direction of the part that is floating free and then returns for stability to the shape that is safe and grounded.

We are usually more at ease with a shape that is heavier at the bottom than at the top. Perhaps gravity is the source for this feeling. A shape that floats or looms overhead may be suggestive of a fanciful or threatening idea.

Dominance may also be expressed by direction as in a group of trees whose trunks are strongly vertical but whose branches change direction to diagonal or horizontal. This directional change of the lateral shapes need not detract from the strong verticality of the tree trunks but may add variety and interest.

A design element located away from the center of a composition may appear to carry as much weight and importance as one that is centered. A shape in the upper part of an arrangement appears heavier than one in the lower part.

Weight is also influenced by size. The larger the shape, the heavier it appears. A large balloon may look heavier than a small rock. A bright color like orange may look heavier than a dark blue, even if both shapes are the same size.

In the same way, in an area covered equally by a black and white shape, the white shape will appear larger than the black. An isolated shape looks heavier and draws more attention than the same shape surrounded by others.

Tension is a dynamic relationship, a directional movement between shapes of varying sizes. Tension can also take place in a stable design in which everything is in balance. Shapes can be imagined to have forces pressing in on them from all sides, forcing the shapes to change their contours. Shapes that are small and closely grouped may show more or less tension, depending on their organization. In the same way, the dynamic relationship between small shapes counterposed by large, strong ones will depend on their arrangement for their strength or weakness. Tension, operating within, around,

Fig. 35. *Isolated shapes.*

Fig. 36. *Tension between two figures.*

toward or away from a shape, is a force that attracts and repels at the same time.

When we talk of tension between shapes we must remember that no tension is actually visible. It is a feeling that we contribute mentally or emotionally. That is one of the reasons why some people see a push and pull among shapes in a composition where others do not. If we think of the design as a magnetic field, the spatial tensions between shapes may be more readily sensed.

Emphasis

By its nature, emphasis assigns more importance to some parts and less to others. When all parts are equally emphasized, the result usually lacks conviction and resolution.

Emphasis by contrast is a particularly useful principle for tapestry designers. Contrast brings the shapes to our attention and emphasis holds them there. Emphasis balances parts of a design on which our attention has been focused, against other parts which are less important. Different designers, reacting to the same stimulus, will emphasize or subordinate different parts of a design, depending on their determination of what is important and their objectives for the final resut. Emphasis achieved by location, i.e., situating the most important parts of the design where our attention is to be focused, is another means of signifying importance. See the last chapter on "Nine Weavers — Nine Approaches" for examples.

Dominance is a factor of emphasis. It may be expressed by a line, shape or texture which dominates by size, emphasis or repetition. A composition in which two visual entities are equal is usually considered less interesting than one in which there is a

Fig. 37. *Emphasis on the wheels by location.*

dominating force. Contemporary art in which space or shapes are evenly divided demonstrates the challenging problems which artists set up for themselves to solve opposing principles.

A continuous even flow of a repeating motif or theme may become monotonous, and only opposing movement and direction can add interest and excitement. In weaving, this generalization is particularly apparent because of the interlacement aspect and patterning that are an inherent part of weaving construction.

Movement is an essential principle of design as it is an essential characteristic of life. A shape that is

Fig. 38. *Movement in static objects.*

static cannot actually look as though it is in motion. It is the tension and direction within the shape and its surroundings that suggest its activity.

Without movement, actual or implied, there is no life in the work no matter how technically well woven. A landscape that involves horizontal "hills and valleys" techniques can appear to be static or alive, depending on its design. Some of the devices that implement movement are diagonal lines, overlapping shapes, hatching, tension between vertical and horizontal shapes, shapes that narrow or widen and shading which suggests one particular source of energy.

There are also less obvious devices to suggest movement inside or outside of shapes that are more subtle but just as graphic, such as light and color.

Intervals, the spaces between repeated units or shapes, whether equal or unequal, may also suggest motion. Large intervals can break up the rhythmic flow between shapes and can be used as pauses in movement passages. Equal intervals will result in a much more static or relaxed impression than unequal ones which break up the ongoing activity.

Repetition is a rhythmic aspect of movement providing a sense of comfortable recognizability similar to symmetrical balance. The equal distribution of an overall repeat may be totally present, partially present or subtly suggested and still offer the visual and emotional satisfaction of a refrain. Randomness may be compared to asymmetrical balance as a more challenging form of design than reiteration.

Multiplication of shapes even when monotonous can increase energy. The eye will be led just so long before it starts looking for a change or climax. If the monotonous repetition in size or shape changes gradually and subtly the repeated motif becomes an echo of the original but retains the eye's interest.

Repeats may occur side by side, vertically, in dropped or half dropped positions, or in other relationships. These uses of repetition are seen more frequently in screen-printed designs, but offer possibilities to the tapestry designer.

In the repetition of design motifs, the exterior shape ceases to operate alone and becomes part of a rhythmic progression. Since nature rarely multiplies itself exactly, this is one form of expression in design in which objective and non-objective expressions are brought more closely together. As art assumes a greater role in the industrial world of design, repetition assumes greater design importance.

Repetition may also occur when shapes are similar in some respects but vary in others. In a series of repeats, the top part of the shape may be exactly the same and the bottom part alternate in different ways, or each bottom part may be different than its neighbor. The larger the shape that is to be repeated, the less repetitive the result will appear. The eye is more willing to accept small repeating shapes than large ones.

One form of repetition is in the growth of leaves or flowers which increase or decrease in size along a stem. Because of the considerable time element involved in the detailed realistic representation of fields of grain, flames of a fire, pebbles along a shore, bricks of a building, or leaves and branches of a tree, these are better suggested or implied in a repetitive design than in detailed reproduction, precisely woven. It is in the organization and variation of repetition that the dexterity and originality of the designer is challenged.

Rhythm

Rhythm in design is a form of repetition that is not necessarily an exact repeat. It is rather a feeling of ongoing surges that lend it its satisfying effect. Rhythm is co-equal with balance as an organizing design principle. It is one of the first things to which a child responds. Rhythm in art is not just an orderly repetition, but a repeated pulse, phrase of pattern or shape. As soon as one motif is emphasized in a repeated unit, a form of recognition takes place.

When we speak of a design having a rhythm we generally mean some kind of repeated pulsation and flow. It can be a continuous sweep within one shape or between two or more shapes, or the actual shape itself may be repeated.

Rhythm is experienced both as a tapestry design and in the actual bodily movements required for entering and withdrawing a weft. It may be slow, fast, flowing, hesitant, turbulent, rising or falling. Just as the design is determined by these attributes, so is the actual weaving influenced by them.

Rhythm must be a part of the original design

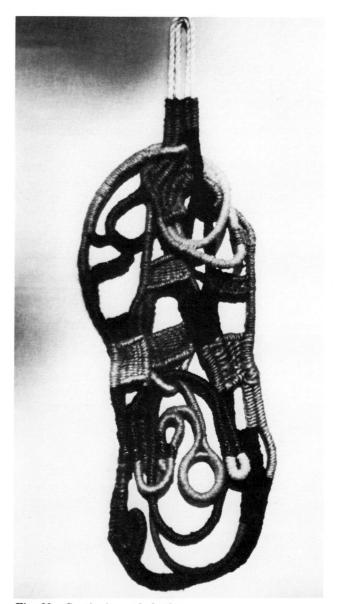

Fig. 39. *Continuity and rhythm.*

since it cannot easily be added as an afterthought. Frequently a rhythmic pulse is present in the weaving activity without our being aware of it, just as it is present in the constant human heart beat or the regular extension and flexion of the leg as we walk.

Rhythm may be subdivided into repetition, progression, continuity and phrasing, but these are rarely found in isolation. They are usually intermixed, interdependent and with emphasis on one or another.

Progressive rhythmic design may increase or decrease in size or shape and may be used to provide relief from plain repetition. These increases or decreases need not be consecutive; their order can be interrupted, resumed or reversed.

Continuity, even if only subtly suggested, is essential to every visual art. This does not necessarily require an uninterrupted theme, but may incorporate variations and transitions as long as the original theme remains recognizable.

The principle of unity requires that all parts of the design are tied together in a satisfying relationship. The integration of all the design components into one composition makes a coherent whole. Frequently unifying elements appear in design combinations whether their inclusion is consciously planned or occurs at random.

Organization through grouping, a form of linear continuity, leads the eye to travel continuously from shape to shape. When a composition is an artistic whole, there is an interplay between foreground and background, shape and shape, variety and homogeneity, where each part enhances and becomes an integral portion of the whole.

The unifying element in a tapestry may be a color or shape or technique or any of the already mentioned principles or their combinations. The singularity of one of the design elements or principles keeps the piece from flying apart. Limiting this connecting factor, such as rhythm or shape or texture, helps hold the piece together so that even if foreign features are introduced they do not overwhelm or destroy the original idea, but add variety and interest.

Losing unity is one of the greatest dangers in improvisational tapestry construction, where each new idea is explored as it surfaces. Improvisational tapestry weaving is a method of letting the imagination move freely, drawing on design experience and technical competence, and determining the next move without long contemplation and consideration.

Proportion

Proportion includes consideration of dimension, i.e. the height, width and depth a design takes up in space. Proportion is 1) the relationship of shapes within a design and their total relationship to the space they occupy, 2) the relationship of one yarn to another in size, color or texture, 3) the relationship between open and closed areas of design and open and closed (solid) weaving areas.

Proportion relates to the relative size of shapes in space. The slightest change in size or the space which they occupy changes the proportions and therefore the design.

Different proportions please different people. It involves a comparative relation between parts or between parts and the whole. Whether arrived at through mathematical calculations or intuition or a combination of the two, the final test is the weaver's intuitive feeling of the "rightness" which comes from ceaseless questioning, observation and experimentation.

The basic concept of proportion can be learned and applied to the outside dimensions of a tapestry or the relationships of shapes within it. The most widely known system is the Summation theory. It starts with the association between one and two, which are added to make three. Thereafter the last two digits are added to make the next one in the sequence: 2 & 3 = 5, 3 & 5 = 8 and so on, resulting in 1:2:3:5:8:13:21:34:55:89:, etc.

Adjacent numbers are good proportions for overall dimensions as well as inner ones. Eighty-nine by 55 could be used for the vertical and horizontal outside proportions and variations of 3, 8, 13, etc. for shape relationships. The proportions need not adhere strictly to the number, and may vary up or down as the design dictates. This system is offered merely as a check. Obviously the work itself will dictate the proportions.

Shapes

The essence of composition in art is the disposition of shapes in space. The interplay among these shapes involves forces, pressures and movement resulting in the dynamics that hold the whole piece together.

The terms form and shape are frequently used to define each other. Traditional definitions distinguish between form as being three dimensional and shape having two dimensions. I prefer to define shape, either two or three dimensional, as having both contour and depth. Form is used as in art form or sonata form, to indicate category and content. It is a style or manner of presentation of an idea.

Tapestries are built up in spatial shapes. Every moving or static object has a shape that takes up space. Mobile human shapes move in, around, over and under other mobile shapes such as automobiles or immobile shapes such as houses. Shapes are an integral part of our existence.

Sensitivity to visual shapes and colors enhances our understanding of ourselves and our environment. Some familiar shapes hold our attention momentarily, but we pass by most others as though they do not exist.

No matter into how many parts and shapes a design is broken up, what is seen first is the total effect. Then the eye starts moving around and dividing up areas as suggested by the fragmentation.

Edges and outlines are the customary means for defining shapes. In other art media these outlines become important in their own right. In weaving, because of the interlacement technique required for outlining, there is more of a tendency to work in

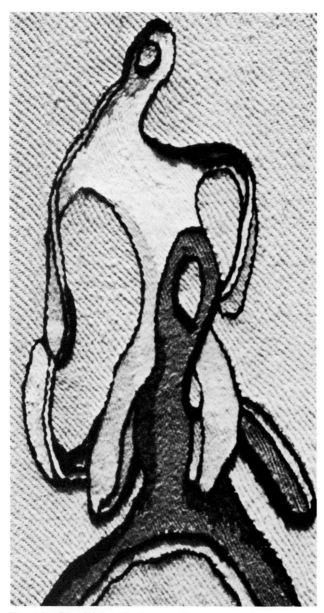

Fig. 40. *Simplifying the human figure.*

shapes. As we work with these shapes, we begin to distinguish among them by using different textures and techniques which in turn lose their individual importance in the service of the whole.

Exaggerating or simplifying shapes is one way of symbolizing them. The change in the shape becomes an emotional symbol to which we can relate. Specific descriptions or duplications tend to limit such feelings.

Shape implies some degree of recognizability; otherwise we call it shapeless. In design it does not matter whether the original shapes are recognizable or not. Frequently shapes not originally intended to be recognizable become so through an unconscious effort to relate them to something. There is a compulsion to read into a shape some recognizable object or story line. Psychological tests like the Rorschach are built on this principle, so that what we see in an ink blot presumably reveals our inner selves.

Since tensions between shapes increase as they approach each other, this relationship may be used to convey feelings of anxiety or disturbance. The space between the shapes may seem to be squeezed, or a top shape pushes down on a smaller bottom shape.

By themselves, solitary simple shapes do not necessarily suggest an image or a point of reference. A circle or sphere, a cube or square, a pyramid or triangle or a free-form splash, have no top or bottom or sides. It is when we place them in some context that they take on meaning.

Shapes placed close to each other do not necessarily make better design than those that are separated. There is a kind of strength in widely separated units in a composition that is totally different from closely related units. In this instance the negative spaces (discussed later) take on significance.

Shapes may have:
— inner or outer surfaces and a configuration
— strong emotional associations
— elements of similarity which tend to group easily and logically

Shapes may:
— occupy space and represent spatial relationships
— interlock or interlace
— overlap, showing clearly that one is in front of or behind another
— penetrate, oppose, surround or squash each other
— shrink, grow, repeat, change position, remain recognizable or change to the point where they depart completely from their origin

Shapes may be:
— open or closed or a combination of the two. Open shapes may bleed off of the edge of the tapestry as though they continue on beyond its

limits. Closed shapes are contained within the tapestry edges although they may touch them.
— transparent so that we have the impression of looking through them
— flat, solid or filled
— representational or abstract or any combination of the two
— closed, giving a feeling of solidity and compactness, or open, in which case the surrounding space mingles with the partially closed shape, both being essential to the total concept
— touchable, having weight and texture
— curved, having no sharp angles so that they appear softer and more giving
— impermanent as in clouds and waves

Shapes that have volume may also have mass which can take on different shapes. They can be solid as a rock, be fluid and subject to change like water, hang in suspension like clouds, or grow and explode like a bomb. Mass objects are the opposite of skeletal frames. A boulder may be presented as a mass or in the framework of an outline.

A person may be thought of as a shape or a group of related shapes, part of a crowd, moving about in space, containing an innumerable number of small and large shapes. At first glance, all these shapes may appear overwhelming, but may be reduced to recognizable ones that can be organized and managed.

Space

As shapes we exist in space. We sit and lie on objects that take up space and drive in three-dimensional objects that move in space. We arrange three dimensional objects in space around which we move.

It is difficult to perceive unlimited space. The concept of space becomes more apparent when boundaries are added, thereby creating shapes. Subjective interpretation of space depends on one's experience. What appears small to one person may be large and endless to another.

Space is not only an enclosed area, but it surrounds objects and should not be confused with distance which is defined in terms of depth. Space has no limits and changes subtly with each different perception. The sense of space is intensified by the juxtaposition of shapes.

Shape and space are inseparable. Shape makes space conceivable. The more the shapes converge, the more the space is compressed, the more tension is created. Newton's Third Law states that "for every action there is an equal and opposite reaction." Once this concept is applied to tapestry design, we see that the more shapes that are introduced into a given space, the more pressures are built up.

Fig. 41. *Shapes and interrupted space.*

Space is the medium in which color and shape are present and perceivable. It does not exist solely to be filled. The opposite of filled space is not empty space, but rather the relation of time and space in the total area.

Space, like shapes, may be broken up, molded, disconnected, increased, altered, compressed or organized. It may be enclosed by a contour or extended beyond the limits of the piece.

Ideas about space have not remained static. The Expressionists changed shapes in space to express emotions. To them, space was an aesthetic device with which they could unite shape, line and texture.

Positive and Negative Space

Negative space is as important as positive space and not simply space that is left over. It provides the eye with a rest time, just as the ear requires a silent time. Negative space is the unoccupied but required space within which positive shapes exist. Negative and positive space are interdependent, equally functioning elements both of which have a presence.

The proportions of each of these two constituents must be equally considered. One part of the design must not be read against another. If the designer is comfortable with the design, it does not matter which is the ground and which is the figure.

Positive and negative spaces should set up an interplay in a dynamic versus static form that creates tension, which in turn suggests movement. Positive space may be visualized as enclosure as opposed to the exclusion of negative space. Although shapes are considered positive as compared to the negative space around them, they may also exchange these positions.

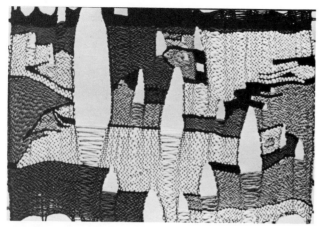

Fig. 42. *Positive and negative shapes.*

Size

Although our tendency is to use human scale as a measure for size, emotion and direction, our attitude towards size and space is constantly being conditioned by the world around us, from atoms which are shrinking, to the limit of outer space which is expanding. The human body is the constant against which relative sizes are perceived. Those sizes or shapes that are larger than ourselves are seen quite differently than those that are smaller. As the size of an object diminishes, it becomes more personal as opposed to the more public larger-than-self pieces.

When there is a variation in size that is unusual, e.g. when a human figure is larger than a house, it is assumed that there is a distance between the closer figure and the house that is further away. This is also true for those representations in which the position of shapes closest to the bottom margin appear closer to the observer than those in the upper portion of the composition.

IV
ADDITIONAL DESIGN CONCEPTS

Part 1: Tapestry Design in a Third Dimension; *Three Dimensional Structures; Bas-relief; Perspective; Linear Perspective; Aereal Perspective; Color Perspective; Scale Perspective*. Part 2: Illusion in Tapestry Design; *Art and Illusion; Illusion of Contour; Subjective Contour; Illusion of Irradiation; Illusion of Contrast; Illusion of Space; Illusion of Shape*.

Part 1: Designing in the Third Dimension

Three dimensional structures

One of the major ways that handweaving has progressed from its original classic form is in its use of three dimensions. Fiber is being accepted as sculpture despite the difference in materials used in the two media.

Many shapes that are actually three-dimensional are drawn in a two-dimensional plane, suggesting the third through the addition of shadows. One shape is partially hidden because it lies behind another suggesting depth and dimension. In considering depth we must decide whether we actually wish to show it clearly or by implication. Depth may be depicted in three ways: by size, overlap or perspective.

Projection is an amplification beyond the two-dimensional plane. Artists have explored many devices to suggest shape/space as a third dimension on a two-dimensional plane. Since it cannot be actual as in sculpture, an illusion of supporting armature has to be created.

Protruding shapes, whose surfaces reflect light from different angles, create an interplay of light and shadow by virtue of the additional dimension of depth. The surface texture must be considered in relation to the entire piece, whether it is to be consistent with it or draw attention by opposition.

Three dimensionality demands technical solutions far beyond those of two dimensional work. Three dimensional constructions impose the use of different, perhaps more rigorous materials and at the same time involve more technical limitations. Weight, stress and joining are critical to permanence. Because they are surrounded by space, fabrication problems must be solved to push the material beyond usual structural requirements.

One of the decisions with which the weaver is faced at the outset is how the work is going to be viewed, i.e., will it be seen from one specific point in space or will we feel that we are looking at it from within, seeing the design all around us? Will we be seeing the work as though we are standing directly in front of it, from one or another side, or walking around it? Will we be seeing the design as though it has no depth or will we appear to be seeing all the sides and perhaps the top as well, simultaneously? Will we see the work as though we are looking in through a window from the outside or out through a window from the inside?

Designs in two dimensions have been re-exploring the roots of spatial illusions. Renaissance artists were challenged to produce three-dimensionality through some aspect of linear perspective derived from the principles of geometry. Cubists accepted self-imposed restrictions on their medium, creating illusions of depth, but avoided modelling with light and shadow. The Cubists analyzed shapes, broke them up and reassembled them into new totalities. Emphasis moved from representation to design, texture and shape. Cubism and its derivative "isms", in which co-existing sides of a shape are presented simultaneously, have become part of contemporary terminology.

Another means of creating an illusion of a third dimension and one used more frequently by fiber designers is called chiaroscuro modeling. It is a way of using light and dark without regard to a specific light source. Shape modeling in weaving, similar to that used in painting, emphasizes the shape, disregarding the logical light source which would put all light planes on one side and all dark planes on the other. This technique draws attention to a specific area without regard to traditional rules of perspective.

Unlike the flat plane of two dimensions, three dimensional composition employs constantly shifting light relationships. Each plane and contour takes on a new form both from within itself and in relation to the rest of the work, as the weaver and observer move from one viewing position to another.

As weaving becomes more three dimensional, the observer has to focus differently. In nature, the eyes start at one or another end, the closest or farthest part of a shape, and move towards the opposite side. In a shape that has three dimensions, the eye must adjust to the total shape at once.

Three dimensional shape is surrounded by air like the human torso or a piece of sculpture or a tapestry that hangs freely from the ceiling or is self-supporting from the ground.

Shading and shadows impart depth and volume to objects or designs by creating a distinction between the different planes. It is not necessary that it be a realistic representation of the light direction,

Fig. 2. *Hatching outlines the bottom, larger shape more boldly, and the upper, smaller shape more subtly.*

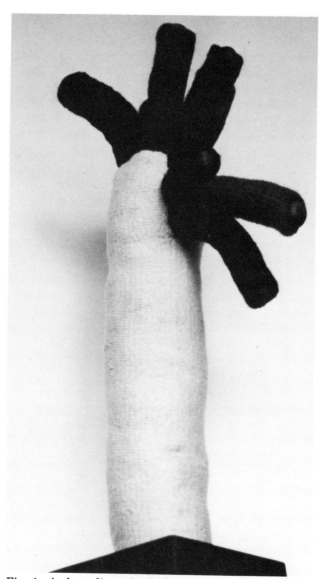

Fig. 1. *A three-dimensional shape with wooden armature concealed in the trunk, wire supports for the finger-like projections, and wood knobs at their tips.*

Fig. 3. *Overlapping shapes.*

especially as subtle shading is one of the more difficult techniques to achieve in fiber. Hatching, in which darker colors are used to delicately outline a shape as the background moves away, is one of the techniques which best suggests depth around a shape. Roundness is aided by shading inside the outline but not touching it, with colors woven darker at the edges and lighter towards the center.

Overlapping makes it possible for more than one shape to occupy the same space. Transparency occurs when overlapping shapes do not block each other out but each is seen as though through the other. The same space is shared by more than one shape on a plane, giving the impression of another dimension.

Unlike sculpture, we do not have the choice of cutting away to reveal the shape within the material, nor do we use tools such as a chisel or hammer. Our fingers are our tools and we become ambidextrous, using them to pull, push and poke.

In works of more than three dimensions, the observer contributes the additional dimensions which cannot be seen.

Bas-relief

Bas-relief offers the weaver an expression midway between traditional flat-plane tapestries and sculpture in the round. It offers a shape-in-space form that casts light and shadow in new roles.

Fig. 4. *The bottom, horizontal shape protrudes 3", the top overhang 4", and the three vertical shapes 5".*

Fig. 5. *The bas-relief shape in the center is double woven and supported by a strong linen warp.*

Whereas sculpture in the round may be viewed from any point, bas-relief can only be seen from the front. Either type of shape may be open or closed, but both require some form of armature for support.

Sculptural fiber shapes, whether in the round or in relief, are less explored by fiber workers, perhaps because of the soft and non-supportive nature of fiber. However, fiber can be supported by various materials such as sponge rubber, wool or cotton stuffing, plastic polyurethane, cardboard, plywood or wire.

Because of its attachment to a background, bas-relief has less problem of support while still offering an almost unlimited opportunity to investigate three dimensional shapes. Contemporary shapes in which hollow areas are juxtaposed with solid ones are more difficult to achieve in fiber if they must use their own support than if they are supported by a background wall.

Relief sculpture almost always casts shadows so that it is not necessary to incorporate them into the weaving. In high-relief there are greater shadows than in low relief, which does not project out as far. In low relief the design may be more complicated and detailed since smaller shadows are cast. The third dimension takes on a palpable form when we can see in as well as up, down and across.

Perspective

The rules for the strict perspective system with which most of us are familiar were established in the fifteenth century. They are based on a linear perspective in which objects appear to decrease in size as they move away from the viewing point.

In linear perspective the horizon line is determined by the level of the eye and its distance from the center of interest. The "vanishing point" is where all parallel lines seemingly come together on that horizon. Since the vanishing point seems to exert a visual pull, it acts as one of the determining forces to set the mood of the work. There can be more than one vanishing point in a composition. A path is established which the eye follows as it moves from one to the other. The use of a changing viewpoint can be a device for emphasis of one or another part of the design.

Linear perspective involves the seeming closing in of vertical shapes in the distance, although we know that they actually remain parallel. Not only do the lines seem to meet, but they also appear to rise. In the same way curved lines below the eye level appear concave while those above the eye level appear convex.

The sculptor creates figures or shapes without having to take this phenomenon into consideration, since the viewer can walk around and see the work from various positions. To achieve the same effect, the two dimensional artist must foreshorten the subject.

Just as we take liberties with design, so must we also feel free to alter perspective. We reduce our effective creativity if we are restricted by the traditional rule that lines converge at a point on the horizon and shapes diminish as they recede into the distance.

Although it is important to be familiar with the mechanical rules of perspective, the requirements of the idea and design must be our first consideration. If it is necessary that the work appear to be viewed from different eye levels or sides at the same time to create a better design or interpretation, then mechanical perspective rules must be abandoned. The addition of different eye levels in one design has been found to add increased feeling of three dimensionality and calls for more than superficial acceptance on the part of the observer.

Various clues suggest the relative position of shapes. Larger indicates closer, and smaller indicates further away. We know that actually the shapes may be the same size, but if they are shown that way a conflict arises. Another spatial clue is overlapping, in which the closest shape appears as a solid which interrupts the contour of the shape it is partially blocking out.

The size and shape of a human being does not change essentially, but may seem to do so under dif-

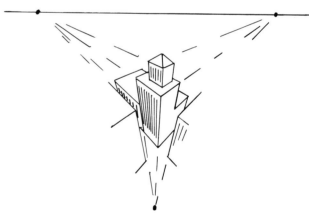

Fig. 7. *A three-point perspective looking down and up. Each set of lines has its own vanishing point.*

Fig. 6. *All parallel lines meet at the same vanishing point.*

Fig. 8a & 8b. *The sides of the shape in 8a meet sooner after a dip in the road that is further away. In 8b the dip in the road is closer and the sides appear as though they are concave.*

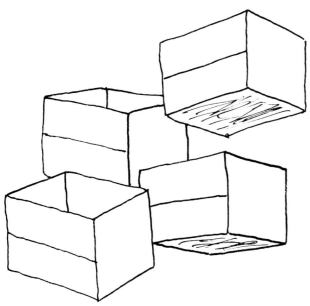

Fig. 9. *Although the eye level is the same, each of the boxes has a different vanishing point. The bottom and third boxes are viewed from above. The second and top boxes are viewed from below.*

Fig. 10. *Rules of perspective are disregarded for the sake of the composition.*

ferent conditions. It may be seen from above or below, near or far, horizontal and vertical, bent or twisted, or small or large in relation to other objects. In contemporary art, the eye may be guided in every direction disregarding horizons, eye level and meeting points.

Aerial or atmospheric perspective is based on the seeming change in color and distinctness of objects viewed at a distance. Because the atmosphere is difficult to depict in fiber, it is used less frequently by weavers. Haze, fog, wind, rain and smoke which are part of the artists' repertoire are not easy to translate into fiber.

Atmospheric perspective blurs the details of the design and decreases their importance as they recede into the background. A hatching technique may be

of some help in this form of perspective, where the hatching angles decrease in size and the colors move towards the neutrals.

Color perspective uses color to accentuate spatial illusion. This type of perspective is a major contribution of twentieth century artists. Cezanne, a Post-Impressionist painter, presented light and color as solid and lasting with three-dimensional qualities.

Scale perspective was one of the earliest methods for suggesting a third dimension. It placed the subject or shape to be emphasized at the bottom of the total design with the implication that the upper part was further back and less distinct. Space depth was ignored and the emphasis was placed on positioning the center of interest in the most eye-catching position. This form of perspective, distorting scale to draw the eye in the desired direction, is used by advertising artists and can be successfully adapted to tapestry design.

Part 2: Illusion in Tapestry Design

Art and illusion

There is a dramatic quality to illusion which challenges the imagination. Most of us are familiar with the illusive devices that help create a sense of depth, distance or dimension, but hesitate to incorporate them into the fiber medium. Visual illusions are a phenomenon of awareness through sight. They are all clues to relationships between shapes in space.

1. When one part of a shape is covered by another, the covering one appears closer and the covered one appears further away.

2. Darker shapes appear to have more solidity than lighter ones.
3. Distant shapes appear fuzzy because of the minute particles in the atmosphere which blur the light between the eye and the shape.
4. The farther away a shape is on the ground, the higher it appears on the visual field. This is based on our visual relationship to the ground: we sight above it.
5. The closer a textured surface is, the clearer and more three-dimensional it appears. The farther away it is, the smaller and smoother it appears.

In optical illusions the eye recognizes relationships but interprets them incorrectly. Therefore optical phenomena can be used to manipulate space and shape so that straight lines appear curved, space diminishes or increases, and shapes change their configurations. On a flat, two-dimensional surface there is no projection into space, nor does the surrounding space penetrate the surface. There is no sense of depth except as an illusion. Illusion is a kind of internal accounting or organizing for which color and shape become the artist's tools.

Scientific studies have determined that there are large cross-cultural differences that result in the same illusion being experienced in different ways or to different degrees. For the tapestry designer it is also important to recognize static illusion not involving movement.

Gestalt theories suggest that "closure" is a need to complete a shape in which there is an incomplete part, whether in contour or on the surface. The illusion does not have to be of a material nature or have a visual presence.

Illusions of contour

A semicircular shape closed by a diameter appears more circular than one that is left open. It also seems to have a greater radius. It follows therefore that if the design requires a less round and more open appearance, with the ends seemingly further apart, the shape should not be closed by color or outline but may be left open with subtle hatching interconnections inside the half-circle. In the same way, shorter arcs of a circular shape appear flatter than longer arcs. In three equal squares, with the top and bottom of the center square removed, the center area loses its square shape and appears higher and narrower.

Illusion of subjective contours

Subjective contours or lines are the names given to certain designs which appear to have clearly visible contours although they do not exist. In the example of the triangular shapes, the contours appear continuous even though they are not. The white of the inner and outer areas are identical but the inner triangle appears to be more intense. In the example of the dots, we tend to organize them into a triangle even when they are not equidistant, although the effect is increased when the distances are equal. The imagined lines take on a real presence in the visual experience.

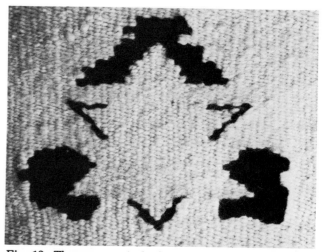

Fig. 13. *The contours in both triangles appear continuous even though they are not.*

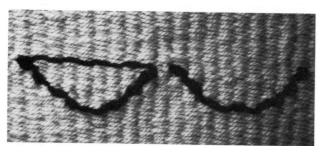

Fig. 11. *A closed half circle appears more circular and smaller than an open one.*

Fig. 12. *The center, open square appears higher and narrower.*

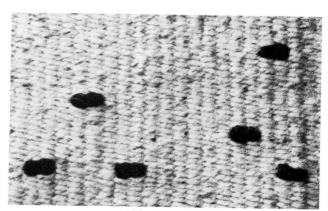

Fig. 14. *The two sets of dots tend to organize themselves into triangles.*

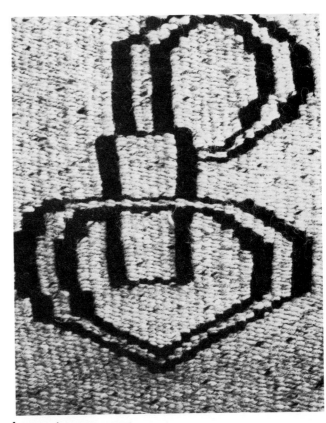

Fig. 15a & 15b. *The missing contours are not actually seen but have a strong presence.*

In the Figure 15a example of rings and a rectangle, both rings appear to complete themselves behind the black shape. In Figure 15b the missing contour of the upper ring is not actually seen, but has a strong presence.

The area bounded by the subjective contours usually appears to be brighter than the background even though they may be exactly alike. The area within the shapes bounded by the subjective contours appears as an opaque surface superimposed on the other figures.

Another aspect of subjective contours is the appearance of transparent subjective surfaces. Here, again, the eye completes not only the contour but fills in the surface as well.

Short line segments generate their own completion, as may be seen in the example where the separation takes on a curved effect in the center.

Subjective surfaces appear to be superimposed on other shapes that look brighter than the background. It is possible that the brightness of the surface is due to contrast enhancement. Such intensification is generally found when a light surface is adjacent to a dark surface.

Subjective contours may be explained in terms of partial activation of contour-detector cells in the visual system of the body which have a tendency toward completion.

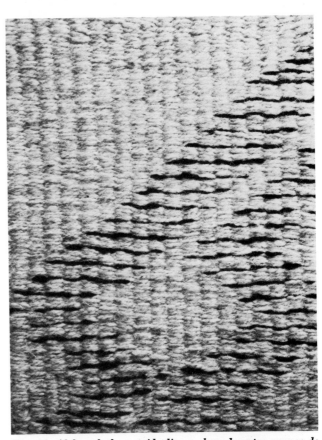

Fig. 16. *Although the outside diagonals and center curves do not exist, they generate their own completion.*

Illusion of irradiation

When a white shape is placed in front of a larger dark background, it will appear larger than it actually is and seem to radiate light in a glow around its edges. A small dark shape against an intense light ground will have the opposite effect. These illusions are called irradiation. It is as though one change takes place at the expense of the other.

Illusions of proportion

There are times when the design cannot be changed for reasons of proportion, inter-relationships between shapes or some parts having already been woven. A new shape may then be made to appear larger or smaller by changing the color value, or its contours.

A shape can be subtly subdivided vertically without destroying its outside contours. It will then appear taller. This subdivision can be accomplished within the design itself or through a weaving technique or texture which will make the subdivided areas look thinner. The same shape can be made to appear wider without changing its outside contours by using a basket weave or long floats.

A thin, horizontal, longish shape will appear wider if a hit-and-miss interlacement is used and will appear shorter if it is broken up by one or more small shape irregularities or if the weave is interrupted by changes in texture.

Illusions of contrast

Shapes adjacent to larger ones appear smaller and those adjacent to smaller shapes appear larger.

Fig. 19a. *A shape with smaller ones near it appears larger.*

Fig. 17a & 17b. *One shape is elongated by a division, the second by weave.*

Fig. 18. *A hit-and-miss weave widens the shape.*

Fig. 19b. *A surrounded shape appears to decrease in size.*

Either of these may be used to alter the appearance of shapes without disturbing the basic design.

A shape with smaller shapes near it will appear larger than if it is surrounded by similar sized shapes. If the center shape is surrounded by another shape, it will appear to decrease in size and importance.

Illusions of space

There are some designs which may be viewed from more than one angle. This is more true with black and white and complementary color designs which appear to exchange positions. Sometimes such compositions seem to vibrate without our control.

Strategically placed angles can make parallel lines appear to bend. The size of an angle can change the appearance of the length of a line as well as make it look as though it is changing direction.

A line or stripe appears longer when in a vertical position than in a horizontal one. This is an error in perception in which the missing factor is supplied by the imagination.

Illusions of shape

The position of a shape can change its effect. The number "8" as usually printed has a smaller top half than bottom half, although we are not conscious of this difference. However, when the number is inverted and repeated, the difference is clear: 8888 .

A shape that is filled, whether by color or subdivision, appears larger than the same shape left empty. A shape that is subdivided horizontally will appear wider than the same shape subdivided vertically.

The number of possible illusions increases with the complexity and number of shapes and backgrounds. The more geometrical the shape, the more geometrically inspired optical illusions become possible.

For the tapestry designer who wishes to pursue illusion in design, the bibliography on page 166 lists references in art and science literature which may be adapted to tapestry design.

Fig. 20. *Depending on their relationship, angles and lines can seem to change.*

Fig. 21. *A filled shape appears larger than an empty one.*

V
COLOR — ITS CHOICE AND EFFECT

Color; Combining Creativity, Color and Weaving Techniques; Subjective Choices; Relationship of Color to Subject; Modeling and Grading with Color; Personal Color Expression; Color Harmonies; Pure Color Fibers; Primary Colors and Triads; Faber Birren's Triangle.

Color

The weaver has fewer guidelines for color use than the painter. This opens an intriguing albeit occasionally threatening color vista. Everything the eye sees is in some color. Shapes are recognized because of the difference between their color and those surrounding them. Yet color, and fiber color in particular, is a subject in which we have had the least education and are most likely to be influenced by tradition-bound concepts.

We cannot avoid the influence of color even if we should wish to do so. We must, therefore, start thinking more as professionals and less from the bias of past limited instruction or color trends set up by others. Unless we step outside of our learned or acquired likes and dislikes, our color palette will remain anemic and dull.

Exercises in color use in other media are not always transferable to weaving. Basic principles may be learned by making samplers, but it is in the application of these principles to a work that they become truly understood. It is much more beneficial to produce a spontaneous, even if not fully realized, work than a routine color sampler. The learner develops an approach and attitude at the same time as color sensitivity.

Colors do not require as much decision-making in representational compositions as in abstract designs. If a color is not in keeping with what we expect to see in a recognizable shape, it is attributed to the eccentricity or lack of color training of the artist. As shapes move away from recognizable images, it becomes more important to investigate and work with color as such.

Combining creativity, color and weaving techniques

Most sources that deal with color in the creative visual arts tend toward a subjective rather than a rational approach. In handweaving, the bias has been toward a strict adherence to traditional doctrine. My own experience as a student, practicing weaver, and teacher suggests that color is one side of the triangle that prepares a tapestry weaver; so that aesthetic and creative sensibilities, color technology, and weaving techniques are all learned at the same time.

General color principles, as discussed here, are specifically geared to the needs of the weaver and the nature of fiber. Color relationships differ for pigment (subtractive color) or light (additive color). In working with fiber, color considerations will differ for yardage, wearing apparel, household goods such as linens or upholstery, or wall hangings and tapestries. It is probably true that some people are born with a greater sensitivity to color and that no discussion will teach color discrimination to those who do not have it. But willingness to put aside prejudices, and openness to new presentations, plus constant practice, will result in a marked growth of color awareness and understanding. I use the term color as an all-embracing visual experience derived from light. I include black and white with colors, although they are not part of the color spectrum.

To make color do what we want it to do requires not only understanding but mastery of the mechanics of color relationships. With color, more than any other design factor, individual feeling is the final guiding principle. Color perception and our ability to see color kinships which are constantly changing with each change in our environment is a selective process. Our color perceptions, likes, and dislikes are a subjective process, and their refining is part of the maturing that goes on throughout our lifetimes.

Subjective choices

Color choice is highly subjective and broadreaching. For some people, a certain color dominates and consciously or unconsciously some form of that color choice appears in all their work. If the choice is red, then blue or purple or whatever color is used will tend to lean towards red. Subjective choice also generally appears in other areas such as design orientation in terms of horizontality or verticality.

Visual arts evoke a response of feelings and/or emotions through the use of shapes and colors. If we eliminate color we have cut ourselves off from an important source of possible inspiration. We rarely see one color alone. It is always affected by those colors surrounding it or adjacent to it.

Criteria for absolute aesthetic values have never been established, as only that which can be measured can be agreed upon. Artistic standards for colors are not absolute, and individual color perception is highly subjective; we cannot, therefore, make definitive statements about "good" or "bad" color.

There is no one appropriate color for any one subject. It is how the color is used that makes us feel more or less comfortable with it. A color scheme for any tapestry must please the weaver first and foremost. It must also be relevant to the subject of the tapestry. Actually both of these requirements are the same, as it would be difficult to accomplish one without the other.

We must rethink our approach to color areas which dictate boundary lines. Colors have dimensions and directionality of their own which condition their shape if we permit them to do so. Color combinations and harmonies or disharmonies depend almost entirely on what we have been taught or have seen in our immediate environment, which is usually based on what our parents and teachers were taught and what they then taught us. They tended to avoid sharp contrasts with such adjectives as "agreeable", "harmonious" and "attractive" to define their judgements.

In practice, colors that are not usually considered harmonious, that "clash" or "repulse" each other, are excellent devices for expressing ideas which require such meanings. Matching and harmonizing colors serve learning purposes, but it becomes too easy to slip into a pattern in which they are the only usable combinations. It is meaningless to designate any color as beautiful or ugly. It depends on the other colors that are used with it, the amount of each color, its movement, value, saturation, etc. The eye has been taught to move smoothly from one color, tint, or shade to another. It does not like to jump, which so-called conflicting colors ask it to do.

Relationship of color to subject

Relationships between a color and an idea or an object become established and accepted. Colors are called blood red, butter yellow or pure white. In other variations of the color-object relationship, color is used as a symbol such as red for danger, yellow for cowardice and white for purity. A slight change in the color such as adding orange to red, or to yellow, or black to white, may change its reference completely. If such object or emotion-related colors are used, then the creative emphasis should be placed elsewhere than on the color, as the already established color-object relationship may be too difficult to overcome.

Our concern is with the reaction of one color to another rather than whether they harmonize or match or go together. Orange by itself appears one way. Orange abutted against blue looks different. How much is color affected by shape? Black looks black until a blacker black is brought close to the first one. Sometimes black looks blacker if it is next to a very dark blue. Much depends on the area or size of juxtaposed colors. If the areas are large, like a large checkerboard, strong differences in value and hue will cause startling visual effects. The same colors in very small amounts may cancel each other out as their individual strength diminishes.

To some extent, the more different colors concentrated in a given area, the less threatening or disturbing is their combination. When just a few colors are used that we feel cannot live together, their discord becomes evident. If these same discordant colors are mixed together with many others, their inability to get along with the others is tempered. Proportions of individual colors are also easier to determine when there are many colors than when there are a few. The medieval tapestries of the sixteenth and seventeenth centuries are excellent examples of this principle.

Modeling and grading with color

By modeling with color we mean changing the color or its lightness or darkness as the shape appears to be turned away or toward its source of light, thus producing a sense of depth or dimensionality. Modeling with fiber color is as possible as modeling with pigment color. It is important, though, to clearly differentiate that which weaving can learn from painting and that which does not apply because of the difference in the medium. If we persist in trying to impose a painterly approach to fiber, we do handweaving a disservice and place a huge obstacle in the path of our progress.

For example, in painting, lines may be used to contain or bound color areas. Lines superimposed on these color shapes sometimes break up and change them considerably. This line concept may be part of preparing a cartoon but it is not a major functional weaving technique. An outer border of a shape which is dark and cold, placed against a color that is light and warm, eliminates the need for a separating line. This line is not necessary when the contrast between the two shapes is clear and distinct.

In fiber it is quite difficult to grade subtly from light to dark or dark to light within one color or a group of colors used as a single weft unit. Unless the fiber has been specifically prepared for such a gradation, this is more easily accomplished with exact control and timing in the dye pot or in spinning.

Adding or subtracting mathematically, i.e., using a group of perhaps ten strands of the same color and adding a darker one, may work if the addition is closely related to those colors already in the core. If the addition is much darker or lighter, the first pick of the changed unit will be obvious. The only way I have found to gradually enter or smudge a color in is to include a single strand of the new weft in a hit and miss fashion for several picks before it is added to the total weft core. The effect of the sudden addition is thus dispersed.

If it were possible to have fibers in all colors, shades and tints, it would also be possible to set up mathematical rules for multiple color organizations. Since we don't, it is the skillful choice of those fiber colors that may be bought or that we dye ourselves that will enable us to achieve the desired effects, using our own color selection and association to create individually satisfying work.

Personal color expression

There are several ways of making color decisions. If one has no personal choices and has never really explored color or is afraid to do so, one can pick a favorite painter or teacher as an example and try to match fibers as close to their color combinations as possible. Some weavers move more confidently among the available yarn colors, choosing subjectively. The work of weavers of this group is often easily recognizable, since their designs and shapes may change but the colors frequently remain the same. A third group intuits the desired result and chooses a different color treatment to suit each subject. The idea dictates the placement and use of colors relative to each other, their values, proportions, textures and rhythmic relationships.

Weavers, as other artists, can take brush in hand and with a few strokes reproduce color charts and exercises to act as a guide. They must then, however, take the next step and translate these charts into fiber. Beginning weavers with limited capital for yarn purchases frequently work in reverse. They choose yarns that are appealing or from those that are available and then try to calculate what can be done with them.

Fine tapestry color combinations can seldom be reduced to any known color theory. It is the interaction between the yarn colors, as well as the visual vibrations that they set up that produce an equilibrium that pleases our eyes. The traditional color harmonies become less sufficient for our color needs as we discover that unswerving devotion to such theories may lead to banality and neutral choices that defeat our purposes.

Basic laws of color, form, proportion and rhythm are the foundations of Johannes Itten's concept of art education. Itten is particularly alert to the visual effects of simultaneous contrast. Much of the following discussion on color is based on his belief in spontaneity and personal expression supported by adequate knowledge, discipline and training. These ingredients apply as well to the use of fiber color in handweaving.

Itten bases his theory of color expression on the subconscious perception, inspiration and experience of each colorist. Color effects are more in the eye and feeling of the colorist than in the laws of physics or chemistry. Some can use color well without studying accepted theories. Others require the foundation of color systems upon which to build their compositions.

Many theories and systems have been conceived to chart the wide range of colors. Sir Isaac Newton (1642-1727) pioneered the color circle and determined that color WAS light. He related the number of colors to the seven then-known planets and to the seven notes of the diatonic music scale. Others found three-dimensional figures would better represent the intricacies in color gradations and combinations. Herman VonHelmholtz (1821-1894) determined the differences between light and pigment theories and recognized the different ways in which we see colors. He was the first to explain color blindness.

Ogden Rood (1831-1902) devised a double cone paradigm with white and black at either apex which became the model for the two best known colorists. One of them, Albert H. Munsell (1858-1918), based his system on a sphere, adding the dimensions of hue, value and chroma, and the other Wilhelm Ostwald (1853-1932), developed a double cone of measurable proportions of hues plus black and white. Many contemporary artists follow the color development of Faber Birren (1900-), whose color triangles are composed of 13 hues with nine steps between black and white.

While providing us with important models, the color principles of Ostwald and Munsell, on whose systems we rely so much today, have proved limiting for the weaver. Their generalities and rules of harmony and beauty simply do not serve us today, except as shackles, and there is reason to believe that there will be great changes in our views about color in the future.

Color harmonies

Everything we see is the result of light. Brightness and color help the eye discriminate between shapes and boundaries. Color and shape help us distinguish and identify, and both act as media for expression.

Many color combinations used by artists do not fit into any of the recognized color systems. The term color harmony implies that the colors "fit together" somehow — leading to a simplistic conformity which may be satisfactory for matching parts of a clothing scheme or a living room, although such homogeneity is often dull and unimaginative. Tapestries based on such color schemes may be peaceful but would probably be as dull as the clothes or rooms. Artists reject such conformity in other media, realizing that many so-called harmonies are expressions of passing fashion.

Nonetheless there is a body of work which, when studied and understood, can guide our efforts toward some form of personal color expression. There has to be some organization or else we will be awash in a mishmash of color.

Weavers have resorted to trial and error color methods for years because the theories they were offered did not relate to the medium within which they were working. Making color choices by trial and error is, however, a slow, painstaking and often frustrating process since the weaver cannot overlay as the painter overpaints. The tapestry weaver must unweave or take out each pick individually as well as those picks in shapes that overlap the undesirable ones. It is necessary, therefore, to become familiar with the various color systems and adapt them to our own needs.

Pure color fibers

The uniqueness or differences in the colors each of us sees is the result of the organization in each individual's eye and the resulting recognition in the mind, none of which need be related to the chemical makeup of pigments.

Just as humans can easily discriminate eight steps between black and white, they can also discriminate eight steps between each of the primary colors. These steps do not have universally accepted names, although when we mention a color like turquoise, we can usually agree what it looks like. In the eight steps between yellow and blue, for instance, there are several shades of leaf-green, which has more yellow, and sea green which has more blue but retains some recognizable yellow. There is also some turquoise which has lost almost all of its yellow. These may all be considered pure colors or hues, totally free of black or white. Pure colors, though, are rarely seen in our everyday environment or in fiber.

Each pure color may be graded up to white or down to black in eight distinguishable steps, and it is these gradations and non-pure colors from which we have to choose in most commercially dyed fibers. When we experience difficulty in finding a particular color, it is usually because we are rarely offered pure colors as choices. Because of the peculiarities of dye chemistry, there are certain colors which are difficult to dye in a pure state. Searching for a true red which contains neither orange nor blue is usually a fruitless task. A deep navy blue fiber is always difficult to find. Add to this all of the modifications that may occur when a color's complement or white or black are added, and the search for pure hues becomes even more formidable.

In their desire to go beyond the limits of commercially available fiber colors, more and more weavers are familiarizing themselves with and learning how to use synthetic dyes. Another good solution, although not usually available to beginning weavers, is to have an accessible dye house which understands the needs and requirements of weavers, who will work with them in supplying them in large or small quantities. Through experimentation, many weavers have attained interesting results by overdyeing already available colors. After some experience, they are able to control the results.

The use of color and what may be evoked with its infinite combinations and variations is gaining recognition by contemporary tapestry weavers, but our understanding of the properties and refinements that are possible in color in fiber is at an early stage.

Primary colors and triads

Most weavers eventually arrive at their own ways of organizing colors. There are, however, some recognized systems which can be used as reference. Beginning with Sir Isaac Newton and followed by Ives, Munsell, Ostwald and Prang, all have some terminology in common upon which we base our use of color. The Prang color system and the color wheel with which we are most familiar use the three primary colors of red, yellow and blue. The color wheel is really a spectrum shaped into a circle for the sake of convenience in visualizing color relationships.

Primary colors are not related. They are distinct and in opposition but at the same time need each other. One strong red shape can bring out the red components in the colors around it. They are unique in that they cannot be created by mixing other colors, but can be mixed with each other in varying proportions to produce other colors, and if a color wheel is spun around to visually mix all the primaries, they will each absorb a part of the light spectrum and appear together as black or brown.

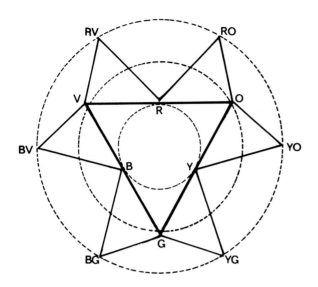

Fig. 2. *The color wheel.*

A triad is composed of three colors an equal number of steps removed from each other on the color wheel. The most easily recognizable triads are:
1. red, yellow, blue
2. orange, green, violet
3. red-orange, yellow-green, blue-violet
4. yellow-orange, blue-green, red-violet.

The first triad appears most forceful and direct, the second more refined and discriminating, the third more violent and startling, and the fourth appears in our eyes to have an oriental quality.

Any number of triads may be found on the color wheel and each has its own quality. In the red-orange, yellow-green and blue-violet triad, the red-orange which is close to the yellow-green offers a warm relationship. The blue-violet moves from the

red-orange, from warm light to cool shadow, and the yellow-green acts as a passage between the warm and cool extremes.

The primary triad of red, yellow and blue is classic, strong and aggressive and is one to which contemporary artists return again and again. Individually, each of these colors is strong and when two of them are mixed, the resulting tones have considerable color and strength. In equal proportions, these three can become jarring; but when the proportions and positions vary or when they are separated by neutrals such as gray or if one color is emphasized more than the other two, they can be striking. This triad may be found in many old tapestries, but their brilliance has faded with time which is one of the reasons we are not so startled by them.

A tetrad is composed of four colors which are three steps removed from each other on the color wheel as red, orange-yellow, green and blue-violet.

Although yellow is the lightest color on the color wheel, the circle is arranged with red at the top because it is the one with which we are most familiar.

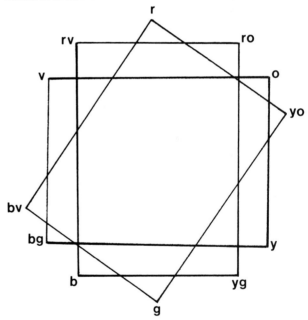

Fig. 4. *Three tetrad harmonies.*

Color wheels are usually shown in segments as though red is distinctly separated from yellow. Actually, there is a continuous blending from one to the other, one color merging into the next without a break. If we think of colors from this perspective there are many more variations on color relationships than we might ordinarily consider.

Faber Birren's triangle

The well-known colorist Faber Birren developed his color triangle based on principles arrived at by Michel Eugene Chevreul (1786-1889) who, while

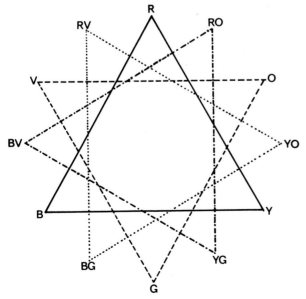

Fig. 3. *Four triad harmonies.*

directing the dyehouse at the Gobelin Tapestry Works, investigated the laws of visual color mixtures. Birren's principles of tints, shades and tones can be of use to the handweaver. He says that considering white and black as colors, they may be used in the four following ways:

1. Combining black and white results in gray.
2. Combining white with a color results in a tint.
3. Combining black with a color results in a shade.
4. Combining white and black with a color results in a tone.

The sequence of the passage from a pure color through its various tints into white is one which seems to be satisfying to the human eye. Perhaps because it is so often found in nature, this progression has become a frequent choice of artists. There is a freshness in the transition which is appealing and comforting. Weavers find the discrete subtle movements of clear color to tint difficult to achieve unless the graded tints have been anticipated in the dyepot. They must frequently content themselves with

the more abrupt use of the hatching technique to move from red through pink to white.

The passage of a color through its shades as it darkens into black offers a depth of color and richness not obtainable in the tinting sequence. The smooth movement of color to black seems to be easier to achieve in fibers than its opposite, color to white.

In the Birren triangle, color moves through tint to white on the right, through tone to gray in the middle and through shade to black on the left. The base line takes us from black through gray to white or back.

The tint, tone, shade sequence across the middle is considered one of the most discriminative, expressive and yet delicate, going beyond just adding white for tinting and black for shading. A color appears purer by being highlighted rather than whitened, and shadowed rather than blackened. This delineation of subtle movement from light to dark or the reverse is not easy to achieve in pigment and even more difficult to carry off in fiber, but well worth the effort.

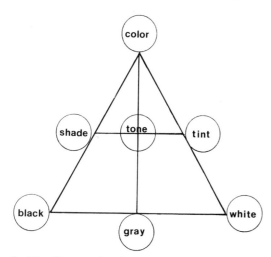

Fig. 5. *The Birren triangle.*

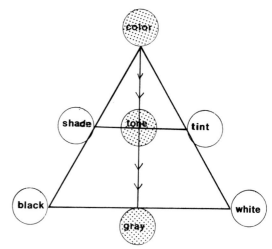

Fig. 7. *Color to tone to gray.*

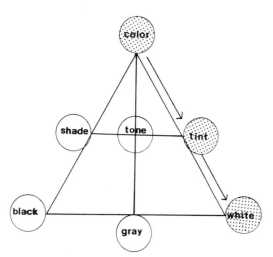

Fig. 6. *Color to tint to white.*

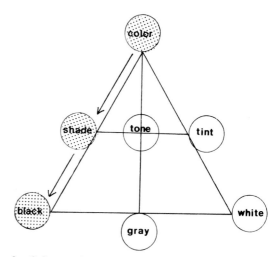

Fig. 8. *Color to shade to black.*

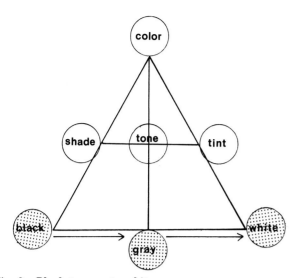

Fig. 9. *Black to gray to white.*

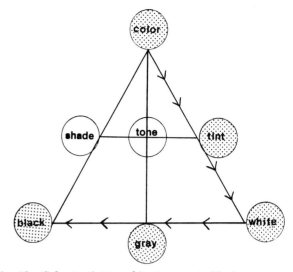

Fig. 12. *Color to tint to white to gray to black.*

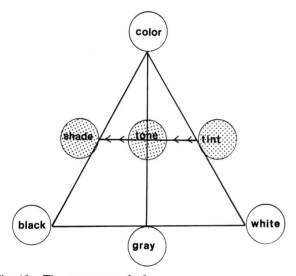

Fig. 10. *Tint to tone to shade.*

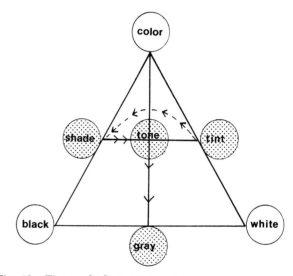

Fig. 13. *Tint to shade to tone to gray.*

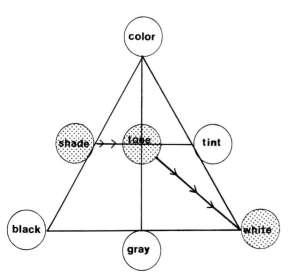

Fig. 11. *Shade to tone to white.*

In the shade, tone, white progression, the lighter value is pure and the deeper value grayish, the exact opposite of tint, tone, black. An example of this is a rich shade of green, which, whitened at one end of the gradation, gives a somewhat unearthly effect.

Color to tint to white to gray to black is a classic harmony that works particularly well when a pure primary or secondary color is used.

Tertiary colors result from mixing primary and secondary colors. For instance, purple and orange produce rust, green and orange produce citron and green and purple produce olive.

Tint, shade, tone and gray blend with tertiary colors in a limited way that offers combinations that appear more achromatic and neutral, creating a subdued quality. This sequence is useful for woven landscapes in which receding distance is an important element.

Light values in color are measured by numerical ratios. These ratios are difficult to achieve in painting unless the painter starts out deliberately planning a work that will only contain pure colors such as blue and orange, knowing that blue has half the numerical value of orange. In fiber, since we rarely have pure colors available to us, light value ratios are almost impossible to control. As soon as the purity of a color is altered, its light ratio changes. The most that can be said for this principle in weaving terms is that smaller areas of pure color tend to assert themselves and from this, interesting effects may be achieved. Choices of color areas are better made by their color intensity than by their mathematical ratios.

VI
COLOR — ITS CHARACTER

Hue; Value; Saturation; Weaving with Natural Colors; Black, White and Gray; Mono-chromatic Color System; Analagous Color System; Complementary Color System; Split Complementary Color System; Light; Brightness; Gradation; Dominant Color System; Simultaneous Color Contrast; Luminosity; Transparency; Hue Temperature Illusions; Movement in Color.

As our understanding of fiber color increases, our terminology becomes more refined. It is generally agreed that color has three basic properties. There is accord on the first two, hue and value. The third is called saturation by some and intensity by others.

Hue

Hue is the name given to a color in its purest form and the term that distinguishes it from other colors. Mixing one with another will result in a new hue. It is the first feature of a color that we notice. Those hues that are closest together on the color wheel are considered most compatible.

When we first start using colors it sometimes seems that we have used up all the colors and there are not enough new ones available. It is only through continued experimentation with the possibilities within each hue that we realize that the opposite is true, that working with the values of each hue gives us an inexhaustible palette.

Colors are rarely used or seen alone. They relate and/or contrast and their perception is so compelling that sometimes they appear entirely different than expected. When two different colors are woven alongside of each other the difference between them will be intensified by their contrast. If the two colors are more alike than different, they will not affect each other as much. If the two colors are more strongly contrasted, there is more interaction between them.

The fiber artist uses material that has color *in* it rather than color *on* it. Some contemporary experimentation with color and fiber has led weavers to consider color fields, completely ignoring content and design, an approach which would not have been thought of a few years ago. New aspects of the relationship between color and the eye are being explored. There is an indication in current research, for instance, that the physiology of the eye is directly affected by thoughts, feelings and emotions. When an unpleasant sight is seen, the pupil of the eye is thought to contract, admitting less light. When something that is agreeable is seen, the pupil of the eye opens wider to admit more light.

It is difficult to imagine a shape without color. The Impressionists elevated the role of color from being subordinate to design. Color has come to assume an equal if not foremost position. Traditionally, though, color has been subservient to shape in that it imitated that shape or filled it out. Rocks were thought of as gray, therefore they were painted gray, disregarding their three dimensionality and striations which gave them their rock formation. The late Renaissance painters were most skillful in copying what they thought they saw. Many of today's painters are more concerned with the use of color itself than in their photographic ability to copy.

The relative importance of light, color and shape has gone through several phases, starting with light functioning in a subordinate position primarily to reveal shapes and color, through the period when color assumed an independent existence, through light functioning to reveal color, to the present where light and shapes are considered one and the same.

This approach to color is not just a passing fancy. Color has ceased to be used merely as a decoration and has become inherent to design. It is therefore important that weavers working with color take the time to determine whether their preferences are solely conditioned by their upbringing or are mature personal choices.

It is, incidentally, a fantasy that women have different color preferences from men. As the entrenched conventions of the past are broken down, so do color preferences between the sexes disappear.

Value

Value is a term used for the proportions of light and dark reflected from a surface, ranging in scale from pure white at one extreme to the blackest black at the other. Changing the value or lightness or darkness of one or more colors may make a whole group compatible, which it might not otherwise be. Adding white, black or gray raises or lowers the value of a color. This is particularly important when we take into consideration the over and under interlacement in weaving where the same fiber is brightest as it reaches its most reflective position before starting to bend again.

We can control value change by the amount of white, black and gray which is added. This will also cause a change in hue. For instance, the color green can be achieved in several ways. We can mix blue and yellow or we can create an entirely different green by adding black to green, thus lowering the value and changing the color. Actually, the black acts as though it were blue to achieve this effect.

In weaving, value transitions may be abrupt or smooth; but they must be planned and not happen by chance, or their usefulness is reduced. We relate sharp value contrasts to concepts such as exactness, precision, vitality or enthusiasm. Values that are less sharp, that move toward grayness, suggest such terms as indefiniteness, formlessness and vagueness. Strong contrasts suggest strong determined movement. As the contrast becomes weaker the movement slows down or ceases altogether. Value may thus be as important as a tool as color or shape or texture.

Every color has value, light or dark or any degree in-between. Our awareness of the contrast in colors is heightened when their values are similar. Imagine, for instance, placing deep purple or blue next to black, and then next to white. It will seem more related to the black — because of similarity in value — even though the black and white are of the same intensity. The relation of a color to black (darker), or white (lighter), is an indication of a change in its value and not its hue.

Saturation

Saturation, or intensity, or chroma, all refer to the degree of purity of a color. A color is diluted, or less saturated or intense, when its complement or black or white is added. Different colors having the same value are not necessarily at their highest point of saturation, and vice versa. For instance, when they are in their most saturated state, yellow and orange are higher in value than saturated blue or violet.

Most color combinations take into consideration the saturation of each color used. The general rule has been that very few strongly saturated colors should be used together. As the saturation in inindividual colors decreased, the number of colors which were permitted increased. Observation of contemporary use of color, though, proves how successfully such rules have been broken.

Unlike the painter, tapestry weavers cannot in-

crease the saturation of a yarn color by adding more layers of the same color. The addition of more picks or ply will increase the bulk but will not change the saturation. For the weaver, the use of the theory of saturation is most applicable in the dye pot. Once the yarn has been dyed, its intensity remains the same. Nor can we use transparent colors. The closest we can approach the painting technique of layering or overpainting in weaving is to use a film or filament that is transparent as a second layer on top of a ground layer that has color.

While intensity changes are more easily made in the dye pot, a very fine (thin) gray or green yarn added to a field of red will suggest some of the same effect. Of the six colors of the wheel, a pure yellow is more readily found in fiber than any other. Most greens look more yellow or more blue and most reds lean toward orange or violet. Weaving with a yellow-blue adjacent to a green-blue will produce a different effect than the use of yellow, blue and green individually. In the first combination, blue does not appear alone, permitting a more gradual color movement. In the second combination, the movement is not smooth but rather an abrupt break between colors.

Weaving with natural colors

It is believed that the addition of one or more neutral colors such as beige or light gray will help almost any color scheme. They are also reputed to help weld bright colors together. Like any other general rule, this applies in some instances and not at all in others.

There is a large range of white and off-white that attracts handweavers. White has a pristine or primitive quality, which unless used carefully and in proper proportion can become pallid. By themselves, various whites are usually not enough to sustain a piece. There has to be some intrinsic interest other than added textural differences. Confining color to the limits that pure white and related whites offer, or adding so-called neutrals, is frequently resorted to by handweavers intimidated by colors.

Colors in nature follow their own laws of sequence and balance. Colors in nature and in pigment are not identical, and their sequences, mixtures and balances are usually quite different from those in fiber. They are rarely flat and totally of one hue; and they tend to be textured, containing an intermingling of hues.

Black, white and gray

Black and white are considered colors by some and not by others. For our purposes, since they are used in producing shades or tints of colors as well as being important in their own right, we consider them and use them as colors.

Black and white are extremes of darkness and light and tend to dominate compositions in which they are used in large amounts. They can be very effective when used in discrete proportions. Although white is closer to the warm colors, it is actually a cool tone and black, absorbing the most light, is a warm tone.

In pigment or fiber, a white shape on a black ground looks larger than a black shape on a white ground. White has a way of overflowing its boundaries and black has a tendency to contract. An example of this phenomenon may be seen when you try to decide the size of a tapestry on a colored wall. If a white sheet is used as a gauge, the tapestry, which is not white, will look much smaller. In the same way, yellow shapes look darker on white ground and more brilliant surrounded by black or dark colors. Red will look darker on white and have very little brilliance, whereas the same red may become luminous when placed on or next to black. This effect is generally referred to as simultaneity and suggests that one way of thinking about weaving a project could begin with color which would then generate the shape. This is not the approach to which most of us are accustomed, but it offers an interesting alternative.

Black and white are respectively of lowest and highest value. If the weaver wishes to achieve the effect of a true black, a color difficult to obtain in fiber, no strong color should be placed adjacent to or cutting through it because the black will take on that color's complement and lose some of its blackness.

Gray has always played an important role for painters, but its use has not been as significant among fiber artists. By itself, gray may be lifeless; but it is instantly altered by an adjoining color since it depends on its neighboring colors for spirit and individuality. Any color may be lightened or darkened by adding white or black for light and dark contrasts. The weaver achieves this in the dyepot or by adding a specific amount of white and/or black fiber during the weaving process. The effect is, of course, entirely different, and the desired end result is the guide as to which approach is to be taken.

There is a tendency among beginning weavers to use many colors in one piece of work because their visual threshold has not been stretched to the possibilities within each color. As the weaver develops color sensitivity as applied to fiber, the number of colors used in one piece tends to diminish and gives way to more subtle interplay.

Color is seen in its greatest intensity in the first fraction of a second of the first look. Immediately thereafter the intensity decreases rapidly. It follows, therefore, that neutral areas in a design reactivate the intensity of color sensations. In the same way,

low intensity colors such as grayish blues become more apparent when placed next to neutral gray. With pure gray we need only consider its value, as it has neither intensity nor hue. Gray acts as an illusive leveler of all color contrasts and absorbs, accepts or changes, depending upon its adjacent color.

Gray is warmer or cooler depending on the ratios of the adjacent colors. It will tend to be cooler if more blue than orange is used. If more orange than blue is used, it will tend to be warmer. If the gray is mixed out of black and white alone it will likely be neutral. Understanding the sources and uses of gray expands the weaver's palette in a way that is all too frequently overlooked.

One of the solutions to the competition among colors in large areas is to separate them with neutral shapes or borders of gray or black. The leading in stained-glass windows is an example of this effect. No matter how unrelated the separated colors, each retains its own value and intensity because of the separation.

Some artists consider gray to be an enemy of all color because it robs them of their color. Gray can be warm or cool, depending on its use. It becomes warmer and softer when it is next to beige and cooler and harder when it is next to black. The so-called earth colors behave in similar ways. They vary from the faintest off-white to the deepest browns, including the various colors of woods, stones and earth. The major quality they all share is a lack of vibrancy. This includes ochre, sienna, umber, earth reds and charcoal blacks.

The result of mixing colors with grays in pigments or dyes may be very useful. For instance, subtle olive tones result from mixing yellow with different grays. Although juxtaposing colored yarns doesn't result in this sort of mixed color, certain grays, when placed next to certain yellows, will result in an olive cast.

Spinning color discs in varying proportions is the classic way of demonstrating color mixtures, the assumption being that the demonstration will be followed by exercises in mixing pigments to achieve similar results. If colored fibers are spun (by gluing them to rotating discs) the resulting color mixtures will be quite similar to the colored paper mixtures. In fiber, however, the application is totally different. Once the fiber is dyed, colors will not mix unless they are blended in the spinning. We must therefore think of fiber colors as juxtapositions of color.

Monochromatic color system

Colors may be combined in two ways, those that are related and those that contrast.

The first classification includes monochromatic

colors, which rely on changes in value and intensity within one color, and analagous colors, which are close to each other on the color wheel and have a hue in common. The second classification includes complementary colors which are opposed to each other and split complementary colors in which one color combines with the hues on either side of its complement.

Monochromatic color schemes can be boring or exciting, depending on how they are used. Mixing a single color with various proportions of black and white produces a wide range of color tones which belies the supposed limitations in the use of only one color. The value or variations of a basic color can change a single color system from dull to pleasing. There can be an organization of a strong contrast of intensities and values or a subdued graying with a strong contrast. There can be a smooth gradation of tones that lead to or away from the most intense hue.

There is a proclivity, especially in contemporary geometric shapes, to weave large flat areas in one unchanging monochromatic color scheme. Theorists generally classify as monotonous such use with no value relief, intensity or color gradations in pigment. In weaving, interlacement and texture encourage the use of such unchanging color areas. Weaving within a monochromatic system can be a challenge for exploration of the possibilities of one color which is not present when other colors are added.

Analogous color system

Analogous colors are adjacent colors that enrich and strengthen each other. They always have one hue in common with usually one color predominating, supported by two colors that lie on either side of

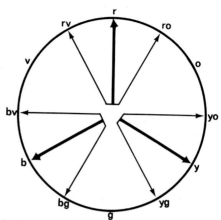

Fig. 2. *Analogous color system and primary colors.*

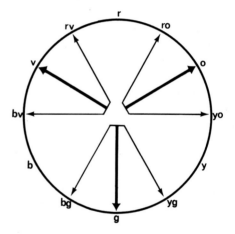

Fig. 3. *Analogous color system and secondary colors.*

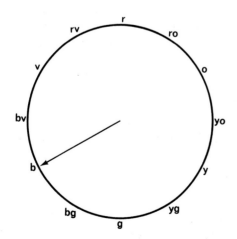

Fig. 1. *Monochromatic color system.*

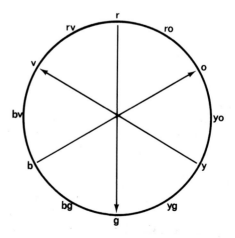

Fig. 4. *Complementary color system and primary colors.*

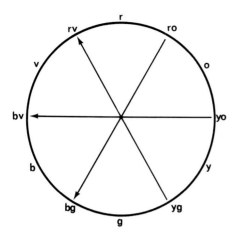

Fig. 5. *Complementary color system and secondary colors.*

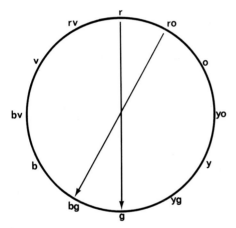

Fig. 6. *Double complementary color system.*

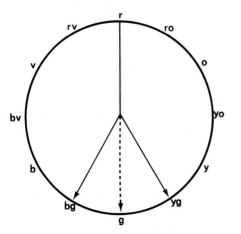

Fig. 7. *Split complementary color system.*

it on the color wheel. Colors that are close to each other appear to reinforce one another through visual oscillation which adds richness and depth. Some analogous relationships are more interesting than others, but all lack a varietal aliveness which can be supplied by opposition.

Analogous color schemes are most useful for fiber workers when the major color is some version of one of the primary colors, red, yellow or blue.

1. Red with red-violet and red-orange
2. Yellow with yellow-orange and yellow-green
3. Blue with blue-violet and blue-green

Secondary colors, orange, green and violet behave in the same way:

1. Orange with red-orange and yellow-orange
2. Green with blue-green and yellow-green
3. Violet with blue-violet and red-violet

Such arrangements are frequently seen and are among those with which most people are ordinarily comfortable. The relationship between analogous colors tends to get lost in large color areas but is more apparent in smaller ones. The affinity between orange and red is much clearer when these two colors abut each other in many places than when there is only one place where they meet. The same two colors next to each other in small areas, such as spots or short lines, cancel each other out unless they are separated by a ground color.

In fiber it is difficult to duplicate the flame glow of a red poppy or the gleam of polished metal. Even the closest fiber colors do not approach the original. The skillful use of analogous colors, however, makes it possible to approach their richness and vibrancy.

Complementary color system

Complementary colors may either complement or contrast. If there is a doubt about the true complement of a color, one has but to gaze steadily at it until the eyes are fatigued and then look away at a white or gray ground. The afterimage takes a few moments to reach its full intensity and then starts fading away. Even though the complementary afterimage is always paler and quickly disappears, it is a useful clue.

When the results of mixing two complementary pigments is gray, they are accepted as complementary. With fibers which cannot be mixed, as in paint, we must rely on the visual afterimage. Complementary colors have opposing effects on each other. Orange and blue may be clashing and disruptive or at the same time brighten the intensity of their opposites. When the intensity of two opposites is low, this enhancing effect may not be as obvious, but it is present nonetheless.

When two complementary pigment colors are mixed, they cancel each other out. When two complementary fiber colors are mixed together in equal amounts, as on one bobbin, they agitate each other, do not mix, and each appears with less strength. When the same two complementary colors are adjacent to each other in two shapes, each brings out the richness of the other. Each color has only one complement and the amazing appearance of the after image points up the physical need for the eye to achieve an equilibrium.

After weaving and looking at large areas of yellow, orange or red, we instinctively reach for some blue or green. If the smaller areas of blue or green appear too brilliant, their effect can be modified by separating them with neutral colors such as beige or a soft gray, although it is sometimes a challenge to remain with a strong color scheme.

Comfortable color combinations remind us of recognizable relationships and rekindle pleasant memories. We are content with certain complementary colors, but accept, although only for certain occasions, red and green in Christmas ornaments because of our familiarity and emotional response to their combination. Yellow and purple, which are equally complementary, are less easily acceptable to us because our culture has not used them to such an extent as familiar symbols.

Complementary colors in shapes that cut across each other, as compared to those that are stationary and isolated, appear to be in motion and their activity is intensified. Using complementary colors in more subtle relationships, such as in a hills and valleys composition, will make the composition come alive, as compared to one using pale colors and neutrals.

In each pair of complementary colors there is one warm and one cool color and this opposition in temperature can be reduced or increased depending on how they are used in terms of degree and position.

Opposite colors tend to add brilliance and purity to each other without any apparent change in hue. Analogous colors, on the other hand, influence each other. With yellow and orange side by side, the violet afterimage of the yellow will tend to swing the apparent hue of the orange toward red, while the blue afterimage of the orange will make the orange appear greenish. With red and violet, the green afterimage of the red will make the violet appear bluish, while the yellow afterimage of the violet will swing the red toward vermillion.

A composition that uses opposing colors in one part may provoke dramatic tension, while in another part of the work, analogous colors may satisfy the eye's need for completion and balance. When one color is present the eye desires to "complete" it by calling up its complement. It is a form of fulfillment as well as an expression of opposites.

A few inches of woven yellow next to a few inches of woven purple will bring out the intensity of each, whereas if the same two colors are wound on the same bobbin or in a butterfly and entered as one weft, a striated effect will result with neither color being put to its full use. While the two opposites are being wound together, they appear to blend because of the speed with which the yarns are moving, but as soon as the motion ceases they return to their original color state.

When two complementary color yarns that are similar in type are woven together as one weft in a shed, they may be entered either as parallel to each other or twisted around each other. In the first instance they will appear as narrow lines. In the second, if the twist is consistently clockwise, they will appear as a right diagonal twill. A counterclockwise twist will look like a left diagonal twill. In neither case will they blend. If these colors are yellow and violet, neither will change in hue, but the intensity of the yellow will decrease. If the violet is finer than the yellow, it will gray the yellow a little. If more violet is added, the graying process increases but the yellow never actually blends with its complement. If the proportions are reversed and more yellow is added to the violet, the same holds true. No matter how much yellow is added, the violet fibers will remain violet. Even with eight or more strands of violet and one strand of yellow, the yellow will not merge with the violet. It will retain its own hue although weakened in intensity.

Not only may colors be complementary, but there is a duality, an opposition as between romantic and classic, objective and non-objective, negative and positive. Compositions that encompass opposition are more likely to have a dynamic equilibrium creating a more vital whole. Opposing colors, with their strength and vibrancy, intensify dynamism which can be achieved in few other ways.

Complementary colors do not have to be exactly opposite each other in their position on the wheel. Each of the two or more colors may have more or less of the adjacent color or black or white in them and still be considered complementary. Actually this pairing of opposites of more subtle complementary colors is one of the best tools the fiber artist has and leads to split complementaries which are even better tools.

Split complementary color system

Split complementaries are a color and the two that lie on either side of its exact opposite. Yellow-green and blue-green are the split of green which is the direct opposite of red. This is a more subtle opposition than the direct one, red to green and is particularly applicable in fiber where the direct opposite is sometimes harsh.

Split complementary colors offer somewhat different qualities than those of direct opposites. The triteness of the exact color wheel opposition is avoided while at the same time the "opposition" interest is sustained.

The more subtle the colors, the more split complementaries are involved and the greater the number of colors that must be considered. It is at this point that proportions of colors and accents are most important. Equal amounts of split complementary colors of equal value might be an interesting challenge as an exercise but are very difficult for the weaver to achieve, even if an experienced dyer is standing by to provide them. Using the same yarn and type of dye, different colors are absorbed in different proportions and their values become unequal. Using certain colors as accents, rather than in equal proportions in split complementary systems, is one solution.

In split complementaries, the intensity of the fiber color is decreased because the color on one side of the color wheel is opposed by the two colors on the opposite side. Since they don't mix as pigment would, they never cancel each other out to become neutral. The two hues on either side of the color that has been split are equal in quality to the true complement and its opposite, as both sides of the split contain the true complement.

Blue is the complement of orange. Its split complement is blue-green and blue-violet, both of which contain blue. In fiber, if both the green and the violet have a strong blue component, we approach actual mixing, as in pigment, as closely as possible and achieve effects which orange and blue alone cannot. The presence of the green and violet softens and subdues the intensity of the pure orange.

Split complementary colors offer an intermediary step. A blue sky that has a faint tint of red-violet and/or blue-violet, its split complement, will appear much more blue and less flat. The split does not have to be confined to the exact color on each side of the complement. The two radii of the split can move on around the circle to the next colors. In the case of blue this would be red and yellow which make orange in pigment. In fiber, however, these have moved so far apart that their affinity is lost and we have a color triad in which the three hues are at about equal intervals.

Light

Every surface or shape has the faculty of reflecting and absorbing light. Since each surface has a different spatial position with respect to the light

In essence, sight is more than pure sensation. It also involves the organization of light rays in the mind into significant proportional entities. As light rays enter the eye, the mind organizes the nervous impulses that they trigger. The transparency of air, the brightness of light, and the light-splitting quality of the fluidity of water are among the most difficult concepts to achieve in a tapestry.

The "color" of the light completely changes the appearance of a fiber color. Light appears white when all visible radiations are present in an equal intensity. If certain parts of the spectrum are missing, they will not be reflected and what is seen will vary according to the missing parts. It is important to recognize that the electric light bulb casts a yellowish warm light as compared to the cold light usually cast by fluorescent light so that colors appear different under each.

Obviously the fiber surfaces that face the light rays will receive and reflect the most light. As these recede from the light, they get darker, although the color is the same. The light reflected from an object comes directly from the surface without any change of color. The light that penetrates some of the surface of the object has some of its rays absorbed in its passage. Weavers' problems spring from the absorption and reflection which are multiplied many times because of the variety of yarns, their different bulk, ply, spin and dye and the interlacement of the weave.

Objects reflect light to different degrees with sharp borders causing an edge to the light and round objects creating a gradation of light. Objects in front of each other block the light, casting shadows, and small objects scatter light. Irregular surfaces like woven ones scatter light in minute amounts in all directions.

In other media light is used much more in interaction between highly absorptive and reflective materials, on incised and raised surfaces, on edges and on transparent and perforated areas. In weaving this use of light is mainly limited to large or small slits.

Brightness

Brightness is a function of both intensity and value. Colorists who are concerned with pigment insist that the brilliance of a color should not be confused with saturation or purity. These differences are not so clear in fiber use, especially today when we combine so many different fibers in one yarn that accept or reject color in different ways. With certain dyes a fiber mixture of cotton and linen will result in the linen accepting a more brilliant color than the cotton, which remains lighter and duller. So much depends on the type of fibers that are mixed and the type of dye used that no hard and fast rules concerning brilliance can be laid down.

In rayon and wool combinations, the wool color will usually be deeper and darker and the rayon color will be lighter and shinier. When several different wools are blended into one strand, or several different wool fibers are plied together, or different plied wools are used together, the only rule that can be applied is the sensitized choice of the weaver.

If the weaver is working on only one project, the color choices do not have to be as well organized as if other versions of the same project are being woven in other color combinations which must have similar relationships. If more than one color combination is offered, then the original colors must be chosen to anticipate the same effect of brilliance and contrast in each separate version.

The amount of light that reflects off a surface determines the brightness of a color. It is sometimes difficult to distinguish between the brightness and illumination of an object as these may be the properties of the object itself. The brightness of an object depends on the distribution of the brightness values of the total area.

A white shape in a tapestry does not depend on the amount of light it reflects so much as on its brightness relationship to the shapes around it. A white shape surrounded by light grays and beiges will not look nearly as white as it would if surrounded by other darker colors or black. A bright white shape in a satin weave or of silk or mercerized cotton will reflect more light and will therefore not require as much contrast with its surroundings as a textured white shape woven in wool, which absorbs more light.

Luminosity appears as an inherent property of the surface of a lighted object. It is as though the surface is like a transparent film through which the color of the object shines.

Designs for tapestries may be organized as either being lit from some obvious source such as the sun or a lamp or as though bathed in light without any specific source. When these light sources are confused, the effect of the work may be decreased. Weavers must, therefore, be clear in their planning. When an arch shape is meant to be seen as if in a third dimension, the additional dimension may be suggested by a shadow which would be cast by a distinct source of light. The same shape will remain flat in appearance, like a hole in a design, when the light is all-pervasive and does not appear to stem from any one source or direction.

When light is obviously coming from one distinct source, various degrees of shadows appear and some places are lighter than others. Weavers can use these shadings and highlights, which may not be correct from the point of view of the laws of illumination, but which better serve their purpose.

Many classical Renaissance tapestries used the device of overlapping trees, flowers, animals and people to create depth. The gradual lightening and darkening of the same plane without relation to the light source and with contradiction to light rules is a well known technique. Buildings are darkened next to the sky, shapes are darker than their surroundings, regardless of the light source.

In choosing colors for a composition, holding two yarns alongside of each other will offer a suggestion of the result; but it is necessary to weave a few picks of each before their real effect will be apparent. Light falls and reflects quite differently from unwoven yarns than it does from interlaced ones, especially if the warp is visible in the net result.

Gradation

In gradation, colors pass more or less imperceptibly into each other. Purple and orange are contrasting colors; but if red is placed between them, running from purple-red through red-orange, the two outside colors, purple and orange, are drawn together and become more compatible.

Gradation from dark to light or small to large is one means of suggesting movement. Gradation makes full use of the value scale. Graded steps form a natural order for shapes to enlarge or diminish in size as well as for colors to lighten or darken. Combining gradation and repetition is a useful design tool in weaving where one shape grades down in size and becomes lighter in color as it recedes.

Dominant color system

A dominant color system uses a single overall color to draw other colors together. It is as though a group of unrelated colors is infiltrated and tied together by one other color. In painting this is frequently accomplished with a transparent wash. With fibers, we cannot overlay with a transparent color, but one color may be added to a group of other colors to help tie them all together.

There is a natural law of harmony in which those colors that range around yellow such as orange, yellow-orange and yellow-green are said to adapt easily to tinting or lightening. The closest that this law can be approached in weaving is by using these colors as weft on a white or off-white warp which remains exposed to some extent. Assuming a 50/50 cloth or close to it, a contrast is achieved rather than a thinning of the colors. The only one that appears a little lighter is yellow, and only if the yellow is low in saturation.

On the other side of the wheel, colors such as

red, red-violet, violet, blue-violet and blue are enhanced by a dark warp which brings out their brilliance. Of course, when the weaving has a weft face, the color of the warp is of negligible importance. In a weft-face tapestry, the color of the warp must be considered when a heavy warp has visible fibers which extend out beyond the weft covering. On such a warp, like a very rough linen, even the most brilliant weft will be somewhat dulled.

Some wefts are blends or plies of different fiber types which do not take dyes in the same way. For instance, in a wool-rayon blend dyed with an acid dye, the wool will accept color readily while the rayon accepts very little or none at all. In such a yarn, the part of the fiber that is not compatible with the dye type being used will remain white or a shade of gray and have a softening effect on the color, making it appear like a pastel. Heather yarns are a common example of this effect; the kempy fibers in the wool yarn remain white, giving a "frosted" appearance.

When a colored light is thrown on a design that already has some colors, a chromatic light effect results and different colors are affected in different ways. The weaver can simulate this effect by adding the same color in each shed in which the other colors are entered. The color that is added to all the others acts as a harmonizing agent, making it possible to use colors that would otherwise be considered incompatible. The added color must be subtle and the yarn fine, or else it will overpower the other colors instead of influencing them.

Simultaneous color contrast

No object can be considered to have an intrinsic color. With each different light the color will appear to change as the light changes at different times of the day. Each pair of eyes will see it a little differently since no eyes see things the same color and no two brains interpret them in the same way. Artists work with the illusion of simultaneous contrasts, but this contrast is of limited use to the fiber artist.

One of the ways in which simultaneous color contrast may be used offers the weaver an opportunity to make a limited number of colors do the work of a larger number, by judicious placement of adjoining colors. The same two colors will give one effect when placed next to each other and appear quite different when separated by other colors. It is a contrast effect in which the visual stimulation of one color brings out a reaction to its opposite.

The appearance of hues is subject to considerable change even under constant conditions of illumination. The awareness of this phenomenon is important to tapestry weavers whose shape colors will be strongly influenced by the ground colors that surround them.

Simultaneous color contrast depends to a great extent on the size of the colored areas, the smaller ones evincing a stronger contrast. Colors that are placed in front of a neutral ground appear stronger than they really are and the reverse is true when a neutral shape appears in front of a strongly colored background. Thus a yellowed blue appears more blue surrounded by a clear yellow and more yellow when surrounded by blue. A green shape placed on a yellow ground will appear much bluer than the same green placed on blue, which then seems to have much more yellow. The ground color is affected as much as the shape color.

This illusion is particularly useful when gray takes on the complement of the color to which it is adjacent. More than any other color, gray seems to accept complementary colors. The same gray area will appear darker on a lighter color background and lighter on a darker color background. Different tints and shades of the color appear stronger on their edges where they abut another color than in their centers. The edges tend to modify or darken when they are next to another color or another shade or tint of the same color that is lighter. They tend to look lighter where they are next to a darker area.

Luminosity

The transference from tint through tone to black or gray is one of the few ways to suggest a luminous quality in fiber. When gray is contrasted with a color instead of shaded with the addition of black, the lighter value of the tint and the deeper value of the gray create a subtle contrast. The effect is of an opalescent flickering light. The warm colors become luminous, and the cool colors recede into the background in grayish tones.

Adding white produces a tint and reduces saturation but increases luminosity. Adding black shades a color and adding gray neutralizes it. Luminosity is reduced in a shaded or neutralized color.

A shape appears luminous when it is lighter than its background or than other shapes in its background. Even somewhat dark masses appear illuminated when surrounded by darker masses.

Shadows are minimized or eliminated and the source of light appears to come from the shape that has the appearance of being illuminated. The glow starts at the light source and decreases as it spreads. Rough surface textures also decrease the glow, and inversely, hard shiny textures increase it.

In the Impressionist approach to painting, colors are comparatively bright and luminous with the boundaries of the shapes seeming to hatch into each

Positive and negative spaces are clearly delineated in this tapestry taken from a photograph of a wall with peeling paint. 55" x 47"

The trees were woven in a hit-and-miss soumak which gives this landscape a three-dimensional effect, increased by the arrow-like shadows. 33" x 33"

A landscape is suggested despite the non-realistic shape. Supplementary warps were added after the tapestry was woven on a fly-shuttle loom and then stretched on a vertical one. 50" x 62" x ½"

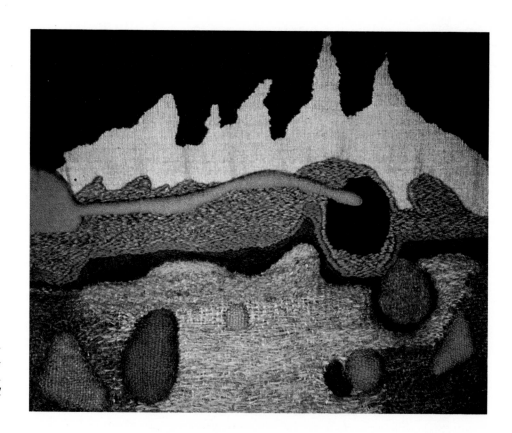

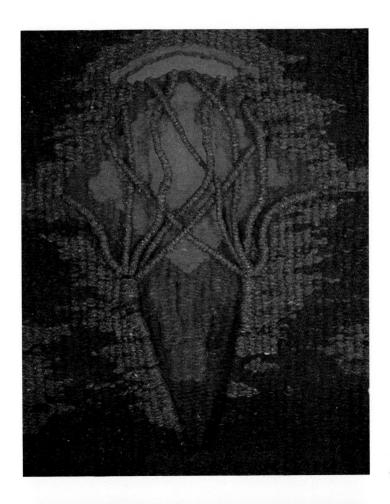

The wrapped, charcoal interlacing adds to the glow of the surface behind it. 40" x 28"

Both layers were woven separately on the fly-shuttle loom. The back layer was stretched on a plywood backing and the upper layer was cut up into different shapes and attached at different levels. The effect is that of exploding stripes. 71" x 60"

other. There are few distinct boundaries of light, and often luminous colors blur as they move in and out of each other's shapes. The centers of the color areas are almost opaque, with the luminosity occurring as the colors meet and intermingle. Although this is very effective in weaving, the approach requires considerable firmness in the use of color in the hatching area where a fiber color must be blended when by its nature it resists blending.

The most characteristic style of modern painting is in shapes and designs that are rendered in pure unchanged colors which are quite luminous but also textureless.

Luster effects occur when the quality of illumination is changed by choice and arrangement of colors. A lustrous color is a very bright color that stands out from the surrounding colors. Ordinarily the weaver would choose a fiber that reflects light, like silk, but it is possible to simulate a lustrous effect with wool by organizing the colors in a very subtle ascending order from the darkest to the lightest. The lightest color occupying the smallest area appears to shine out. This effect is strengthened with primary colors as long as the lightest and brightest areas are kept comparatively small and pure and the contrasting colors are held very dark or black. Dark colors should be somewhat larger in area, keeping the background subdued in the medium color range. A very small amount of white in the smallest shape will emphasize the lustrous impression.

Colors appear more luminous when contrasted with gray rather than black or a deep shade. Gray is the antithesis of pure color; therefore the effect of luster is enhanced by an overall impression of subdued light. It is like a star which glistens brightly because of the surrounding darkness. The background is kept suppressed and the bright area is kept small.

Luminosity is most easily obtained through the use of a metallic thread. Without this built-in reflective quality, the result may be achieved in another way. The area to appear illuminated must have the purest color, the highest value or brightness, and the smallest size. The light source should be evenly distributed as a background that centers the interest on the desired area. Strong contrasts detract from this effect. The general rule is to keep the entire illuminated shape lighter than the ground on which it is to be imposed. The desired effect is as though the shape is seen through a fog in the early morning before the sun rises.

Luminous bodies such as the sun are visible because of their own inner luminosity but nonluminous bodies are visible only because of the property they have of reflecting the light that falls on them from luminous bodies. The light of the moon

is diffused through the atmosphere when the air is full of moisture.

One of the ways to suggest a light-reflecting luster without actually using materials in which they are inherent, as in cellophane, is to add a few touches of intense color, blended or hatched into duller, less intense colors. The brighter colors will then appear more lustrous by comparison. Another way is to surround a small area with its complementary color and then with darker colors. Pastels such as pink or lavender lend themselves more easily to this effect.

Transparency

An illusion of transparency is created by the transmission of light so that shapes are seen as though through an intervening material such as a piece of colored plastic. The outline of the shapes remains clear, but the colors change their quality.

Transparency achieved by Renaissance painters, who depended on glazes and scumbling over forms built up with white, is not possible in the woven medium. The closest we can approach this effect is in the juxtaposition of various colored small planes that produce an illusion of transparency and depth through color relationships. The painter can also leave minute intervals between color areas unpainted. For the weaver, the unwoven warp in this instance is not equal to the canvas and cannot therefore be considered in the same context. If small uncolored areas are woven in white to resemble an unpainted canvas, the effect is entirely different from an unpainted canvas.

A transparency effect cannot be achieved in fiber as it is in pigment by spreading a wash of one color on top of another. True, a mesh fiber layer may be superimposed on a more solid ground, but the effect is of an opaque imposition, not of a see-through transparency. The closest weavers can come to achieve this effect is to use colors and their shades and tints as they would appear if overlapping transparent material were superimposed on parts of the design.

There has been little research on the changes that take place when an almost-transparent fabric of one pure color is placed over another fabric of an equally strong hue. The same two strong hues woven pick-and-pick or hatched will look entirely different. They remain as individual hues and the smokey, gauze-like effect of the overlay is lost.

Hue temperature illusions

A guiding principle in hue contrasts is the illusion of temperature. Colors are sometimes given temperature values such as warm and cool or hot and cold. Temperature extremes of the color wheel are generally considered to be red-orange and blue-green. When a warm tone is placed on or near a cool one, the warm tone appears warmer and the cool tone appears cooler. They are also said to suggest movement with warm ones seeming to move forward and cool ones seeming to recede.

In general, art theory suggests that warm colors be used in smaller areas against cooler colors in larger areas, although I have seen the reverse used with stunning results. As warm colors appear close and cool colors more distant, it follows that the warm colors should be placed in front of the cool ones. This phenomenon of warm versus cool colors loses its effectiveness as all colors recede in the distance where they pale and gray out the further they recede.

Red and blue fibers have warm and cool color contrast. As long as a considerable degree of those colors remains in the fiber mixture, they continue to contrast. As light or dark fibers are added, their contrast diminishes to the point where it is quite possible to have a pale red and a dull blue which have lost their warm and cool qualities and at the same time their contrast and movement. Grays with a bluish cast are called cool grays and those that contain a trace of red or orange are called warm grays.

Warm and cool colors may change their warm and cool feeling depending on the colors with which they are contrasted or in which way they are used.

Movement in color

A gradual change in adjacent colors suggests movement as the grading takes place from darker colors toward lighter ones or the reverse. It is the organization of the colors and design that encourage the eye to move along. This is true of passage from color to color as well as subtle gradations within a color. Movement in color, which changes imperceptibly, is among the more difficult effects to achieve in fiber.

Simple additions of the next shade or tint are not sufficient to accomplish this. Distinct lines of separation where one color ends and another begins will interfere with the movement. Starting with many strands of one color and dropping one to add the next shade or tint works for a while, but the mathematical dropping and adding ceases to give a smooth gradation at a certain point and other ratios and combinations must be used. (See Hatching and Seeding.)

Yellow is the closest color to light. Any color organization that leads toward yellow suggests movement toward light, and any color organization that passes through the color wheel from green to blue to violet suggests movement away from light into shadow.

Each time another yarn is added, as long as it is in the slightest way different from those which are close to it, or those of which it is to be a part, it will be perceived differently than if it were alone. It and its neighboring yarns alter their color relationship with their physical relationship.

There are those who hold that color is as basic to the human being as fire and water. Freedom to use color released from conventional restraints is, to the weaver, just as basic. It may be a form of effrontery to equate a degree of color freedom with emotional freedom. But it remains undeniable that color is of major creative importance.

Explosion behind and barbed wire in front, enclose the bloated human figures. 50" x 38".

Above: *The male shape remains recognizable despite its distortion. 48" x 32". At right: Minimal use of black suggests a calligraphic effect. 42" x 40".*

Three figures, brown, black and off-white, are woven in a hit-and-miss soumak. Supporting rods are embedded in a redwood stump. 7'6" x 3' x 2'

VII
TAPESTRY LOOMS AND WARPING TECHNIQUES

Horizontal and Vertical Looms; Harnesses; Beaters; Warping Different Shaped Frames; Warping Tapestry Looms; Nail Frame Looms; Starting and Ending the Warp; Selvage Reinforcement; Small Frame Looms for Sampling.

Horizontal and vertical looms

Chaining, braiding, plaiting, wrapping, twining, knotting and similar construction methods are not weaving techniques and so do not necessarily require a loom. Weaving, or interlacing, requires the use of some type of loom. It may be the most primitive support, acting only as an anchor point from which the warp ends are pendant, to the most sophisticated construction. The choice of a loom depends on the purpose to which it will be put, whether for learning, production or improvisation or research into a particular technique.

Regardless of how they are secured, all warp ends require some type of rigid material from which they are suspended or to which they are attached. Tension must be maintained, even if one end of each warp end hangs freely held under tension by weights. The most primitive structure, whether a simple frame, metal circle or tree branch, is a loom upon which warp and weft may be interlaced. Even a cardboard frame may be used as a loom.

Any design can be woven on any loom although some designs are more suited to one type of loom than another. The complexity of a loom, the number of parts and their possible manipulation, do not determine the suitability of a loom. In fact, many built-in enhancements and their manipulation act as deterrents to the free flowing creativity of the weaver-designer.

Looms are basically divided into two classes, horizontal and vertical. The horizontal loom whose harnesses are controlled by levers or pedals must have a minimum of two harnesses to make a shed, but may have any number beyond that. Warp ends are usually threaded through heddle eyes held by harness bars. A beater containing a reed through which the warp ends are sleyed may be part of the equipment of a horizontal or vertical loom, and may hang from a castle and swing freely, be attached to a superstructure, or be hinged near the floor.

A horizontal or low-warp loom may be used for many tapestry designs and has two major advantages and disadvantages. A horizontal warp with which the weft is interlaced is visible for the short distance that it remains horizontal, usually about 12″. In order to view a composition that is larger, the weaver must release the tension and roll the cloth beam back with the consequent problem of reestablishing the warp to its exact previous state. The second disadvantage is working at and seeing an interlacement horizontally which will subsequently be hung vertically. The shapes, colors and light reflection change with the plane.

The two major advantages relate to the harnesses. On most looms other than small table looms, the pedals are operated by the feet to raise and lower the harnesses or move them forward and back to create sheds, leaving the hands free to manipulate the weft. The second advantage is the pattern creating function of the harnesses and heddles. Only plain weave is possible with two harnesses. Each additional harness increases the pattern possibilities. Such patterns may be blown up to become the center of interest or given less importance as a background for shapes that are incorporated into them. (See twilling in Chapter XI, Part 1.)

Basically all harness loom systems act in a similar way, as shed-making devices. On the vertical loom in figure 1 the harnesses move horizontally and are controlled by a pair of foot pedals. It has a cloth and warp beam and a ratchet and pawl for tensioning. The vertical loom in figure 2 incorporates more refinements, a vertical, sliding beater and additional sets of pedals.

Among the smallest vertical looms is the lap or table-supported "I" frame loom. Although smaller looms are comparatively less expensive and easy to assemble, they must, like all other tapestry looms, be constructed so that they will not torque or collapse, no matter how much tension is exerted by the warp.

For large, vertical looms, various systems of gears, levers, ropes and turnbuckles are used to hold the warp under tension. Some of these are so heavy and bulky that they are built into a permanent position by being lashed or nailed to the floor and ceiling.

There are several very practical reasons for using vertical looms for extra long tapestries that will hang on high walls. Woven in the same direction it will hang, a loom somewhat higher than the full length would be required. Such a high loom is not practical from the standpoint of the working conditions of the weaver who would have to work from a very high scaffold for the upper part of the tapestry. The alternative is a vertical loom that has warp and cloth beams around which the warp moves while the weaver remains at a fixed level. If the tapestry is designed to be turned 90°, the weaving area on the loom would have to be at least as wide as the tapestry's vertical dimensions.

Traditional high-warp tapestry looms are used more by weavers trained in the European tradition than in the United States. They are frequently designed and specially built to meet particular size and strength requirements.

If the design elements are vertical, like standing figures, elongated trees and bushes, borders or tall buildings, the slits between the shapes and the background will be longer than usual and the overall construction will be weaker, even when sewn together. Straight selvages will be more difficult to maintain because of the weakened structure.

Among the most important considerations is the greater light reflection on the horizontal ridges than on vertical ones. Whenever possible, tapestries should be woven on the same plane as they will be viewed.

No matter how the loom is constructed or warped, the warp ends must be held in exact alignment. If this structural condition is not present, the top and bottom of the warp must be secured by chaining or twining to act as warp spacers before the weaving starts.

The warp support may remain as a permanent part of the tapestry or the work may be completely removed from its support and hung by other means. If the former method is used, the relationship between the support and the content of the tapestry must be maintained. Using an extreme example, the effect of a delicate gossamer-like work will be destroyed by hanging it from a heavy piece of wood or metal. If its support is visible, i.e., if it extends out from the sides or the top, it must be in keeping with the rest of the work. A found piece of wood like driftwood may be the easiest and least costly from which to suspend the work but may also not relate to the texture and idea of the tapestry. The possibilities

Fig. 1. *The Crisp "Tina" Tapestry Loom. Crisp Woodworking Concerns, Ltd., Portland, Oregon.*

Fig. 2. *The Crisp "Ruthie" Tapestry Loom, Crisp Woodworking Concerns, Ltd., Portland, Oregon.*

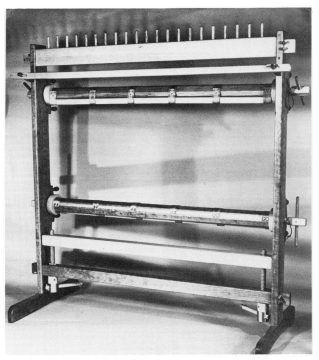

Fig. 4. *The Crisp Gobelin Tapestry Loom, Crisp Woodworking Concerns, Ltd., Portland, Oregon.*

Fig. 3. *The "I" frame loom. This loom is among the smallest and easiest to make.*

Fig. 5. *Jeff Glenn constructed this high-warp tapestry loom based on a design by George Davis. It requires a continuous warp and both the upper and lower beams and the heddle bars are adjustable.*

of plastic, metal and hidden supports of other materials have yet to be explored in greater depth.

Among the supports which are more visible and control the outside shape of the work are permanent contours such as metal or wooden circles, ovals, frames or boxes. These shapes may be totally covered before the warp is added or parts of them may be left exposed if that is more in keeping with the theme of the piece.

Harnesses

The advantages of an automatic shed opening control have been mentioned. The disadvantages are less obvious. There is a tendency to use the threading and sleying order of such systems without further exploration of different ways of entering the weft within the same piece of work. There is a strong predisposition to remain within the existing pattern.

Any variations require leaving the warp without any shed and changing the weft entry by forcing it over and under different warp ends that are not within the threading and sleying order.

Although some weavers prefer to pull and release heddles, I find it much easier to eliminate all additional sticks, rods, swords and heddles and simply use my fingers to open the shed and beat in the weft. There is less clutter, there is nothing to pick up, insert, remove or lay down. For me this method is faster, and just as important, encourages a freer expression of design than one in which the warp ends are controlled in predetermined sequences.

Rigid heddles are sometimes used on tapestry looms. These are designed to create a shed by a system of alternating long and short slots. When the alternately threaded warp ends are raised, one shed is formed and when they are lowered, the opposite one is opened for the next pick.

On a back-strap loom or on some traditional vertical looms, a loop or heddle, usually of strong smooth string, is looped around alternating warp ends. This results in one stationary warp end and one movable end encircled by a string heddle on either side of it. The second set is called movable because it may be drawn toward the weaver by grasping the string heddles in the design order. The first shed is created by a shed rod, dowel or a flat, smooth piece of wood. The shed may be enlarged by the weaver reaching through the heddles and grasping the warp ends in front of the rod. The second shed is created by the weaver pulling the heddles forward. When the weft has been entered into the second shed, the heddles are released and the warp ends which they encircle are returned to their normal position. With this technique only one hand is free to enter the weft since the other is holding the shed rod or a group of heddles.

Other types of horizontal looms were used in the eighteenth century, and some are still in use. For wide tapestries small sections of pedal controlled heddles, in small harnesses about 2' wide, are individually raised and lowered by two pedals. The cartoon is cut or divided into vertical strips and laid beneath the warp. The weaver works from the back of the tapestry, the face being next to the cartoon. In this way several weavers can work at the same loom on the same tapestry at the same time, as all weavers have complete control of the two sheds in the area in which they are working.

Fig. 6. *The Mailes Vertical Tapestry Loom. This loom uses a staggered nail system, eliminating beams, harnesses, rods and heddles. The sheds are created with the fingers and most of the illustrations in this book were woven on it.*

Fig. 7. *The Crisp Heddle Bar Tapestry Loom, Crisp Woodworking Concerns, Ltd., Portland, Oregon. The sheds are achieved by rotating the heddle bars.*

Beaters

Many weavers do not use any beater other than their fingers. The motion is more like a pressing down rather than beating. Actually, a coordination is developed in which one motion accomplishes two purposes. As one hand is freed as it passes the butterfly to the other hand, it holds the weft that has just been entered and keeps it from being pulled up too tightly. The same hand presses the weft down to settle it into place. Some harder wefts require additional beating, but generally the pressure of the hand with the fingers spread on the last pick is sufficient. Depending on which side the butterfly is entered, it is passed from hand to hand in the open shed, leaving one hand free to adjust and press the weft down.

Various types of hand held beaters have been developed over the years, but many homemade ones are as good or better than those sold. A wide-tined fork whose tips have been filed off has the advantage of additional weight. It may not be as aesthetic as the wooden ones, but the teeth do not splinter after a little use and because of their width, the tines do not split the warp ends. A large, tapered pin called a fid, a nautical device, is an excellent tool to push down weft or separate warps.

Hand held beaters are available in various shapes and sizes. These must be picked up and put down for each beat. Single point beaters or pin-beaters must also be strong and smooth.

Some weavers waste a considerable amount of time beating harder and longer than is necessary. The last pick springs back to some extent, no matter how much it is beaten in. Actually, its major function is to hold down the closest previously entered picks. There is a point beyond which no amount of beating will further compress the weft. It is sometimes preferable to use a softer weft that beats in more easily than a hard twist weft which requires ex-

cessive beating. For most purposes the weft should be left with some spring remaining in it.

Warping tapestry looms

Production methods for warping vertical looms are not too feasible, so most warps are planned separately for each tapestry. However, warping directly onto or around horizontal beams or a nail frame loom is a faster method than transferring the warp from a warping frame where it was measured and put under tension, to the loom, as in the Columbian back-strap method. The Navajo method is somewhat similar in that the warp is first put on a warping frame which is then lashed to a loom frame.

Calculations for warp yardage requirements on vertical looms are similar to those for horizontal looms. The length of the warp is multiplied by the number of e.p.i., times the width of the warp in inches. If the selvages are to be reinforced, the additional ends must be added to the total. Here, as in any warp calculation, overestimating is always safer than underestimating.

There are several methods for warping frame looms, most of them depending on the built-in, or lack of built-in, arrangement for keeping the warp aligned. A continuous circular warp may be wound around the upper and lower horizontal bars with the warp spacing held by notches on the frame or by the alignment being secured with twining or chaining the back and front warp together above the bottom bar and below the top bar. With this method the back warp may also be left unwoven, but it is wasted and interferes with weaving on the front warp. The part of the warp that loops around the frame cannot be woven on and must be accounted for when estimating warp length. It should also be remembered that if the frame is to be used again, the warp will have to be cut loose when the work is removed. In another method the frame is constructed in such a way that the upper and lower bars are removable and may be slipped out of the warp loops around them. All loom constructions, large or small, simple or complex, must be able to withstand the tension necessary for weaving interlacement and weft beating.

For tapestries that are longer than the loom, dowels or rods may be placed behind the warp which passes over the top bar and under the bottom bar. Additional lease sticks are inserted between them to control their tension. When the weaving reaches the point where the warp must be lowered, tension is released by removing the lease sticks. After the warp has been moved, the lease sticks are reentered and the previous tension reestablished.

Lease sticks may be used in the same way on a warp that has become too loose for interlacement so that the weft cannot be sufficiently beaten down.

Fig. 8. *Various types of hand-held beaters including a wide-tined fork, different sized and shaped wooden combs and small pin beaters, and two fids.*

This may result from the warp material being too elastic and stretching, or not being held under sufficient tension as it was being put on. Two lease sticks inserted into the two sheds on the upper part of the warp will provide enough tension until the interlacement has taken up some of the slack. The diameter of the sticks determines the degree to which the warp can be drawn up.

The figure-eight method of warping creates a cross between the top and bottom bars as the warp is wound around them. This method has all the limitations of the continuous, circular warping plan. Both are more useful for small frame looms where the warp may more easily be moved around the bars. On a large frame loom both of these warping methods are impractical. In any case, the warp cross should be pushed down to the bottom before the weaving starts. If it is left to be resolved later, it will interfere with the sheds, all the way up the tapestry.

On looms that have a warp beam directly above a cloth beam, the warp hangs vertically in a straight line and the weaver sees the work progress as it will appear when it is hung on the wall later. In another version of this method the warp is rolled around the warp beam from the front and is received by the cloth beam from behind so that the work is woven at an angle. The disadvantage here is that although the weaver can see the whole face of the work between the two beams, the angle is not the one at which it will be hung and constant accommodation must be made for this discrepancy. A similar handicap is present on some small tilted frames supported by a stand. The tilted face is desirable for work such as embroidery where both hands must be able to reach behind or under the frame. This is not a requirement for weaving, and such frames should be tilted to a vertical position for viewing.

Variations in texture, heavy, lumpy yarns next to fine, smooth ones will not roll up equally on a cloth beam. In traditional rugs or tapestries, where yarn variations were confined to color, the weaving was accepted smoothly and evenly. Considering the great variations in current fiber use, this type of loom is less practical.

In those warping systems where the warp is movable, the weaver sits at a comfortable height and the warp is moved down as the weaving progresses. In those systems where the warp is not movable, the weaver must adjust the weaving position to the place where the work is going on. On a very large tapestry the weaver frequently starts by sitting on the floor or on a very low stool or bench. As the height of the weaving moves up the warp, the height of the stool is raised until the weaver must, if the tapestry is very long, first stand and then sit and stand on ladders or specially built platforms.

Another method of covering the warp with weaving from the bottom to the top gives it, in effect, four selvages. Each tapestry warp loop is linked with a dummy loop both at the top and the bottom. These are cut away when the work is completed. The dummy loops are put on like ordinary frame loom warp, either around the bars or around nails, and are the correct length to hold the weaving warp under tension. If each warp is interlaced in the weaving, the top and bottom selvages will hold like the side ones. If the warp ends are used in double units, each loop must be caught with the first and last pick. The usual twining or chaining system across the dummy loops will hold them equally separated and aligned.

A dummy loop system may also be used as a design or color device. In this case the warp loops are no longer extraneous to the tapestry but are integrated into the body of the work.

It is important that the weaver sit or stand with the eye level at the fell. If the eye level is much above or below, the angle at which the shapes are being woven will not be correct. Considerable distortion occurs when sight and working height are not the same. This is particularly true when the cartoon is hung directly behind the loom and the weaver must sight the contours of the shape through the warp. Seen from above or below, there may be a difference of two or more inches between the cartoon shape outline and the weaving shape edge. In addition, working above shoulder height is much more tiring for the arms.

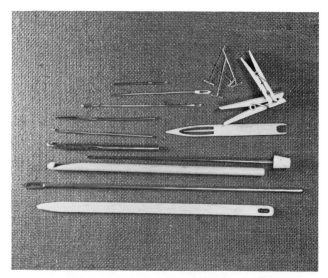

Fig. 15. *Other tools include a flute cleaner, a flat scissors, long wooden and metal needles, different sized metal and wooden crochet hooks, a short, blunt-end embroidery needle and T-pins.*

Warping different shaped frames

Weaving frames need not be limited to rectangular shapes. However, warping on curved shapes can present slippage problems. There are three ways to overcome this difficulty. A thin colorless glue can be applied to the frame to keep the warp in line. However, sometimes the glue seeps through and becomes hard and reflective. The second method involves using lark's head loops or buttonhole stitches around the curved frame. These may start slipping when the length of the warp ends shorten as the sides of a small curve are approached.

The third and probably best method is to prewrap the frame. This may be done with the same color as the warp or a different color yarn. The warp can then encircle the frame once and move across the intervening space to the other side. With this method, the warping can be discontinuous or continuous and the number of e.p.i. can be controlled and varied. Prewrapping holds the warp in place and offers some resistance to help keep it under tension.

Warping a horizontal loom for a tapestry is no different than warping for any other textile project. The type of tapestry dictates the type of warp, threading order and the e.p.i., and the braking system controls the warp tension.

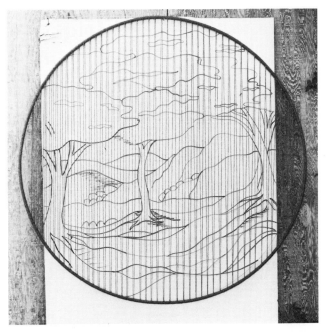

Fig. 16. *A warped circular frame hanging in front of a cartoon by Lynn Murray.*

Tension

Although no exact rule can be given for warp tension, it must be consistent and constant. Tension varies with personal preference and the type of warp and weft as well as the e.p.i. The tension of the warp also increases as more and more of the warp is interlaced. Many tapestry weavers have at some time found themselves forcing the weft into a very small shed opening at the top because all of the elasticity in the warp has been used up. At this point, and also if the fell is so close to the top that it is difficult to enter the weft, a long needle with a large eye may be able to get in where the fingers cannot. Such a tool tends to pull the selvages together and additional bubbling or slack must be left in the weft to counteract this tendency.

Calculating the amount of weft that will be required to cover a given area is similar to warp calculation. The number of p.p.i. is multiplied by the width of the warp by the inches to be woven, and the total inches are then converted into yards. As weft yarns are usually given in yards per pound, it is easy enough to estimate the number of pounds of yarn required to cover a given area. Here, too, it is much safer to overestimate than to underestimate.

One way of expediting weaving time is to use two, three or four warp ends as a warp unit or bout. The weft can then also be multiplied, with the number of ends depending on the type of yarn. This will not produce a fine grained surface, but offers a wider choice of weft movement as the warp end units can be subdivided and used in different organizations. More than one weft may also be used in the same pick and, although the rib organization is disrupted by the breaks in the warp unit, another design element thereby is added.

Nail frame looms

For most purposes, I have found that a large adjustable frame with a staggered nail system, supported by a strong, rigid structure is best. It offers more freedom to the contemporary weaver for wider personal expression, as well as lending itself to strict traditional techniques. The upper and lower horizontal bars may easily be moved to various positions, adapting to any length warp without warp waste. Different lengths of horizontal bars may accommodate various tapestry widths.

The staggered nail system makes a large variety of p.p.i. possible. As it passes over each nail, each warp loop is an individual entity, and may be grouped with others, used as a single or double unit or skip some nails entirely. Warp loops can be moved in any direction at any time, or removed entirely when the construction calls for such elimination. The nails also offer the opportunity to add supplementary warp at any time, in any warp grouping; nor need warp ends always be put on in the same direction. A nail arrangement makes it possible to

Fig. 9. *The first step in making a butterfly. A tail is left hanging in front of the palm before the weft is looped around the thumb and index finger.*

Fig. 10. *Continue wrapping the weft in a figure-eight.*

Fig. 11. *The figure-eight is removed, retaining the crossed center.*

Fig. 12. *The weft is wrapped around the core of the figure-eight.*

Fig. 13. *The last wrap is raised by the forefinger. The weft is torn and the short tail is passed through it from left to right.*

Fig. 14. *A completed butterfly.*

Shuttles, bobbins and butterflies

Traditional boat shuttles are more likely to be used on a horizontal loom than on a vertical one. They are generally filled with background weft, bobbins and/or butterflies holding the weft for the main shapes. Stick and rug shuttles may be used on either type loom. They are made of plastic or wood and are available in a variety of shapes and sizes. Those that are flat have notches with a V or U shape cut into both ends. If there are two sides, a bar near each end separates them. The double-sided shuttle holds more weft but requires a larger shed to pass through. Before these shuttles are entered into a shed, the weft must be unwound for the full width of the pick or the selvage will be pulled.

I rarely use a shuttle of any kind, preferring butterflies which release the weft as they are passed through larger or smaller sections. Butterflies may be passed through small or large sheds, have practically no weight and will hang from whatever place in the tapestry they are left without unravelling. They are quickly and easily made and have a built-in release control. The more weft in the butterfly, the longer the weaver can work without starting a new one. There is, of course, a point at which a butterfly may be wound into a figure eight that is too bulky to pass easily through a shed.

If a bobbin is used, some arrangement must be made to keep the weft from unreeling. There are bobbins made of wood, plastic or cardboard with a notch that holds the unreeling weft.

To make a butterfly, a fairly long tail is left hanging in front of the palm between the thumb and index finger. The weft is wound behind and around the thumb and small finger in turn in a figure eight. The

larger the spread between the two fingers, the larger the butterfly and the longer it will last. When it is large enough, the figure eight is removed from the hand, carefully retaining the crossed center. The feeding end is then wrapped around the crossed center several times to secure it but not so tightly that the loops will not release easily. If the end, after being torn, is wrapped around the crossed center several times, and passed from left to right under the last wrap, the whole butterfly will unreel without any knots. If the tip is passed from right to left, a knot will remain at the end. A single weft, small knot will not matter. If many wefts are wound together, such a knot at the end will have to be opened up or cut away. The last wrap around the cross must be secured in the same direction as the end that is being pulled. Many butterflies may be used at the same time without tangling and unreeling, as gravity keeps them in a straight line.

Weft that is too thick or bulky to be made into a butterfly is left to hang in a long length and used as needed. Here the nail arrangement with which I prefer to work serves another purpose as well as warp separation. The nails of the upper bar are used to hang long weft ends or butterflies out of the way until they are needed again.

There are other tools borrowed from different mediums which I have adapted to tapestry use. A large tapering pin called a fid, a nautical device, is an excellent tool to push down or separate warp ends. A flute cleaner that is more than a foot long and has a large long eye at one end is stronger than a similar sized wooden needle and will not bend or break. Different sized crochet hooks and long heavy embroidery needles with blunt ends are also useful.

put warp loops on so that their direction is changed while still retaining the required tension.

If longer warps are needed, i.e., longer than the height of the loom, the warp loops may be continued past the nail around which they would ordinarily return by being looped around other nails or supports that are further away. In this way some warp ends will be much longer than others and, although still retaining their tension, be available for other uses such as supplementary warp, as weft, or as fringe.

This staggered nail system permits the weaver to sit or stand at any height in front of the loom or walk around behind it to weave or mend or clean up any part of the tapestry at any time. Almost all of the techniques and tapestries illustrated here were woven on this type of loom.

Although different arrangements are possible with a single row, a double row of staggered nails, spaced at ½" intervals, allows a greater variety of e.p.i. organization. The nails on the upper and

Fig. 17. *A three-tier platform.*

lower horizontal bars are slightly angled away from each other so that the loops are secure and do not slip off.

Another advantage of the nail system is the possibility of starting the weft directly above the upper of the two bottom rows of nails and weaving right up to the first row of nails on the top. If the first and last two picks interlace the warp loops, an automatic control keeps the loops from slipping through into the weft. Weaving a beginning and end on the tapestry eliminates the need for a hem at one or both ends. In actual practice I usually weave two picks, one in each direction, catching the loops from both sides, resulting in a stronger edge that holds well after the work has been removed from the loom.

Six or eight penny finish nails, 2" or 2½" long, allow the warp loops to slide off with a small pull and without too much strain. If the tension has increased and the warp has become so tight that it cannot be slipped off, either horizontal bar may be loosened by unscrewing the bolts on the sides, and the loops slipped off the nails.

A plumbline ensures the exact verticality of the first warp end. All subsequent ends follow in order and are correctly aligned.

Additional suggestions

With the nail warping system, broken warp ends or ends that have knots or thin or weak places that should be reinforced are easy to mend. A small knot can be pushed to the back of the tapestry. A weak spot may have a reinforcing end added to it from the upper to the lower nail. The additional end may be interlaced at the weak spot, later cut away and the tails mended with the other weft ends.

Warping may be started with a small loop around the first nail and ended the same way around the last nail. Interlacing the beginning and end of the warp around unused nails is another way. The second method is preferable because it leaves a little warp for tension adjustment at both ends.

As a loop of warp is passed around the next nail with one hand, the previous loop is held in place and under tension with the other until the next nail has been looped. Regardless of which warping arrangement or how many e.p.i. are used, each warp end must be placed and held under equal tension. If, after the whole width has been put on the loom, a discrepancy is found in the tension, it is much better to start adjusting from the center out to the closest selvage than to start at one selvage and adjust all the way across. Tension may be checked by running the fingers across the warp as though across harp strings. One quickly becomes sensitive to unequal warp ends that require adjusting. If by some mis-

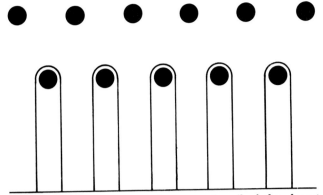

Fig. 18. *The warp is passed over each nail of the closest rows.*

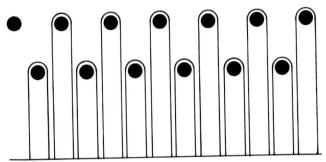

Fig. 19. *The warp passes over the nails in both rows, upper and lower.*

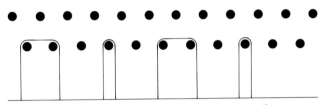

Fig. 20. *The warp is grouped and skips some nails.*

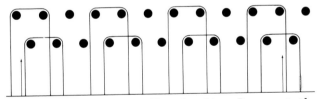

Fig. 21. *The warp is grouped in units of two. It moves to the right on the closest rows and returns to the left on the farthest rows.*

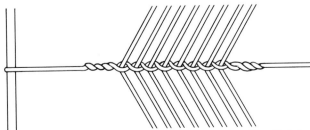

Fig. 22. *The warp is put on in a V turned on its side. Twining holds the center to the upright bar.*

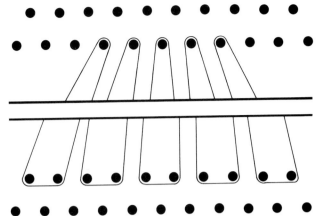

Fig. 23. *The warp is put on in a fan shape—wide at the top and narrow at the bottom.*

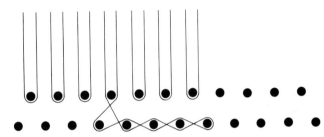

Fig. 24. *Two warp ends are lengthened by twining them around the lower row of nails.*

chance, after weaving has started, one warp loop becomes looser than the rest, it can always be moved to a higher or lower nail or adjusted with a rubber band. See Supplementary Warp for further discussion on the use of rubber bands as extenders.

Planning ahead for finishing

Whether woven on a horizontal or vertical loom, shrinkage must be considered in a tapestry as well as in other textiles. Loss of an inch or more may not be too critical on a large piece. However, if the tapestry has been commissioned to fit a particular space and has shrunk after being taken from the loom, it may legally be rejected. It is necessary to become familiar with the different rates of shrinkage resulting from different weaves, e.p.i., p.p.i., and types of yarn.

Generally the rule is that the finer the warp and the more e.p.i., the less it will shrink. Tapestries are rarely washed or commercially cleaned. Cleaning usually results in minimal shrinkage, if any. Whisking lint and dust off of tapestries should be discouraged. If such material must be removed, use of a blower on a vacuum cleaner is preferable. The suction end is too likely to suck up loose fibers.

Selvage Reinforcement

Whether or not to double the selvages on a tapestry is purely a matter of personal preference. I almost always double or triple the outside warp ends for additional strength and width control. The rare exception is when the warp is a heavy linen or wool which is strong enough by itself to withstand the abrasion that the selvage ends receive and does not require reinforcing. Increasing the number of warp ends at the selvage creates a small ridge. The outside ribs appear slightly rounder than do those next to them. I do not find this objectionable in most tapestries and prefer it to a distorted or irregular selvage.

Small frame looms for sampling

As a general rule it is not advisable to weave samples on small frame looms. The rhythmic body, arm and hand movement that is one of the gratifying aspects of tapestry weaving is not possible on this type of loom. Design and color concepts cannot be developed and are hampered by containment within a small frame unless the whole idea belongs in a miniature. The best use for small looms is for quick sampling for techniques and color relationships.

Even for small sampling I prefer to use a small area on a large loom. Color and technique trials may easily be unwoven. The small loom trial is out of context with the weaving that has already been done and still must be transferred to the larger loom for confirmation.

If a small loom is used, the "I" shape is preferable because there are no side bars to interfere with the hands as the shed is made and the weft is entered.

Some weavers find that the bottom rows of nails become a nuisance as the weaving progresses. The weft tends to get caught on them and repeatedly needs to be freed. A narrow board the width of the warp may be placed across the nails and tied into place as soon as the weaving has progressed 2″ or 3″.

VIII
THE CARTOON

Using a Cartoon; Sketching; Marking the Warp; The Grid; Drawing a Cartoon

Using a Cartoon

A cartoon is a drawing of a design. It may be the exact size of the original, slightly expanded, or more often, enlarged to the full size of the tapestry. Most tapestry weavers copy a cartoon by weaving directly over it on a horizontal warp or in front of it on a vertical warp.

Exact copying of a cartoon raises certain problems. As work progresses it needs to be resolved on its own terms. Exact duplication may negate the original reason for the choice and a particular approach or design may no longer pertain. The weaving may become like painting by the numbers or as in the classical tapestry, weaving by the numbers or making a rug by hooking colored yarns to prepainted canvas designs. Blowing up a small cartoon may give a high degree of fidelity, but what was a good design and color on a small scale may not necessarily work in the enlarged space.

Not all small sketches or drawings profit from expansion. Scale must be considered. It must also be predetermined from what angle the work will be viewed. Certain designs are possible if it is to hang at eye level and be seen from a short distance. Some are automatically eliminated if the work is seen from above or below or from a greater distance.

A small woven rendering of what you expect to weave rarely solves the problems of the enlarged version. A small cartoon, blown up, is often just that and does not solve the problems of the design shape ratios of the larger version. The sense of the total whole must be maintained and the individual, contributing parts must relate to a larger concept. When the final work is presented, it is in its totality, not as an assemblage of parts which may be individually interesting but do not work well together.

If the usual historical procedure is followed, the composition is first drawn or painted on a small scale, then translated into a full-scale pattern or cartoon and then translated again into a weaving. The term cartoon is not limited to weaving. It also refers to a full scale design for painting and other art forms. In the past, most artists were unfamiliar with weaving techniques, and a cartoon designer acted as intermediary between the painter and weaver, trans-lating from one medium to the other. The weaver was a worker who executed but did not create.

Present day weavers are usually a combination of artist and weaver, making their own cartoons, weaving them, and having the prerogative of changing the cartoon and color as the work grows. Although many tapestries are mirror images of a cartoon, details are immensely enriched in the over and under fabrication as compared to a flat picture plane. Because a cartoon is prepared in one medium and woven in another, it will never appear the same. We cannot sketch in fiber.

Sometimes weavers are blocked by inability or lack of training to draw shapes as they appear to them, as art students draw from a model or a still life. Many artists have similar problems and have found ways to suggest shapes in other than representational configurations. Outlines of body shapes, primitive or childlike representation, stick figures, bodies abstracted into geometrical shapes, parts of bodies, and many more, all have been effectively used.

Sketching

Although many weavers do not think of themselves as artists in the sense of being able to sketch easily, they can learn to sketch well enough for their own needs. We are, after all, only interested in a cartoon as a basis for the design of our tapestry. In itself, the cartoon is of little importance.

Those who feel that they cannot draw or design can carve, cut, model, tear or paste. All of these are excellent ways of designing a cartoon. It does not have to be drawn and it does not follow that someone who cannot make a satisfactory drawing must be eliminated from tapestry designing.

Rather than be blocked by what we think is our lack of artistic ability, let us try other approaches. We are surrounded by newspapers and magazines filled with photographs and advertisements suitable as a basis for design. We are, here, not concerned with personal likes and dislikes. We are only interested in eliminating the unimportant and insignificant parts of the composition of the picture and emphasizing the more important shapes, directions and movements.

Using old newspaper or magazine illustrations, we can outline freely and unhesitatingly over major shapes. These act as quick and inexpensive exercises to train the eye to see shapes and organizations where they had not been seen before. The hand moves quickly and freely without dwelling on the artistic merits of the sketch.

A photograph of several athletes in a moment of confrontation must contain, by its very nature, large shapes that have direction and movement. With few exceptions, most illustrations can be used for sketching exercises. After short periods of such activity, the eye starts seeing and the hand responding in new ways. The illustrations no longer relate to the text which they accompany but become the possible basis for a cartoon.

Since we can play with this way of drawing without observation or criticism by another person, years of inhibitions and fears of incompetence may be forgotten in the flow of quickly outlining shapes. As confidence grows, we start seeing dark shapes versus light ones, filling in the very dark ones heavily, the gray ones less heavily and leaving the light ones empty.

We have, without realizing it, started to think in terms of dark and light shapes, eventually leading to color. These and other such self-assigned exercises are a way of freeing ourselves to explore further and expand into tapestry cartoons.

The most unlikely sources will often yield the most suggestive departures for design and subject. Street scenes, buildings, interiors, wildlife, sports, people, animals and almost anything one sees in endless combinations, are sources for ideas. By eliminating details and extraneous matter and outlining the remaining shapes, the basis for a design appears. If the resulting design is unsatisfactory, it can be changed. For some people, placing a mark on a clean sheet of paper can be very inhibiting. Starting from an already simplified design is much less threatening. If a soft undulating design is desired, it is sometimes much easier to start with an illustration of rolling hills that can be translated into a hills and valleys design. Buildings and city streets are obviously good sources for geometric shapes, and athletic events and animals for movement and rhythm.

The guilt that some weavers experience using such source material is unfounded. Over the years, artists have accepted and used variations on these approaches without questioning them, an approach particularly helpful to weavers who, unless commissioned to duplicate some design exactly, rarely follow their original ideas to their conclusion. They tend, rather, to change the design as the work demands, as it grows under their hands, and design as they weave.

In the Gobelin tradition, various shapes are carefully drawn and numbered rather than colored. This eliminates any doubt in the weaver's mind as to which colors are to be used for a shape, as each

Fig. 1a & 1b. *Street scene of men with hats laying cement.*

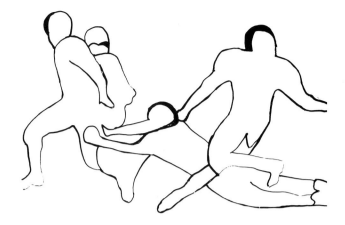

Fig. 2a & 2b. *Athletes in motion. When abstracted, the movement remains but the figures lose their humanity.*

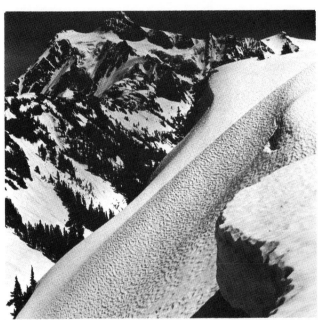

Fig. 3a & 3b. *A winter scene with a strong diagonal broken up on the left side.*

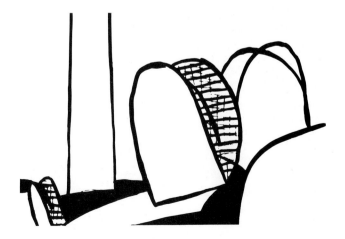

Fig. 4a and 4b. *The superstructure of a submarine loses its identity and becomes a strong contrast in black, white and gray.*

Fig. 5a & 5b. *Landscapes tend to retain their hills-and-valleys but are an excellent source for over-drawing.*

Fig. 6a & 6b. *The torso without the head was rotated three times for a rounded, graceful composition.*

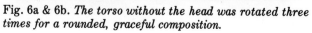

Fig. 7a & 7b. *Abstracted once, the bridge was still too busy.*

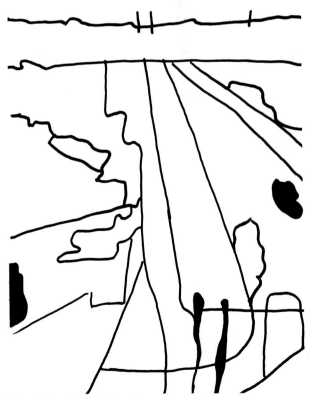

Fig. 8. *Further abstraction makes #7 weaveable.*

number refers to a specific color. The same numbers refer to the same color throughout the tapestry and for other tapestries as well.

It is not always necessary to fill each total shape in the cartoon with color. If the whole composition is clearly visualized, only the adjoining colors need be sketched to suggest how they relate to each other. We know that fiber colors will not be exactly the same as those in the cartoon and certainly have no texture. We know that for our cartoon the paint or watercolors, colored pencil or pastel, will only suggest the final result.

When a tapestry is woven in the traditional manner, face down, the cartoon must also be reversed, or else what was on the right side on the cartoon will be woven on the left side on the tapestry. All titles, numbers, words or signatures must be reversed as well. If this reversal was overlooked when the cartoon was drawn, a tracing may be made of the major outlines of the shapes and used under the warp while the original cartoon is hung close by for reference.

When we weave a tapestry the result is sometimes different from the cartoon because of the translation into a different medium, cartoon drawing to fiber. Sometimes, even when the work is completed we still are not sure of the result. It is as though the weaving has to age, both within itself and in the eyes of the weaver.

The outline of the cartoon design may be placed behind the warp and traced onto the warp by mark-

large tapestry, a large cartoon may be cut up into long strips, but their relationship to each other must be carefully maintained.

Mirrors were used much more when the work was woven with the face down than they are today when most weaving is woven with the face towards the weaver.

Marking the warp

If the warp is to be marked for the outline of the shape, each end must be held and twisted in both directions while being marked or else the mark is erased through absorption and friction.

To draw a cartoon directly on the warp, the tension must be kept very tight and the cartoon secured

Fig. 9. *This photo was taken during the weaving of #80-2. The small cartoon is on the right. The enlarged cartoon hangs behind the warp. Shapes and colors are indicated but the tapestry was changed many times before it was completed.*

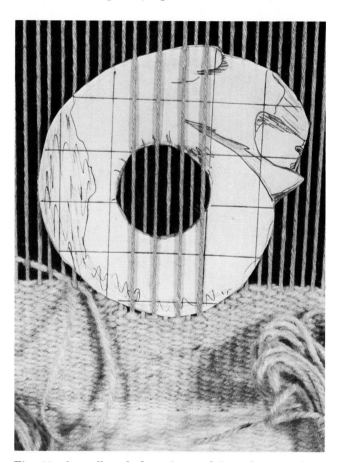

Fig. 11. *A cardboard shape inserted into the warp from which it will be marked.*

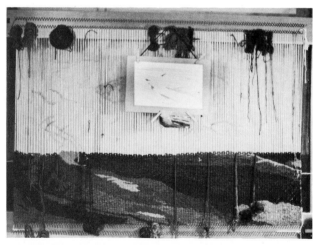

Fig. 10. *This photo was taken during the weaving of #80-3. The small cartoon hangs in front as a constant reminder and colors and shapes are merely suggested. Note the T-pins indicating direction of shapes at the fell.*

ing small points on each end with a felt tip pen. Chalked or pencilled marks sometimes disappear. Once the general proportions have been established, the weaver should feel free to change details. On a

directly behind it. For more complicated designs, it may be necessary to cut the shapes out of the cartoon and mount them directly on the warp and trace the outline. On a horizontal loom a cartoon that is rolled up along with the woven work has a tendency to slip, changing the proportions. The cartoon must be attached firmly beneath the warp and must move forward at exactly the same rate as the woven cloth.

Although there are no exact rules for the rate of shrinkage once the tapestry has been removed from the loom, we know that it is always greater in the length than in the width. Under normal conditions, at least 1" for the warp in the length and ¼" for the weft on the width for each yard should be allowed for any tapestry that is longer than four feet.

If the tapestry must be held to an exact measurement, the cartoon must be drawn and the tapestry woven to include these additional measurements. If the cartoon has been drawn to the exact dimensions, then the weaver must lengthen and widen the work. The stretching can take place on all four sides or the shapes in the cartoon can be slightly increased. The latter is more difficult and must occur during the weaving of each shape, calling for constant adjustments and reevaluation of shape outlines.

The grid

To enlarge a design or sketch or photograph into a working cartoon, some form of grid is used. The grid is the foundation upon which the enlargement is superimposed, whether the exact relationship between shapes is to be maintained or the original shapes changed to expand or shrink as needed. If it is not important that the original drawing be retained, then the grid may be superimposed on it directly. If the original is to be retained, transparent paper may be placed on it and the figure and grid traced.

To make it easier to find your relative position at any time, the squares are numbered in one direction and alphabetized in the other. In this way you can refer to the exact spot at which you are working. Squares C4 and E6 are specific spots exactly in the same place in the tapestry and the cartoon. When a small sketch is squared off and numbered and lettered, it corresponds directly to the enlarged cartoon.

Relationships of one square inch to two, three or more inches are simple enough to expand. If the cartoons do not match in even measurements, the following system may be used: a small sketch is drawn to size on the large one and the grid is extended as required. The same method can also be used for reducing the size of a cartoon.

To enlarge the composition, new horizontal and vertical lines are drawn from the point in the diagonal where they meet to establish the outside dimensions.

Designs may also be distorted by a similar method. The dimensions of the shapes can be extended more in one direction than in another or in parts of one direction than in others. Parts of shapes may also be relatively reduced by the same method.

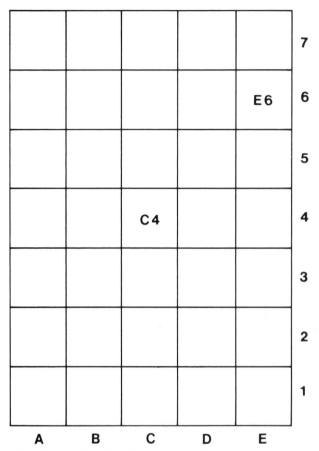

Fig. 12. *A grid with letters and numbers.*

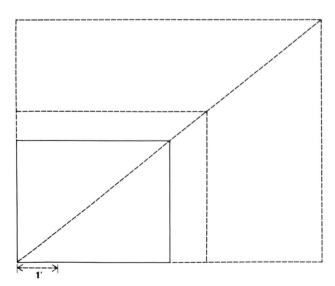

Fig. 13. *To enlarge a rectangle horizontally, a diagonal is drawn through the rectangle, keeping the same proportions. This geometrical method applies to reducing proportions as well.*

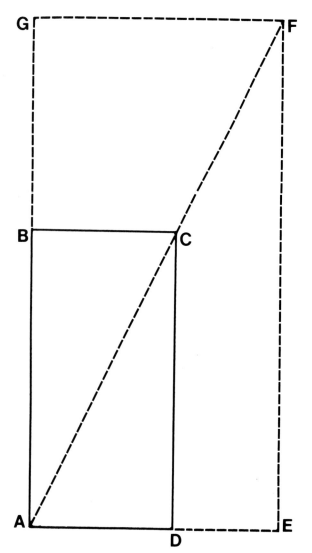

Fig. 14. *To enlarge a rectangle vertically, the same formula applies. AD is extended to E and AB is extended to G. A perpendicular is drawn from A through C to F. The expanded cartoon is now AEFG and the design may be entered upon it.*

Drawing a cartoon

When drawing a cartoon, necessary tools to expedite the process should be at hand: a large, straightedge ruler for the edges and grid, a carpenter's square for exact right angles and a compass for circles. The cartoon itself is a tool that acts as a guide and will, in all probability, be discarded when the work is completed. It is a waste of time to draw in freehand that which may be more quickly and accurately accomplished with proven tools. A camera and various types of enlarging equipment can also expedite the cartoon process. The original can be photostated or projected by an enlarger onto a large grid.

The cartoon, drawn on heavy paper such as brown kraft, should be several inches larger than the intended tapestry with space left on all sides for attachment. It may be attached to a wall with tape or push pins, or stapled to a rod hung at the correct height behind the loom. The additional inches also leave room for some maneuverability if the cartoon is to be held under the warp on a horizontal loom.

Weaving freely without any cartoon or without enlarging an original small sketch is an excellent way to advance and refine our creative faculties, although this way of working entails certain risks. There are no lines or proportions to follow and the woven shapes may prove to be quite different than what was originally intended. In particular, there is a tendency to expand the lower portions beyond what was envisaged, leaving less room for the upper portion of the composition. Dimensions tend to become distorted as we get carried away in the progress of colors in a certain shape and pass the limits that were mentally set. Design limits can be marked on the warp with felt tip pens or small pieces of yarn can be tied to different places on individual warp ends to act as reminders and direction pointers.

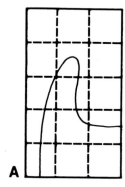

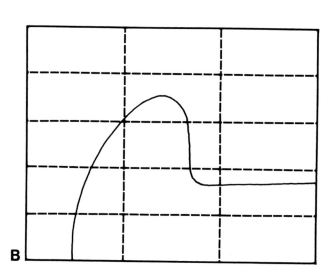

Fig. 15. *The small grid A is 5' x 3'. The larger, distorted grid B is 7' x 9'. The vertical 7' of the large grid was divided into 5 equal spaces and the horizontal 9' was divided into 3 spaces, both similar to the divisions in the small grid A.*

IX
PLANNING, FINISHING AND HANGING A TAPESTRY

Planning; Hanging; Hemming; A False Hem; Rod Support and Framing; Finishing; Fringe; Cleaning Up; Blocking and Pressing; Moth Protection; Fireproofing

Planning

The problems of hanging a tapestry have never been fully resolved. Not only must the theme of the tapestry be determined but the technique, size and weight (types of yarn) must also be considered. The means by which it will hang may be woven into the tapestry while it is still on the loom or be added after it has been cut free.

Hanging

There is some feeling against making nail holes in walls, especially where the tapestry will not remain in a permanent position for long periods and sizes and shapes which will replace it may vary. One solution is to hang picture molding across the width of the wall next to the ceiling and suspend the tapestries from it with flat S hooks and transparent nylon.

A current method is being tried with Velcro®. This system uses two mating tapes, one comprised of hundreds of small, soft loops and the other of minute, flexible hooks. When the two tapes are pressed together, the hooks engage the loops, forming an adjustable and secure closure. The loop tape is bonded to the top of the tapestry and the hook tape to the wall or to a 4″ wide strip of masonite or plywood, which then must be attached to the wall with a liquid adhesive.

Small, metal, saw-tooth hangers, obtainable in frame shops, may be attached to a wooden support on the top and back of a tapestry as they are attached to lightweight frames. These must be carefully centered and can only be used on smaller, lighter pieces.

If a tapestry is attached to a frame the screw eyes must be put in so that the top of the frame remains close to the wall, not angled out from it. Some weavers are experimenting with PVC pipe and similar armatures that have adjustable elbows and lengths. Tubes may be covered by wrapping before or while the warp and weft are added and their round edges must be taken into account as part of the tapestry. See the tapestry (Fig. 18) in the last chapter. There are sources for loom frames other than the conventional canvas stretcher, such as window sashes and door frames, which will remain a permanent part of the tapestry. (See Fig. 10 in the last chapter.)

If the tapestry is to travel, heavy frames and large odd sizes require special boxing and cannot be shipped in the usual way. There are special packing and shipping companies whose business it is to crate and ship works of art to secure their safe arrival. The cost for such services is high and this too must be considered and included in the early planning stages. Such massive pieces are sometimes woven in sections to be joined together after they have been shipped.

Hemming

Traditionally the practice has been to hem all four sides with strips of tightly woven cotton fabric, neatly mitered at the corners. Classic tapestries woven with fine yarns frequently required support to maintain their verticality. Heavier yarns often used by contemporary weavers hold their dimensions more easily and rarely require reinforcement.

If a woven hem is to cover the rod which will support the work, additional inches must be added to the length of the warp. Similarly if the bottom is to be turned up into a hem, those additional inches too must be added to the total.

If the top and bottom of the tapestry are to be hemmed, the area that is turned back should be a continuation of the face design and color. It is good practice to weave at least one inch beyond the turning point so that an extraneous color on the hem will not show on the face. In traditional tapestries rings were sewn to the upper hems and were not intended to hold rods. If the tapestry is to hang from rings, it is important that they be placed in precisely measured relationship to the total width of the tapestry so that the nails in the wall correspond to them. This guards against undesirable folds or sags in the hung work. Rings should preferably be of bone, plastic or wood. Metal may rust and will eventually show on the face of the tapestry.

When heavy, bulky or a wide variety of yarns are used in the weft, the tapestry may rack when it is removed from the loom and the tension relaxed. A weighted rod attached to the bottom or inserted into a bottom hem to let the work "hang out" for a time may help straighten it. Reinforcing steel rods in different weights and diameters are easily available from building supply stores. They may be temporarily lashed to the bottom or inserted into the hem. After a time the warp and weft relationship adjusts and realigns itself and the tapestry will, hopefully, hang straight thereafter.

Hems need not be woven with the same number of p.p.i. as the body of the work. The weft may be beaten in with fewer p.p.i. In this way there will be less bulk at the turn and for the rest of the hem. Selvages may be pulled together slightly by the hem weft so that side openings will not show from the front.

A false hem

If a tapestry requires that it be woven without a top hem, i.e., the face must reach to the top of the warp, a false hem in the form of a strong tape may be basted to the upper back. Its ends should be turned under so that the addition will not show from the

sides. The tape should be sewn on close enough to the top so that when the support rod is inserted, the whole top will not fall forward causing the tape to show. Screw eyes placed behind the bar will tip the top of the tapestry away from the wall. If they are screwed into the top, a transparent nylon may be run through the screw eyes holes and held with lark's heads, holding the work parallel to the wall. If nails can be put in the wall the screw eyes may be hung directly from them.

Whatever support is used must be integrated into the work as though it belongs to it and was not added as an afterthought. Stapling a tapestry to the

Fig. 1. *A False Tape. Strong furniture webbing tape supports the tapestry and the hanging rod.*

Fig. 2. *A redwood support. The small redwood comma is in keeping with the colors, shape and natural linen fringe of this tapestry.*

back of a piece of driftwood or wooden rod which relates neither in color nor size nor texture is out of context and in bad taste.

Warp ends or loops that are turned back and reentered into ribs at the top of the tapestry will narrow it. Threading one warp end back into its own rib will not make any perceptible difference, but if each rib is raised with additional ends, the selvages will inevitably be drawn closer together.

Rod support and framing

It is also possible to lash a wooden support to the tapestry, but this can only be done with a slim rod which will not bend and will not be so thick as to prevent the work from hanging flat against the wall.

Fig. 3. *Lashing. Small holes are drilled into a ¼" x 1½" bat for a flat support with screw eyes in the top.*

Such lashing and all hems must be made inconspicuously so that no evidence of their existence should appear on the face of the work to distract the eye. They are usually sewn on with the same color yarn as the weft. If there are color variations across the width of the tapestry or the weft is not strong enough, a neutral, strong, fine two-ply linen is often used. As a blunt needle is passed through the weft, it should pick up about ½" of weft, rather than just one strand which could pull too tight and show on the face.

For a three dimensional, free-hanging piece that will be viewed from all sides, a swivel may be attached to the top so that the piece will rotate freely.

Few tapestry designs can sustain top warp ends being knotted and allowed to fall where they will. Carrying the ends around the top to the back and securing them individually may be a better resolution.

A support may be woven into a tapestry, but it must be remembered that the face of the support will show through the unwoven warp ends. On a long, narrow tapestry the selvages have a tendency

to curl in and rods are sometimes woven in to hold the selvages straight. If the warp ends, one-half of the e.p.i. (the other half being behind the rod), are interlaced in front of the support, a ridge will result. A dowel is the most obvious support from which to hang a weaving but it is also the most banal. A wooden dowel has no texture and very little color. There are many other supports that are preferable. A hanging device must act as more than a support; it is an intrinsic part of the hanging and must be of a

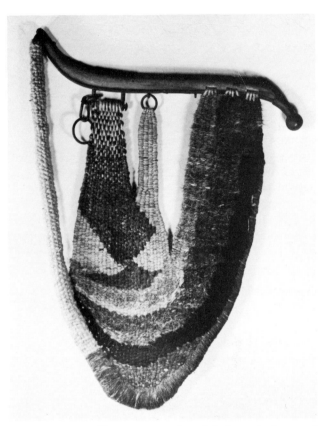

Fig. 4. *A hame. The warp was threaded through the metal bars and holes in half of a curved wooden harness.*

material, shape and color that relates directly to the work that will hang from it. It need not be round; it can be square or triangular. It can be of a grained wood left raw or finished so that the grain shows. It can be oddly shaped like driftwood or deliberately shaped by laminating or steaming.

Dowels look better if they are covered or painted, but the colors must be in keeping with the tapestry. Metal or plastic rods, chair rungs or other found or constructed shapes are possibilities. Such rods may be suspended from the top beam with the warp in the form of lark's heads attached to them at the top. The bottom of the warp may loop around the lower row of nails in the usual fashion.

As part of a more professional approach, some weavers are stretching their finished work on frames or plywood so that they appear more like paintings. The tapestry covers the front and wraps around and behind the frame for several inches on all four sides. These additional inches must be included into the original planning. Even a small, narrow frame requires at least 4″ to cover the sides and a short distance around the back. If not anticipated, a loss of 8″ or more can destroy the composition.

If the tapestry is attached to a surface from behind, it is better to staple it to the support than to glue it. Staples can be tapped down to hold permanently or they can be removed if the tapestry is not exactly squared. Backing such as burlap can be basted or stapled to the back of the work to give it a clean finish. A lining on an unstretched tapestry, however, will have a tendency to pull the selvages toward each other and the work will not hang flat.

All frames must be reinforced or braced, depending on their size, and the rate of stretch on a tapestry must be controlled as it is being attached. Weft picks and warp ends must be held parallel to the horizontals and verticals of the support. If this control is not kept, the work will be pulled out of alignment and the design distorted. The tapestry is turned face down on a large sturdy surface. The frame or plywood is placed on top of it and the centers and corners are secured first. The rest of the

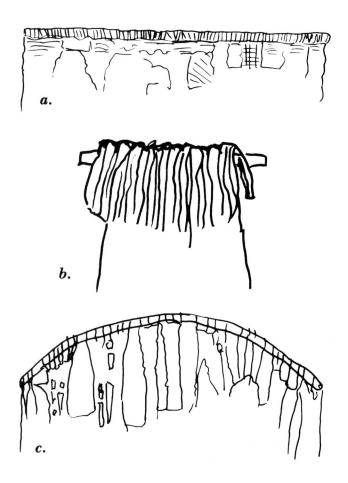

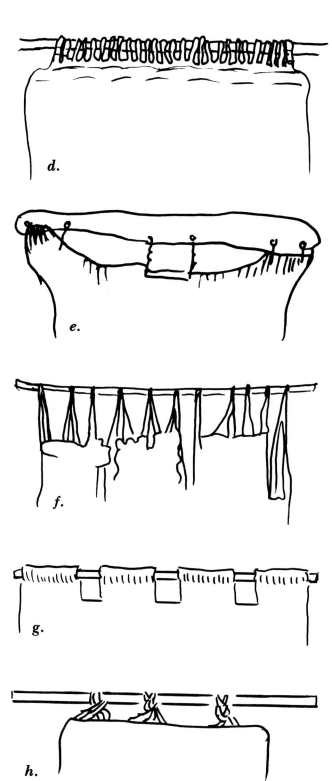

Fig. 5. *Other ways of hanging a tapestry. a) A continuous warp is wrapped around a supporting rod. b) Warp ends tumble loosely over a top supporting rod. c) A laminated wooden arch supports non-aligned warp ends. d) Woven strips encircle a round support. e) A found piece of wood with only six holes drilled for warp support. f) Warp bouts gathered together as they encircle a round support. g) Wide woven strips encircle the support as a hem. h) Warp ends are grouped and braided to encircle the support.*

edges are then fastened to the frame, constantly checking the alignment.

A bulky weft on a tapestry that is to be framed will project out beyond the turned-back edge, breaking the frame line. This is acceptable if a straight edge is not required, but is disturbing if a line is meant to be straight. The extending bulk can be forced to the back, inside the frame.

Sharp corners on a stretched tapestry are likely to poke through unless the tapestry weft is very heavy and well beaten in. Corners can be sanded and padded with a fine but firm material so that the wood will have less tendency to penetrate the corners of the tapestry.

Unless the work has been commissioned or planned for a particular area, it is difficult for the weaver to anticipate where the tapestry will eventually hang. The ideal situation, in which the weaver knows the color of the wall and the source of light, is rare. We must therefore hope for the best light placement with an inconspicuous background.

Finishing

Finishing is included with planning because it is part of that process and not something to be thought about after the work is completed. Finishing is an all-embracing term covering the treatment of a tapestry after completion. This includes such processes as brushing up the nap, closing slits where needed, cutting away extra weft lengths, moth-proofing, surface protection and fireproofing when necessary. All of these may be done while the tapestry is under tension on the loom or after it has been removed. In textile finishing the "hand" and appearance of a fabric may be, and frequently is, entirely changed by the finishing process. In tapestry finishing the appearance of the surface usually remains the same as when it is woven.

Fringe

Knots, braids and fringe are being used less frequently as finishes for contemporary hangings because they often are not compatible with the rest of the design.

On tapestries that do require a fringe, it is generally made from the unwoven warp that has been left at the bottom. At times this warp does not have sufficient bulk or body and looks skimpy. Additional fringe may be added by lark's heads worked over the bottom picks. Such additional yarn may have a tendency to sag unless it is made of lightweight material. The fringe may be reinforced with a false weft secured on the back, brought down inside a rib, crossed in front of a warp end and returned up the next rib. This both reinforces the bottom and secures the additional yarn.

An overhand knot fringe in one or more rows is the simplest one to make. The first row of knots is pushed up as close to the bottom pick as possible. For additional rows the warp in the knots may be divided with the second row of knots falling between those of the first row. On the last row of knots, the first and last group at the selvages are knotted by themselves.

Braids will hang better if they are thicker rather than thinner and they must be in keeping with the body of the work. Skinny little braids hanging from a heavy bulky tapestry look incongruous. If there are too many ends for the desired finish, some may be worked back into the tapestry on the back while the others are used. Wrapping the end of a braid instead of knotting it helps it hang straighter. One of the strands of the fringe can be used to wrap or if the warp is too heavy, one end can be unplied and one ply used alone. If the unplied strand tends to shred it can be strengthened by twisting as it is wrapped, as in spinning. To secure tightly, see the chapter on wrapping. If the fringe is to be left hanging without any visible finish, a blanket stitch may be taken on the back to secure the weft.

Cleaning up

Some weavers feel very strongly that the back of a tapestry should be as free of weft tails as the front. If tails cannot be overlapped in the pick because of bulk or interference with the design, they may be reentered on the back into a rib and drawn down until there is no possibility that they can accidentally be pulled out from the front. Other weavers follow the traditional system and let weft ends hang on the back as they will.

If an end is to be reentered it should be continued horizontally over one more warp end on the back in the same pick in which it ended. It is then drawn down vertically for 1″ to 2″. If the weft tail is long enough it can be threaded through a blunt, large-eyed tapestry needle and reentered. If the end is too short the needle may be pushed down into the rib and then threaded and pulled through. An alternative to the needle, a crochet hook, may be forced up into the rib, a small loop of the tail passed around the hook and the whole pulled down through the rib.

When one weft is exhausted and another is started, the two tails are next to each other with an uncovered warp end between them. This exposed warp end should be covered even though it is only seen from the back. If it is left uncovered, a small hole sometimes appears on that spot, depending on the bulk of the weft. To avoid this possibility, the two ends should be crossed and entered into each other's ribs. In this way, each tail continues in its original direction, crosses, and no hole appears.

If a weft is too heavy to be forced down into a rib and makes a bulge on the face, it can be unplied or split and drawn down in two adjoining ribs.

All slits at the edges of a tapestry must be closed or an opening will appear; the work will not have a straight line at the top and bottom and will show a break where the openings occur.

Long slits that result from straight vertical lines in a design may be left open but more frequently the design calls for their being closed. On a vertical loom the slits should be sewn together while the warp is still under tension. On a horizontal loom this is very difficult unless the tapestry has been woven face down.

The closing stitch holds the two separated wefts so that the closing weft sinks down between them and does not show. The stitching should be secure enough to hold the two sides of the slit together but not so tight that it pulls them out of alignment. Whether the sewing thread progresses in a diagonal that changes direction with each stitch or a one-direction diagonal that is connected by a horizontal is a matter of personal preference.

A third method of closing a slit avoids diagonals and remains within the vertical and horizontal construction of the tapestry. This method is recom-

mended above the other two and is especially preferable for larger tapestries with long slits.

Greek fret is a term used in common in decorative art and architectural design as well as for a particular pattern. Repeated straight line segments are connected at right angles to each other with horizontal lines that are approximately the same length. This closing stitch resembles the horizontal picks as much as possible. Depending on the type of weft yarn, a needle is threaded with the stronger and less conspicuous color of the two wefts and is secured on one side of the beginning of the slit. A knot is usually out of keeping with the rest of the work and the securing should be done by running the needle up and down in several ribs. One side of the slit weft is picked up for about ¼". The closing thread is brought across horizontally to the other side of the slit, carried up through several weft loops and returned horizontally to the first side. The horizontal direction of the sewing thread, as it crosses the slit, parallels the picks of the slit and is less likely to be seen than overcasting with a diagonal stitch behind the opening.

Sometimes certain warps are left unwoven and there are no controls to hold the last few picks at the bottom or the first few picks at the top in place. These picks will remain beaten in for a while, but will inevitably separate from the rest within a short time. To avoid this sag or loosening, they may be secured invisibly using the same color as the weft and the same technique for securing the bottom of a tapestry. The mending weft covers the uncovered warp end of the last pick.

Blocking and pressing

Tapestries rarely require blocking. If a small, light tapestry is not the desired shape when removed from the tension under which it was woven, it may be squared up with a moist water spray but this is at best a questionable practice. Spread flat on its face on a protected surface the tapestry may be pinned into the desired shape. A spray of cool water is sprinkled on the surface and the work is not moved until it is completely dry. Ironing with a hot steam iron on the wrong side of the work, even with a protecting cloth, may flatten the face, show iron marks on the right side and shrink the fibers because of the heat. A tapestry of heavy yarns will not be changed and finer yarns may overreact.

Fig. 6. *Closing stitches. The left row alternates diagonal with horizontal stitches. The right row has diagonal closures. The center row shows the least, alternating vertical and horizontal stitches.*

Moth protection

Moths thrive in warm temperatures of 70° and over. The moth eggs, which are small and pinhead like in appearance, may hatch out in from six to ten days, but have been known to lie dormant for longer periods of time. Moth crystals, moth balls, and moth sprays may be used in yarn or tapestry storage areas but only constant vigilance will afford protection from this pestilence. Moth sprays are more practical for finished tapestries that do not have hems into which crushed moth balls may be tucked.

It is self-evident that the fibers used in a tapestry must be free of moth eggs. Before it leaves the studio, the tapestry should be sprayed on its back and the buyer instructed that this treatment be periodically repeated after it is hung.

Moths are not choosy as to the type of yarns in which to lay their eggs and may be found in jute and sisal as well as wool. Only treated manufactured fibers are free of this problem. Other conditions that can affect the appearance of a tapestry are temperature, humidity and reaction to chemicals in the air.

Mildew also thrives in warm, humid temperatures, and tapestries hung in such atmospheres should be protected with fabric protector sprays. If there is any question about the effect of these sprays on the yarn, they should be tried on smaller samples of the same fibers before treating the finished tapestry.

Although it may be easier to spray the tapestry while it is hanging, the moisture spreads more evenly if it is spread horizontally on a firm, flat surface. If the tapestry is left hanging to dry, overwetting in one area and thereby adding unnecessary weight may distort the overall shape during the drying process. It is almost impossible thereafter to return it to its original dimensions. All tapestries should be mothproofed and perfectly dry before they are moved or packed.

To make a tapestry more rigid, some weavers spray with a stiffener, fixative, uncolored laquer, hair spray or the like. These sprays can have a dulling effect, or depending on the spray, offer a more reflective surface than desired. If the back alone is sprayed it will stiffen the interlacement but will not show on the face. Some weavers are experimenting with mixing mothproofing material with stiffening spray. There is no evidence that the mothproofing is affected adversely by this mixture and it is generally assumed that the effect lasts for about one year.

Fireproofing

It is most important to be aware of the fire laws in public buildings in which a tapestry is to hang. Nothing is more dismaying than to find that a completed tapestry cannot be delivered because fireproofing laws were not known or were ignored. Generally the laws dealing with fireproofing designate the maximum number of people a public room can hold before requiring that all products containing fibers be made fire-resistant.

It is reported that a fiber called Cordoron has been developed, 10% of which, when mixed with wool, makes the whole blend fireproof, meeting fire regulation codes. This fiber has not yet become available to hand-weavers. The mixture of nine ounces borax and four ounces boric acid to one gallon of water in which to soak a tapestry has not proved too successful. Most tapestries are too large to be soaked in such a bath, and when they are sprayed with this mixture, the colors darken and the fibers stiffen, so that they lose their fiber-like quality.

If the fiber dye and the fireproofing chemicals are not compatible, the fiber colors may bleed into each other and destroy the work. Certain cleaning establishments will work with weavers and fireproof yarn before it is woven or after the tapestry is finished.

Professional flameproofing companies not only know the proofing requirements in their state, they also supply verification of their treatment. Flameproofing companies vary in their knowledge of tapestry construction and in their willingness to accept large cumbersome works which do not fit their proofing systems.

The effect of dipping skeins into flameproofing solutions varies with the type of solution and the type of yarn to be processed. Generally the individual fibers become less pliable and if already dyed, colors may darken or become muddy and metallic materials may corrode. If the yarns have not yet been dyed, they will not accept color after treatment in the same way as they would before. Flameproofing solutions shrink different yarns to different degrees, a factor to consider when yarn poundage is calculated.

After flameproofing the fibers may char and glow on being exposed to flames but will not actually burn. However, fireproofing will allow fibers to char when exposed to a flame but not to glow. Watersoluble proofing solutions must be reapplied after washing the yarns. Insoluble compounds such as those used in dry-cleaning establishments not only stiffen and coarsen the fibers but they add weight which may not be significant in small pieces but may be a factor in larger ones.

Hanging materials like wood, metal and plastic react differently to flameproofing solutions. Wood may remain damp long after the rest of the tapestry is completely dry. Plastic, enclosed in a hem, may also retain moisture. In both cases mold can develop, since heavily sprayed fibers retain moisture longer than dyed fiber. Metal tends to rust after proofing treatment and should be sprayed with a rust preventative. Because of the difficulty of proofing very large pieces, many weavers plan their tapestries in sections which can be sprayed separately and attached to each other on the site of their hanging.

X
FIBERS AND YARNS

Properties and Uses of Fiber; Types of Yarn; Warp; Weft; Texture

The properties and uses of fiber

Manipulated by human hands, fiber is silent. For weavers who work on vertical looms there is not even the clack of the shuttle. There is, however, a distinctly satisfying body, arm and finger rhythm as one hand passes the fiber to the other through an open shed. Because we are dealing with fiber which has a predetermined spin and linearity, weaving is a strong physical experience and at the same time a soft tactile one. As other artists we must consider fiber, the material of our medium, with integrity, realizing its inherent properties before we work with it. Fiber has inherent properties: weight, color, body and "hand".

If we "unweave" a woven piece, the fiber returns to its original linear form, sometimes with a slight memory, depending on the type of fiber and how tightly it was spun and woven. Once used, paint or clay or stone are forever changed and can never return to their original state. The true properties of fibers never change from their original state but can only be organized, arranged and manipulated. The thread-like quality always remains. Poured paint may take on a thread-like appearance in pouring or dripping, but once it hits a surface, it spreads and dries. Clay and stone never have a thread-like quality.

Fiber is a soft material that never hardens. The fiber worker does not leave a personal imprint on the material as does the painter or sculptor. It is sometimes possible to recognize the work of different weavers by the way they organize their interlacement or by their choice of color, design, subject or technique, but the fiber itself does not change.

The fiber artist takes this thread-like medium, and organizes and translates it into shapes. Weavers are not limited to over and under interlacement. They may tear, fold, cut, paint over, burn, wrap, mark, spray, or gouge, but the original material remains thread-like in character, regardless of its texture, color or diameter. If fiber is overlayed, the underneath layer will not be visible. The undersurface will not show through unless certain areas are deliberately left uncovered.

The material we work with has weight, thus gravity must be considered. The sculptor is also concerned with weight and gravity, but the materials of sculpture, clay, metal and stone, are in a mass and shape that must be cut away or added to. The fiber the weaver uses has already been spun and probably dyed and will remain so no matter what is subsequently done with it.

Unlike paint, fiber can be held; unlike metal, it has color; and unlike clay or wood, it is thread-like.

With few exceptions, tapestry weavers are generations behind contemporary artists in other mediums. Although the reasons may be valid, most of us are still struggling with designs, cartoons, abstraction versus representation, instead of the use of fiber as an art form in its own right. Contemporary artists feel free to use any materials that will aid in expressing their ideas. The weavers' self-imposed limitation to fiber may be the challenge that will force us to stretch our use of this material beyond any to which it has previously been put.

Different materials affect the appearance as well as change the way in which we perceive a work. Even within a given medium, the same subject and design will appear quite different if woven in harsh materials such as jute or sisal rather than in wool and silk.

Easy accessibility of a certain type of yarn should never be the fundamental reason for choosing it. The idea to be expressed establishes one choice above another. The choice of material is an integral part of the total creative act.

Some ideas are not as easily expressed in fiber as others. Our reaction to a work is strongly affected by the medium in which it is rendered. The same composition executed in fiber is rarely equally well expressed in another medium. The relationship between the fiber, the weaver and the weaving in progress is a very intimate one, more akin to the potter and sculptor than the painter.

Types of yarn

Today's weavers are not limited to the use of natural fibers such as wool, jute, linen, silk, cotton and manufactured fibers such as orlon, nylon, dacron and rayon, but are branching out into copper, wire, leather, rubber, and the like. Fiber may be hard or soft, thick or thin, round or flat, shiny or dull, light or heavy, transparent or opaque, or any combination of these.

An artist chooses a fine hard pencil as opposed to a soft spreading pastel, depending on the subject and how it is to be delineated. In the same way, a weaver chooses the type of yarn and the manner in which it will be used. Using the same type of yarn to depict a wide range of shapes and subjects, the traditional approach to yarn usage, limits the range of expression of those shapes and subjects. By its nature, yarn cannot be expected to have as long a life under normal usage as clay, metal or wood. There are, however, the classic reminders of mummy-bindings and Renaissance tapestries which are still in existence after hundreds or thousands of years.

As we become more sensitive to different fibers we recognize subtle differences such as spin direction, scale slope and surface quality as well as the more obvious features such as diameter, absorption and reflectivity. Despite the increasing number of fibers now available to fiber workers, tapestry weavers depend on the most familiar: wool, linen, silk and cotton.

It is not necessary to use warp and weft yarns that are similar or even related. Different weights, textures, plies and types of warp require different types of weft. It is obvious that using a heavy weft on a fine or loop warp will not work. But reversing the two by using a fine loop mixed with another fine weft for support to interlace with or encircle a heavy warp may, by its contradiction, create an interesting result.

Warp

The choice of warp is determined by the type of design and the techniques to be used. Warp strength must be decided in terms of the overall proportions of the tapestry, the e.p.i., p.p.i., its smoothness or roughness, its tensile strength, its elasticity and recoverability and its ability to withstand abrasion.

Basically there are three types of warp used in tapestries: linen, wool and cotton. Each has its own advantages and disadvantages. Of the three, cotton, sometimes recommended for beginners, is the least advantageous. It has very little body, no resilience or spring and unless tightly twisted, has a tendency to fray and weaken as a result of the weft interlacement packed into a small area. Over a larger space, it makes an inert warp which does not respond easily to finger manipulation.

Although linen has less elasticity than wool, it is, when plied, strong and stable. Because it has less

elasticity it is usually warped slightly looser than wool. As weaving progresses upward, the over and under interlacement takes up any slack so that by the time the top part of the warp is being woven it may become difficult to create a shed that is sufficiently open to accept the weft.

Because heavier linens add body to tapestry construction, they are frequently selected for warp, whether they are to be totally covered or not.

Silk, like linen, has a reflective quality which can be useful as an addition to a group of other fibers. By itself or in a unit of several silks, it tends to be very soft and has practically no body.

Except for particular purposes, synthetic fibers are not usually used for warps, both because they have no elasticity and because of their frequent slick quality. There are no fibers protruding to catch and hold the weft and any weft must be beaten in with many more p.p.i. than would be required for another type of warp. For weft, these fibers may be mixed with others like silk or linen to add other qualities.

Wool, on the other hand, is usually warped a little more tightly, or the warp ends tend to become loose toward the top. On a horizontal loom this is no problem because the loosened warp can always be tightened by pulling up on the cloth beam. However, it is obvious that weaving on a somewhat looser warp in one part and a tighter warp in another will not result in a consistently woven work. The looser warp will sag. Good tension must be established and retained throughout the whole project.

The form that wool takes, how it is spun, can have a tremendous influence on whether it should or should not be used for warp. Wool can be spun so finely that it will almost require a magnifying glass to see its spin, or it can be spun so irregularly that it can be of interest in itself. Neither of these types are recommended for warp except for particular effects.

Because tapestries are expected to have a longer life than other objects made of fiber, it is important to use the best yarns available. Of these, wool is the most versatile and useful. Less than the best yarn may be permissible for students who are learning weaving techniques and whose work is not expected to endure or be sold. Even here, it is better, whenever possible, to become familiar with the best material as one is learning. The struggle for weavers to be accepted into the fine arts is not served well by the use of shoddy materials. Because of its reflective quality silk offers an excellent contrast to wool, but its use as the major yarn of a tapestry is usually prohibited by its cost.

I use and teach with both wool and linen. They respond to the hand by giving way when necessary and return to their former elasticity and position when the pressure is removed. The only limitation to the use of either is that yarn not spun for warp is more loosely plied and not strong enough to take the punishment of being pushed, pulled and rubbed.

Some rug yarns are excellent for warp, others are not. We cannot rule out single ply warp, whether linen or wool. Most fray quickly but some work better than a less twisted two ply, especially if coated with a strengthening solution such as diluted wallpaper paste. A heavier, five to eight ply linen will support a large tapestry but is rough to work with, resulting in torn nails and cuticles. However, it will not stretch as much as a wool warp.

Some warps specifically spun and called tapestry warp are really not warps for tapestry. There are many types of wool that may be used for that purpose. Specifically, we are looking for a smooth two-or-more ply wool, quite tightly twisted. Some so-called mill-ends are comparatively less expensive and fulfill the above requirements.

The sett and weight of the warp is determined by the design to be woven. If there are many small details, then a finer warp with many more e.p.i. will give more design flexibility. The weft may then move diagonally and laterally for shaping in smaller increments. For such a design, it may also be necessary to forego the strict verticality of the rib technique and use the warp ends individually or in units. For instance, if a warp sett is 16 e.p.i. in four groups of four ends each, each group may be used as though it were one end with the weft passing over and under the group. Where the movement of the shape requires a slower rise, individual ends may be picked up or dropped with each succeeding pick. This, of course, requires that the adjoining shapes compensate. The original units may be reestablished in the same order, be split, or new or irregular ribs be started. This technique adds design and textural quality not achieved by strict rib construction. It is, however, preferable that whatever system is used be planned ahead or the weaving will appear to have obvious errors.

Thicker and heavier warp requires fewer e.p.i. with a resulting step-like rather than a smooth appearance of the edges of the shape. With different warps and different setts each choice finds its own accompanying wefts.

Since most tapestries are weft-faced, the color of the warp is not of great significance. Traditionally, warp was off-white, but if it is to be totally covered its color really does not matter. Sometimes, due to differences in the types of weft yarns used, minute parts of warp show between weft picks. Some of the suggestions in the section on color will then apply. If the major weft colors are dark, a darker warp will not show through. If the greater number of weft colors are light, then a lighter color warp is preferable.

If an error in warp calculation has been made, additional warp of the same type of yarn but a slightly different tint or shade may be added since the difference will not be seen.

The thicker the warp ends, the fewer e.p.i. This, of course, affects the overall appearance of the work. Widely spaced warp ends do not permit smooth passage or finely detailed design. Fewer e.p.i. mean fewer over and under interlacements over the same area resulting in a coarser surface. Generally, heavier warps are woven with heavier wefts and finer warps with finer wefts. However, interesting effects may be obtained by departing from these conventions.

Whether the warp and weft are coarse or fine is determined by the design. It must be recognized that the finer the yarns, the longer the weaving time. Financial considerations of time and yarn cost are practical aspects which must not be overlooked.

Weft

Traditionally, a single ply homespun type of wool has been considered the best fiber for weft. It is soft and covers the warp well. It is resilient but does not pull apart under ordinary tension. Limiting the weft to this one type, although of different colors, makes for a conventionally uniform surface that presents no problems in tension and smoothness of adjoining areas. This limitation proves to be very confining in terms of surface light reflection, interest and texture.

If we venture beyond one-ply, soft twist yarn and use whatever type, ply, or twist best creates the effect we are searching for, many problems may arise. The choice that must be made is whether to work with the tried and safe, although perhaps less engaging, or the untried, tension creating, but perhaps more creative and certainly more challenging.

Short wool fibers which reach out in many directions and are crimped and curled expose more surface to accept and absorb dye. Yarns whose fibers are longer, smoother and more tightly twisted expose less surface and do not accept dye as easily. The latter, therefore, reflect more light and their colors appear more lustrous.

Wool has always been the classic fiber for tapestry weaving. Worsteds which are more tightly twisted are usually thinner than other wools and are not used as much for weft. For those weavers who combine many strands into one weft unit, the full properties and possibilities of worsteds have yet to be explored.

Tapestry weavers are now starting to use worsted yarns for weft, finding them strong, consistent, easily dyeable and combinable. They may use six strands of 2/20's as a unit for a medium spaced warp, or 12 or more strands for a more widely spaced warp as compared to one strand for a closely spaced warp.

Traditionally, the weft in tapestries has been finer than the warp. Some of the finest fabrics were counted at 42 e.p.i. to 260 p.p.i. Finer linens add luster and light reflection to a weft, whether used as an addition to another mixture or as a total group. Obviously, if the weft of one shape is a small group of fine linen and the next is heavy and bulky, the second will require fewer picks to cover an equivalent space.

Cotton works well for weft when mixed with other yarns but may be too soft by itself. Unless it is mercerized, its colors are usually duller. Mercerizing increases its strength and affinity for dyes as well as its luster and reflectability.

Silk, the only natural fiber in filament form, is highly reflective with a luster that increases the tighter it is spun.

The amount of twist and the number of ply in any thread will affect its color as will the structure into which it is being woven. Linen has an absorption fiber length of a few inches to one yard and, when tightly spun, has a natural luster and body. A tightly woven linen tapestry will therefore reflect more light and appear more lustrous than one of loosely woven wool. It need not be an either/or situation, however. A few strands of linen or silk added to wool will change the appearance of the weave. The same yarn for weft in a plain weave construction will appear deeper and duller than soumak or wrapping in which the color will seem clearer and purer.

Each year new types of yarns not previously available are offered to weavers. These should not necessarily be used because of their novelty or uniqueness, but they do offer a diversity of effects which may be explored. Among these are various bulk yarns which tempt the weaver for quicker and greater coverage. Because of their fiber alignment, diameter irregularity and increased crimp, they cannot be beaten in as closely and are better for other types of design rather than as a replacement for finer yarns.

Texture

The slightest movement on a two-dimensional surface is the beginning of texture. If we think of texture in this way we see that it is not limited to

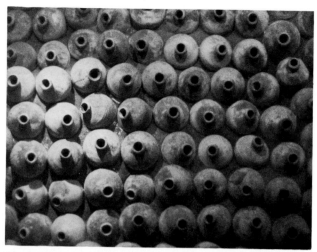

Fig. 1. *Facing in different directions, half-buried pots in a wall in Oaxca, Mexico, create a texture of their own.*

Fig. 2. *Fallen eucalyptus leaves and flecks of sunlight add texture to the roots and trunk of the tree.*

fiber but is all around us. Everything has texture. One of its chief characteristics is its multiplicity of projections reading as an overall surface. Another major characteristic is the way in which light is reflected and absorbed, which is why various types of pile play such an important role. Texture and light also work hand in hand to give life to a surface from the infinitesimal interlacement of fine fibers to the heaviest protruding pile.

Tactile reaction is virtually as important as visual reaction. Up close we see and feel the individual projections. From a distance, although we cannot touch them, we are still aware that the surface is not flat and smooth.

Most tapestries are actually a low relief with projections and recessions covering the whole surface. Weaving interlacement creates texture which may be obvious or subtle. Low relief, middle relief or high relief are determined by the degree to which the projections move away from and return to the plane surface.

Textured yarns have a greater apparent volume than conventional yarns of similar grist. They, like bulk yarns, have a relatively low stretchability and are frequently thrown to the face in a hit-and-miss or soumak technique to make the most use of their surface quality.

Loop yarns are characterized by large numbers of regularly or randomly spaced and sized loops. By themselves, they are weaker and are therefore frequently reinforced in the spinning by a finer, stronger, often different fiber, e.g., wool loops strengthened by rayon. Because of the texture created by the loops, the reinforcing element is hardly seen. The encircling or twining movement of the reinforcing fibers limits the stretchability of this type of yarn which is already partly restricted by the loop construction.

Crimp yarns, characteristically saw-toothed, are harder to the touch and have very little elasticity.

Core yarns are more bulky with a central, more tightly woven core surrounded by loosely spun fibers. This type of yarn stretches easily. Care must be taken to keep it from overextending unnecessarily if the bulky effect is to be retained.

Thick and thin yarns are spun with regularly or randomly spaced finer and bulkier areas. These, too, are frequently reinforced for additional strength.

Two, three and four-ply knitting yarns may be used by separating the ply and using them as though they were singles. Woven in a knitting ply they look coarse. These may also be given additional interest by holding one ply back and pushing the others together, creating small irregular wrap loops around the ply that is held back. The same may be done with yarns in which a thin core acts as a base for

Fig. 3. *Tied to a swivel that is attached to a hook, a weft is held under tension.*

loops or brushed yarns. Thus one yarn serves more than one purpose.

Unplying long units of yarn is simplified by the use of a small swivel. One end is attached to a permanent fixture like a wall hook, with the yarn held at one end by a knot to the loose end of the swivel. Under tension the yarn separates into two units. As the plies are separated, the swivel spins around, releasing the previous spin.

Fig. 4. *The separated plies wrap around both wrists as the swivel spins around, untwisting the weft.*

Space dyed yarns can be used for shading by moving and manipulating those areas where one color grades into another. If the spaces in the yarn are regular, then the exact movement of the shape may easily be followed. If the spacing is random, then some yarn will have to be sacrificed by being dropped behind the warp so that only the section required will be entered into the shed. This yarn may also be used to simulate ikat.

Strength is not as necessary in weft as in warp, so we can also consider yarns which have very little or no spin. These include grasses which, although not continuous, may be tapered and overlapped. Various types of ropes, jute and sisal lose their rope-like appearance if they are unplied. They may also be used singly or mixed with other yarns.

In all of the above types of yarn our greatest concern is with the effect that can be created by their individual or mixed use.

When you have not calculated correctly and there is not enough weft to complete a project, and no more is available, the small remaining amount should be set aside. By adding another texture of the same color, or using a close shade or tint of a similar weft, an intermediate transition area is created with the help of some seeding to avoid a dividing line.

Fig. 5. *A tapestry using space-dyed yarn.*

The remainder of the original color may be then added with tints or shades to extend it.

Flake, nub, knop, loop, spiral and ratine' are all novelty type yarns which can add textural interest. They must, however, be used with care or they overwhelm the design shapes and colors.

An important property of yarn is lightfastness. If a textile made into a garment fades a little after some wear, no great damage is done. A differential fading in a tapestry with colors deteriorating at different rates affects the appearance and may totally change it. Certain colors, like blue, fade more quickly when exposed to direct sunlight. Dye-fast and fade resistant yarns are more available now than they have been in the past.

Luxurious yarns such as cashmere are rarely used in tapestry primarily because of their cost; also we are less concerned with the feel of a tapestry than textiles for clothing, drapery or rugs.

Knowledgeable weavers are constantly searching for new yarn offerings available in a greater diversity than before. Handweaving magazines offer a wealth of yarn sources, both in articles and advertising material. An up-to-date reference file enables a weaver to turn at any time to a yarn which may not have been needed when the samples first arrived, but is perfect for the current project. Although prices, types of yarn and colors are constantly changing, such a file provides a ready basis for reference and comparison.

XI
TAPESTRY WEAVING TECHNIQUES

Part 1: Basic Weaving Techniques; *Tapestry; Slits; Overlapping Weft Tails; Slit Control; Weft Control; Multiple Weft Direction; Hatching.* Part 2: Additional Weaving Techniques; *Single Dovetail; Single Interlock; Double Interlock; Lazy Lines; Hit-and-Miss; Seeding; Multiple Weft Manipulation; Changing Rib and Shape Relationships; Warp Manipulation; Outlining Shapes; Hills and Valleys; Weaving within a Circular Frame; Twilling; Eccentric Wefts; Wedge Weaves; Gauze Weaves; Twisted Wefts; Correcting Errors.*

Part 1: Basic Weaving Techniques

Tapestry

Technique is determined by the subject or feeling and general structure of the work. Tapestry refers either to a specific technique or to a type of mural.

It is not possible in one book to include all or even most fiber techniques or constructions from their inception to final incorporation. As each approach is developed, new problems arise requiring fresh solutions. The following is an attempt to organize and delineate those that may be of greatest use to the searching fiber artist.

Formerly, tapestry technique meant an organization of discontinuous weft-faced, plain weave, rib-like construction. The warp, held under considerable tension, permitted the shed to open but forced the weft to move around the warp to cover it, rather than both interlacing with each other equally.

Interrupted wefts do not have to be different colors. Shapes may be formed with the same color (see Lazy Lines), but the use of different colors for each shape makes them more visible and gives them body. Covering the warp with discontinuous wefts once was considered the only technique permissible for tapestry weaving, but now weavers use any technique that best expresses their ideas, mixing them as needed, and frequently using the warp as an additional design element.

In some of the early literature on tapestry weaving, a whole weft meant what we today define as two picks, i.e., the weft passing in one direction and returning in the other.

To eliminate long slits, the Peruvian method inserted a fine, almost invisible weft from selvage to

selvage after every three or four inlaid picks. The long weft was entered in the same shed as the last inlay pick, which, being of heavier yarn, covered it.

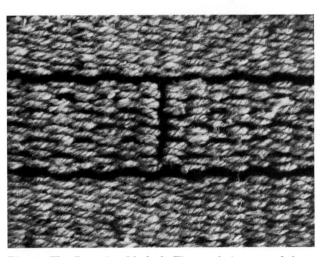

Fig. 1. *The Peruvian Method. Fine weft is entered from selvage to selvage in the same shed with the meet-and-separate pattern weft.*

This is possible only if all the wefts are moving across the tapestry at the same time in the same pick. Today's tapestry designs frequently require a weft from selvage to selvage.

The fly-shuttle is an excellent device for this purpose. Obviously those shapes which do not extend to the selvages must be laid in, but there are often areas between shapes which can profit from this time-saving technique. Stripes can be threaded as part of the warp. Bars can be woven on the fly and the whole may then be removed from the horizontal loom, stretched on a vertical loom and supplementary warp and weft added. The fly-shuttle handle may be hung

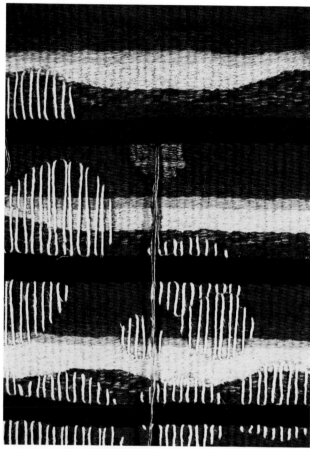

Fig. 2. *Fly-shuttle woven and laid-in shapes. Stretched on a vertical loom after being cut away from a horizontal one, supplementary warp was added and woven.*

Fig. 3a & 3b. *Different Wefts. In 3a, two heavier linen wefts on the right meet-and-separate with three, finer wefts on the left. In 3b, one heavy weft on either side occupies the same space as four finer wefts.*

out of the way when the inlay is required and used again where selvage to selvage weft returns.

Slits

The most traditional and frequent tapestry technique used is within each pick where one weft end meets and turns away from another. Slits occur because the wefts do not connect. Dovetail and interlock are connecting devices. All three techniques have many variations and may be combined in a number of ways.

Slits are often called kilims, also sometimes spelled kelim, khilim, chelim, etc. These terms actually derive from rug construction and are preferably not used when discussing slit tapestry techniques. Tapestry slits may be any length but the longer they become, the more difficult it is to control their edges. There is considerable evidence that the slit was one of the earliest techniques used by weavers in many parts of the world.

Slits are sometimes pictorially called "meet and separate", "meet and part" or "meet and return". This implies that one weft meets another in one shed

and turns back in the next shed, and this is exactly what happens when both wefts are the same yarn. However, when one weft is considerably heavier than the other, the difference in the fell line as they are both beaten in immediately becomes evident. It is therefore sometimes necessary to enter several picks of the finer weft as against one pick of the heavier one. They will still meet and separate, but one weft does this once while the other does it several times to build up to the level of the first.

When a slit moves laterally to the next position between two warp ends in the next pick, it starts a diagonal direction of slits which may or may not be continued, depending on the shape. If the lateral step-wise progression is continued, the angle of the diagonal will be determined by the type of yarn used in the weft and warp and by the p.p.i. and e.p.i. The same one-step diagonal rise in each pick will be sharper with heavy wefts and flatter with finer ones. When the angle of direction is being decided, these facts must be considered.

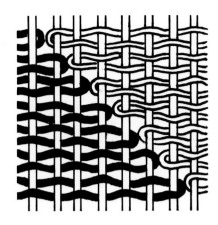

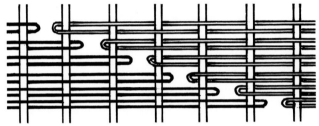

Fig. 4. *Lateral Weft Movement. In the lower illustration the fine weft is well beaten down causing a flatter angle. In the upper illustration the angle is sharper because the weft is heavier.*

A woven structure is weakened when a vertical slit is continued for more than one pick. Similarly, a diagonal slit in which the weft turns back more than one time is weaker than when this occurs just once. However, such weak places are not critical to tapestry structures and may be strengthened by sewing the openings together.

The slit technique as practiced by the Incas produced a tapestry with two finished sides. The end of one color weft and the beginning of the next one were concealed in the short picks of the design.

Some weavers feel that it is easier to keep all wefts in the same fell pick, no matter how many different wefts are in use at the same time. This means that each butterfly or bobbin is picked up, entered in the shed for the design length and dropped before the next one is picked up, a time consuming proce-

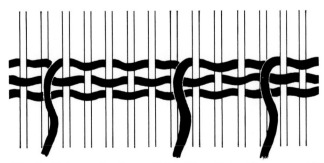

Fig. 5. *Wefts in the Same Pick. All wefts in the same pick moving in the same direction.*

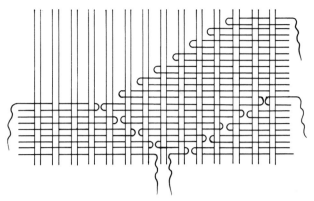

Fig. 6. *Building Up a Shape. A production technique possible only when the shape is narrowing.*

dure. Continuing to build up a shape with one color is a production technique which saves considerable time. Building up one small area at a time permits a clearer visual record as the design develops than is possible when all shapes are woven at the same time.

Sometimes there is a temptation to continue building one shape in one color far beyond the other shapes, a questionable practice for two reasons: the space between the woven and unwoven areas has a tendency to spread as it increases, and the woven warp ends tend to draw together; the second reason involves color and compositional changes that may be made while the work is in progress. A large shape build-up of a very strong color may result in an overwhelming need to dull or change it by decreasing its importance in relation to the surrounding shapes. This is less likely to happen when the other colors and shapes are present as originally planned.

Overlapping weft tails

If weft tails are to be overlapped within a pick, they should be torn rather than cut and the ends feathered out so that they will not show on either side. If the weft has several plies, they may be torn individually into different lengths and the weft ply lengths entered to meet rather than overlap.

Weft tails may be left either hanging, totally embedded in the back rib, or partially embedded. There is little likelihood of ends pulling out to the face with a well beaten-in, fine weft, as is more likely to occur with a heavier weft with fewer p.p.i. Reentering the full length of heavier wefts into back ribs for two to three inches may show a bulge on the face. Partial reentry for security is probably the best solution. Whenever possible, starting or ending weft tails should be entered away from slits or selvages, so they will be less likely to be seen and easier to bury.

When different colored shapes are very small it may be more practical to carry a weft from one to the other behind the warp than to start a new butterfly. Non-structural floats may be left uncut or, if the float is long enough, cut later. It is also more practical to carry one strand of a group of wefts while the others are being used in a pick. Shapes or their contours may be lightened or darkened or subtly changed by floating certain weft ends behind the warp and letting them rejoin the group as required, thus eliminating the need for many separate and different weft group butterflies.

It sometimes happens that the same weft is used in several groups at the same time. Making bobbins or butterflies with different combinations may become very messy. It saves disentangling time and temper in the long run if separate bobbins of the same weft are wound and each used in its own group. As one butterfly is completed, its ends remain together with a single bow hung from one of the bottom row of nails. This group is then conveniently available for the next butterfly without having to single out any one weft from another group.

If a ball of weft is wound on a ball winder, pulling should be started from the inside end. The ball will then remain stationary and will not roll around. This is particularly helpful when more than one weft is being prepared for a butterfly composed of several wefts.

In present day usage of different types of wefts it is sometimes necessary to compare them to ascertain to what degree they will meet and separate in each shed. Interlocking one with the other and twisting them will quickly indicate how many strands of one weft must be combined to equal one strand of the second weft.

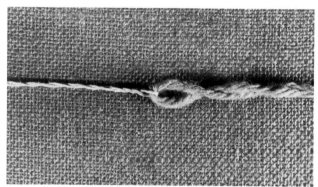

Fig. 7. *Comparing Wefts. Two different weight wefts are interlocked and twisted for comparison.*

Slit control

There is a tendency for internal selvages created by slits to draw together so that instead of two straight lines, a V is formed as the opening continues to spread. Continuous care must be taken so that both sides remain parallel. Even with care, the place where the two must be joined again is likely to create

a sagging arc with the first joining pick. If a long T-pin is entered, with the point catching one selvage warp end and reversing to catch the opposite warp end, the two selvages will be brought together and held. After several picks have been beaten in, the pin may be removed and there will be no visible indication where the two edges were rejoined.

T-pins are also useful as direction indicators of changing shape contours. When many different wefts are used in the same fell and each shape is being individually built up, it is easy to lose track of the directional changes that the shapes take. Repeated referral to a large or small cartoon is necessary. T-pins inserted to point in the desired direction serve as quick reminders as well. See illustration #10 in Chapter VIII.

Weft control

There are usually fewer e.p.i. in a tapestry warp than in a fabric warp. Traditional tapestries are weft faced with the warp set far enough apart to permit the weft to pack down and completely cover it. For this reason we should plan for considerably more weft than in a fabric of more balanced weave. The weft take-up occurs in the arcing or bubbling as it is entered into the shed. Each variation in e.p.i. and type of yarn used in the weft requires its own size of arc or series of arcs and only experimentation will dictate how much weft should be left. Generally, smaller arcs are easier to control and manipulate so that the weft will lie straight, totally cover the warp when beaten in, and not pull in the selvages.

Fig. 8. *Weft Control. The last weft pick before an unwoven area will move unless it is secured. The dark weft on the reverse side barely shows on the face.*

Weft must be entered with such tension that it will position itself in front of and behind alternating or grouped warp ends without disturbing their alignment. This is particularly important with regard to the selvages, which, even if reinforced and under strong tension, tend to pull in toward each other and out again as the upper part of the tapestry is reached. It is both important and sometimes difficult to keep the warp ends in place and the weft entered smoothly without uneven loops on the selvages. Each type of weft has its own elasticity and character and the weaver must adapt the tension as each weft is entered.

In a pick-and-pick weave in which two colors alternate, one color loops the selvage once and does not return until the third pick. The second color remains one warp end short of the selvage. It is left behind the warp and returns on the fourth pick.

It is not necessary to limit the distance that the weft travels in a pick before it is beaten down. Weft may move from selvage to selvage over a comparatively long distance, or in one long arc that is beaten down in small sections. A long arc may be broken up into small arcs or the weft may be entered in small arcs with each one beaten in separately.

For short arcs, beaten in with the fingers, moving from right to left, the sequence is as follows.

1. The right hand holds the weft while the left hand makes and holds the shed open.

2. The weft is passed from the right hand to the left hand through the open shed.

3. The right hand is not taken out of the shed, but immediately presses down the newly formed arc.

This last movement keeps the weft relaxed in front of and behind the warp. At the same time it keeps the weft from being pulled by the left hand as the butterfly is withdrawn. When the weft is on the left, the same order is followed in the opposite direction. With this method the weft is in the correct hand for the next pick without any unnecessary loss of time or movement. Many tapestry weavers develop an ambidexterity in which both hands feed and take from each other equally.

In one way, this manner of handling weft closely

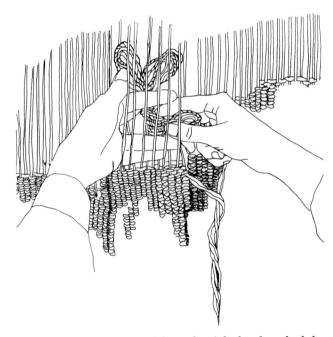

Fig. 10. *The weft is passed from the right hand to the left.*

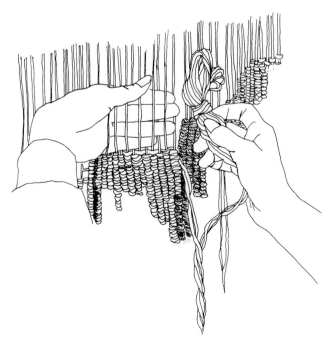

Fig. 9. *Entering and Beating-in a Weft Butterfly, from right to left. The left hand makes the shed while the right hand holds the butterfly.*

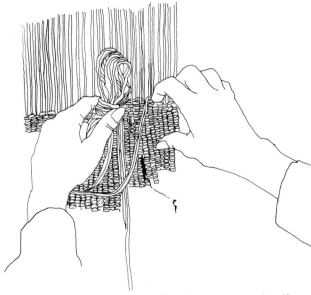

Fig. 11. *The right hand immediately starts pressing (beating) down the newly formed arc.*

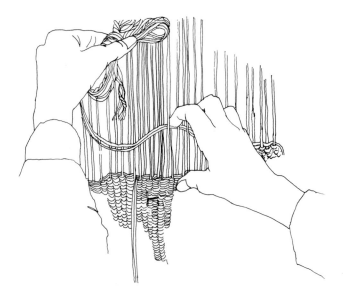

Fig. 12. *The right hand completes the beat.*

Fig. 13. *With the weft in the left hand, the same order is followed in the opposite direction.*

resembles the throw and catch movement of weaving with a shuttle on a horizontal loom. The free hand does the beating, with or without a beater.

If a shed-making device and beater are part of the loom, the same direction sequence is followed, with the free hand manipulating the beater and the feet pressing on the pedals to open the shed. A small, hand-held beater must be picked up, used and put down and cannot have the sensitivity for weft distribution in each pick that the fingers do. Persistent, repeated beating accomplishes very little on a tapestry which, unlike a rug, will not be walked on.

Tugging, tapping, pushing and patting the weft may provide a tactile and kinesthetic gratification but contributes nothing to the construction. On a large work, non-contributing, unnecessarily repeated touching and handling is one of the main factors delaying completion.

The last pick springs back to some extent, depending on the type of yarn and the looseness with which it is entered. Wool, in particular, has this live action, and no amount of beating will keep it in its final place until several other picks are added. Beating or pushing down on the weft affects about four picks. The bottom or first pick has now found its permanent place and the third, second and last pick in turn find theirs as each new pick is added.

On small shapes, the size of the arc is determined by the contours of the shape. On larger shapes, the distance that the hand can comfortably separate and hold the shed open is correct for easy transference of the weft.

Some weavers find different types of rug shuttles useful. I find it unnecessary to wind weft on the shuttle first and then unwind various lengths as needed.

More weft and selvage adjustment is required than in simply pulling out the weft from a butterfly. The amount of weft released from a rug shuttle is controlled by the length of the shuttle, whereas the amount of weft pulled directly from a butterfly as it is being passed through the shed is under total weaver control at all times. For longer arcs, a weft length is usually pulled out before it is entered into the shed and the last bit pulls directly from the butterfly as it passes from one hand to the other.

Using a "crutch" to help hold the selvage at the required width is sometimes considered poor technique. With the many different yarns used for warp and weft and their wide range of elasticity, a "crutch" is more acceptable than having the selvages pull together. See illustration #17 in Chapter VII, where the selvage is held under tension, tied to the loom by a crutch.

Unless a beater is used, different areas may build up to different degrees. It is important that no area be built up in which the shape widens, without at the same time weaving its neighboring shape. After unweaving shapes that have overlapped unwoven areas or trying to needle in underneath an already woven shape, the weaver will quickly understand this basic principle.

Multiple weft direction

If the rise in a design is consistently vertical for all the wefts, then moving them all in the same direction in one pick is not only possible but sometimes preferable, especially for a weaver who is starting to introduce many wefts in the same pick. If all of the weft ends are on the right side of their entry, the one farthest to the left should be returned to the left first. This clears the warp ends for the return of the next weft closest to the left, and so on. When all the ends are on the left of their individual shapes, the next pick should be started with the weft closest to the right.

If only two warp ends are being used for a vertical rise, the figure eight that is woven around them rises more quickly than the equivalent number of plain weave picks over a larger area because of their looping around the warps. If they are to rise at the same rate as the shape next to them, fewer figure eights or more plain weave picks must be used to keep them even.

When more than one weft is used in the same shed and a single-step rise is creating the shape in succeeding picks, the simplest control occurs when all the wefts move in the same direction. If the direction needs to be reversed, each weft will have to pass around the warp end which has already been covered by its neighbor. This is one way to move one warp end at a time, but if more than one warp end is to be passed, the weft in the shed will duplicate a previous weft and there will be two wefts in the same shed at that spot.

Some shapes require more than what one warp end progression will permit. To facilitate this movement, adjoining wefts may be entered in opposition to each other, although this is not always possible. The hatching technique is based on this principle.

Hatching

Hatching is one of the oldest tapestry techniques used to create an illusion of the flow of colors into each other and is an extension of the "meet and separate" concept. Hatching is in the true French tapestry tradition. It was developed as a shaping technique in the eleventh, twelfth and thirteenth centuries by weavers who wished to go beyond placing flat color planes beside each other.

Hatching was also used to suggest three dimensional shapes such as folds and later to delineate skin tones and facial contours.

Hatching is a comb-like process in which two adjoining wefts pass each other and recede in different sheds but do not mix. At a distance, however, they may give the impression of mixing or blending if they are closely related. Although it has been discussed before, it should be emphasized that the "meet and separate" principle must be strictly observed in this technique.

Hatching or "hatchure", as customarily practiced, often involves shading of very closely related colors of many strands or colors in total opposition. When first experimenting with hatching techniques

Fig. 14. *Hatching. Hatching with strong contrasting colors. The cartoon was turned 90° to eliminate the need for too many wefts in the same pick.*

it is helpful to employ strong contrasting colors to see the change of direction as clearly as possible as it occurs. With more experience the contrast need not be as obvious.

There are basically two ways by which a weaver can simulate the blending of colors, either by hatching or shading. Neither of these techniques is comparable to the painter's ability to overlay or blend colors. Because of the strong absorption of light by fiber, the Pointillist technique of very small color areas on another color ground cannot be duplicated in fiber, which does not have the shimmering luminous, flowing surface quality of paint.

Hatching permits the closest possible intermingling of colors, short of using related weft colors in a single unit group. It is one of the few devices which allows the weaver to imitate a gradual passage from one color to another or to tint up or shade down within one color. No matter how subtle the color change, a new color or tint or shade, added to several that have already been entered, will show a line where it has been introduced. If its entry is within a hatching area, the change is still there but is broken up by the coming and going of the colors and the transition is smoother.

Another way to move smoothly from one color to another or from one shade to the next shade gradation is to separate the ply of the new addition and add one ply at a time. At the same time, one ply of the color that has already been in use is dropped. In this way the total weft does not suddenly become thicker at the point of exchange thereby drawing attention to itself. This may also be done with a single ply yarn by pulling out some of the fibers of the ending yarn as well as the starting one. As they overlap in the shed, the two yarns remain equal in circumference to the "before and after" yarns.

Because of the many finger-like extensions, it is much easier to hatch horizontally than vertically. In

example #13, many weft ends would be active at one time if it were woven as seen, whereas only two or three are in use at any one time when turned 90°.

It is not always possible to enter or continue all wefts in the same pick in opposing directions. Because of the various directional changes required in weaving shapes, it frequently happens that the next weft to be used is facing in the wrong direction. At this point there are two alternatives. When the shape calls for a weft to continue in a shed which duplicates the previous shed, it may be torn off, leaving a long tail, and entered in the opposite direction. The other alternative is to pass the weft behind the warp for the required distance, leaving a float which, depending on its length, may or may not later be cut and finished with the rest. If the float is too short for this treatment it may be left in a long loop and cut later.

Traditional Norwegian hatching techniques interlock in one direction, from left to right, or rarely in the opposite direction. Norwegian tapestries were generally woven of homespun weft left over from other projects. The yarns were shredded and respun into heavier singles, unlike the French stranded yarns.

Part 2: Additional Weaving Techniques

Single dovetail

A single dovetail is a structural organization in which two wefts from adjacent areas loop around a warp end which they share in common. Unlike a slit, this does not produce a straight line but a somewhat jagged one as half of each loop penetrates the opposite area. With thin wefts it may sometimes be used as the first lateral advance for a hatching shape.

Two dovetailed wefts sharing a warp end for several picks will cause a weft build-up, and after a few picks a hump will be formed on that warp end. This effect may be used to advantage if it can be incorporated into the design; otherwise it will distort the

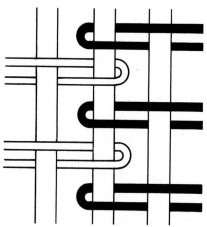

Fig. 1. *A Single Dovetail. Two wefts share one warp, looping it in alternation.*

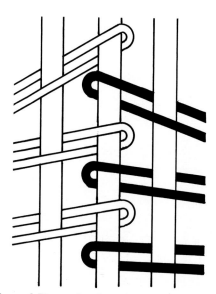

Fig. 2. *Several Dovetails. Several wefts sharing one warp end results in a build-up or lump.*

shape. Pattern permitting, the loops can be passed back and forth between two or more warp ends, decreasing the build-up on one.

Two or more adjacent wefts looped around a single common warp end look like reversed wedges whose size depends on the number of loops of one weft before its adjacent weft is added. Two wefts alternately looped are called a 2/2 dovetail. Three weft loops followed by another three weft loops are called a 3/3 dovetail, and so on. A 2/2 dovetail causes a larger hole than a single dovetail and, unless this is the planned effect, must be well beaten down to close the empty space.

In any type of joining that involves two individual wefts, they must always pass each other in the same order, i.e., the right one passing first and the left one second or the reverse, but with the order remaining consistent.

It is not necessary always to have the same number of loops from each side. If the diameter of the wefts are different, two from the side with heavier weft may oppose three of the finer weft. There could also be a nonuniform dovetailing in which the penetration into the opposite side constantly changes. Two weft ends entered in the same pick in opposing directions could loop around a common warp and return in the same pick. The weft must be appropriate to this technique, as each weft is doubled in each pick.

Single interlock

Interlocking is another way of joining two areas or shapes. Most commonly one weft passes through the loop of the other between two warp ends. A similar but less common use is the combination of dovetailing and interlocking where both wefts link as well as pass around a shared warp end. The build-up here is greater than in the dovetail and is usually confined to specific shape contours that require that effect. Here, too, the order in which the wefts are joined must be consistent. Interlocking is a slower technique but a much stronger construction.

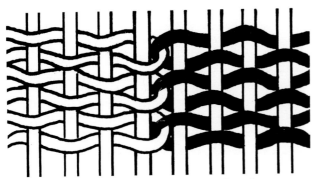

Fig. 3. *A Single Interlock. Two wefts interloop between two warp ends.*

Double interlock

In a double interlock, linking occurs in each pick, once in each direction, and both sides of the joining are not alike. The reverse side of a double interlock most closely resembles the straight line of the slit. The face side has a double loop-like ridge in which the color from the left is looped in the right and the color from the right is looped on the left.

Interlocking and dovetailing may rise diagonally as well as vertically and may also be combined with slits.

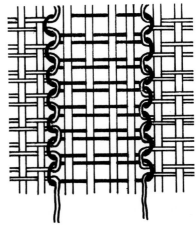

Fig. 4. *Double Interlock. A vertical line of the opposite color borders each color.*

Lazy lines

Lazy lines are discontinuous wefts of the same color. When wefts change direction, the appearance of the surface changes although it is still a plain weave. When the wefts are beaten in, the small slits are barely visible and the surface weave effect is maintained. The total appearance depends on the degree to which the weft is beaten in, the size of the warp and weft, their spacing and the number of direction changes.

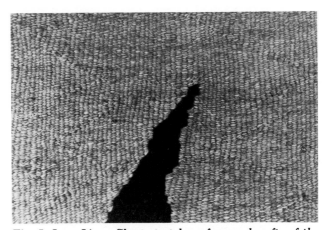

Fig. 5. *Lazy Lines. Short stretches of several wefts of the same color add texture and shorten weaving time.*

This technique is particularly useful when the same color is to be woven in over a large area. If lazy lines are not used, on large tapestries, the weaver must physically move from selvage to selvage if the color is the same all the way across. Lazy lines use several wefts of the same color instead of one. The slits move laterally one warp end in a diagonal step-wise sequence at both sides of the shape. This produces indistinct diagonal lines which may not be suitable if an overall flat color is desired but which, on the other hand, subtly breaks up a less interesting area without introducing more design or color.

Although lazy lines are usually confined to slit techniques, there is no reason why dovetails and interlocks cannot be used as well to add to the textural interest. The weft color stays the same but the overall surface interest is increased.

Hit-and-miss

Hit-and-miss is a way of entering the weft to create a textured, unribbed surface. Most of the

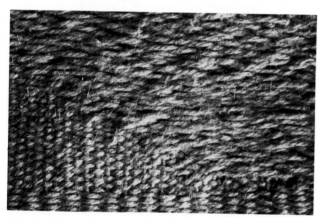

Fig. 6. *Hit-and-Miss. A technique that adds texture and direction in the same or different colors.*

weft is thrown to the face and no weft enters or exits between the same two warp ends in adjacent picks. It is somewhat like a satin stitch without its regular sequence. The weft is passed over two, three, four, or more ends and behind only one end. Selvages cannot be treated in this way and must be interlaced in the usual over-one and under-one manner. If the selvages are not held in a plain weave they will pull towards each other, curling to the back. It is also important that no one warp end is unengaged for more than a few picks. If one warp end is not interlaced for a series of picks, it will have more slack than the adjoining ones and cause difficulties when it is finally interlaced again. This is an excellent technique to cover an area quickly with a heavier weft and creates a rough, heavy surface suggesting a third dimension. This weave is weak compared to the usual interlace-

ment but is quite manageable over smaller areas surrounded by larger plain weave or alternated in a plain weave with a finer weft. For larger areas it may be necessary to reinforce the back or stretch the tapestry on a frame.

Another use for the hit-and-miss technique is as a third element on top of an already woven area. Any type of weft may be used, but the effect is bolder when the supplemental yarn is different from the ground yarn. Two wefts are entered in places that would ordinarily only hold one. The additional weft may be entered in each pick, in hit-and-miss picks, held behind the tapestry as a float and used only as required, or may move (not interlaced) vertically or diagonally on the face of the tapestry similar to a brocade.

Fig. 7. *Hit-and-Miss. A third element, an additional weft is added to an already woven surface creating a third dimension.*

Seeding

Some designs call for a gradual introduction of a color, shade or tint like a wash in watercolors. If the addition is made across the width of the shape in one pick, a separating line will result and the sudden change will be very evident. A new strand may be introduced gradually by being added first over a short distance such as one warp end. This may be followed by the regular weft without any addition for two or

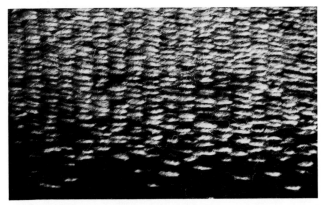

Fig. 8. *Seeding. Adapted from embroidery, this is a good technique for gradual color change.*

three picks. The new strand is then reintroduced for a slightly longer distance in the next pick, perhaps over, under and over three warp ends. Gradually the new weft is added more frequently over greater lengths until it merges naturally and is completely incorporated. The new weft can be entered in individual short lengths with the tails left hanging on the back, or it may be passed as a float behind the warp and brought to the face as needed. The latter is faster and causes fewer weft tails on the back.

Seeding, a term adapted from embroidery meaning small random stitches, may also start with as little as one end being covered in a hit-and-miss fashion until the place is reached where more than one warp end should be covered.

In a group that contains 14 very dark wefts that need to become gradually lighter, a sequence such as the following might be followed:

VERY DARK	MEDIUM DARK	DARK
14	0	0
13	1	0
12	2	0
11	3	0
10	4	0
9	5	0
7	7	0
5	8	1
5	7	2
4	7	3
4	6	4
3	6	5
3	5	6
2	5	7
1	5	8
0	5	9
0	4	10
0	3	11
0	2	12
0	1	13
0	0	14

Much depends on the diameter and kind of yarn used. There are no hard or fast rules or exact mathematical sequences for this method. The brighter the individual colors of the starting group, the more difficult it is to move them in a gradual, imperceptible way. The duller and darker the components, the more options are available for color movement.

Multiple weft manipulation

It is easier to control gradual color changes, shading, and tinting if the individual strands are thin rather than heavy. Dropping one and adding another will not be so apparent. One thin strand may be added for several picks before another is dropped. A group of thin wefts will remain pliant and not become too bulky as the number of strands increase.

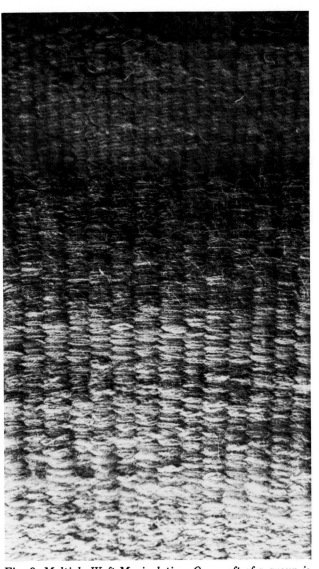

Fig. 9. *Multiple Weft Manipulation. One weft of a group is dropped and the next color is added to control a gradual color change.*

To achieve a smooth flow of color in which a blue becomes lighter or darker so gradually that you cannot see where it happens, as in a painting by Georgia O'Keefe, is one of the highest forms of the weaving technique.

In another form of seeding, the wefts are carried as a group but are manipulated by turning them so that a particular color is permitted to show at some places and is hidden behind the group to disappear in others.

Changing the nature of a single strand by introducing a thin shiny weft like linen or silk, mercerized cotton, rayon or nylon, alters the effect of the whole group by adding a thin reflective element.

Changing rib and shape relationships

The finer the warp and the more e.p.i., the easier it is to create shapes. A loom that has been warped with fine but strong linen may have many e.p.i. which can be used in different ways. The traditional vertical rib structure disappears when the weft uses a warp group as a unit, and splits it in half or breaks it up into whatever increments are required.

Warp manipulation

Widening or narrowing the total shape of a tapestry by increasing or decreasing the number of warp ends by pushing them together in a rib is a dramatic technique in which the flow of the design may start out in a small trickle, gather strength and finally become a broad, bold shape. The opposite takes place when a large, strong shape starts out

Fig. 10. *Changing a Shape. The number of warp ends remains the same. As the width of the ribs decreases the width of the tapestry increases.*

with small, narrow ribs and breaks up into smaller branches with wider ribs. A shape can start large, diminish at a certain point and then reemerge to its original or other proportions, with the ribs following or reversing the changes.

It is possible to change the shapes within a composition while a tapestry is being woven. Only in the classic tradition must the weaving adhere strictly to a rectangular cartoon. As a matter of fact, it is the ability to change shapes, colors, sizes and relationships as the work grows that is one of the greatest creative incentives and weaving satisfactions. More often than not, the growing work calls for changes which could not have been anticipated when the cartoon was drawn. Changes may be made spontaneously or by reorganizing the design on the cartoon.

When a tapestry has been partially woven and the remaining shapes on the cartoon do not feel right in relationship to those already completed, paper or cardboard shapes can be cut, colored and clipped or taped to the unwoven area. These can be rearranged and overlapped until a more satisfactory solution is found. The new design can then be taped to the cartoon or kept loose to superimpose on the tapestry as a check as it is incorporated into the work.

Shapes can be changed on the loom, and can also be changed after the tapestry has been removed from the loom. Edges can be gathered, shirred or pleated. Warp and/or weft can be pulled up so that the weaving puckers. Horizontal bands take on totally different directions when folded, darted, bent or cut. Similarly, outside dimensions and shapes need not remain rectangular or circular.

Shaping a point requires three warp ends. On the first pick the weft encircles the center end. On the second pick the weft moves one end both to the right and the left. On each succeeding pick, one or more ends are added on each side of the center. To reduce the shape, the side ends are dropped in whatever order the shape requires.

There is no rule that says that all tapestries must start and end with the same number of warp ends. If it is necessary to omit some in different parts of the work, it is only required that they be secured in some way, either by being incorporated into the back ribs when their usefulness is over or caught into a top or bottom hem. They may also be brought to the face and their function changed into weft, or they may be added to other warp ends, thickening the ribs and thereby adding a light reflection dimension.

Outlining shapes

Shapes are automatically outlined by their edges. If a contour is to be emphasized, an additional weft that is darker, lighter or in contrast may be added.

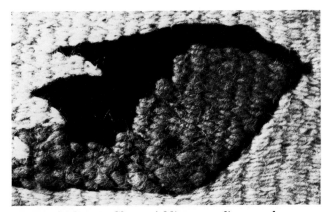

Fig. 11. *Outlining a Shape. Adding an outline to a shape may change its importance.*

The additional weft follows the outline of the shape instead of the usual horizontal weft direction. When beaten in, a single weft will not totally outline because that part of it that passes behind a warp end will not be seen. Two outlining or limning wefts are required to make a clear delineation. The outlining weft need not be interlaced but can float on the surface, held down as needed from the back with another weft. It will not act as a construction element but rather as a decorative one. It separates a shape from the background but belongs to neither of them. An outlining weft may also be floated and tied down on the back of the warp. It will not be visible and its major function is a strengthening one.

Any shape, or a shape within a shape, can be outlined, but the steeper the incline, the longer the float between warp ends, the weaker the construction will be. The most useful place for outlining is in rounded, mounded and angled shapes that rise or descend in 45° angles or less.

Outlining on a steep diagonal often results in a buckling of the interlacement caused by the long stretches of weft not caught by the warp. If this type of construction cannot be avoided, it is helpful if the outlining yarn is somewhat more bulky. A finer yarn can then be used in a zigzag pattern underneath the outlining weft to strengthen it. This outlining technique resembles brocading. The opposite effect is obtained when shapes, outlined with a finer weft, faintly trace or imply a division without a strong dividing line. Another effective outline may be made by avoiding the warp and catching the weft loops of the two adjoining areas. The third weft travels around the shape, giving a different definition than when it remains on the surface without interlacing with the warp.

An outline need not be restricted to one or two wefts. By definition it must follow the contour of the shape but it may change its proportions at different places, acting as a shadow, helping to mold the shape, or adding another dimension. An outline can also change its character by boldly accentuating the edge in some places and disappearing in others.

Outlining a vertical slit can be done by wrapping a single warp end which has been left unwoven between the selvages, although this usually looks quite different from the weaving around it. A figure eight

Fig. 12. *Outlining by Wrapping. On the left, the bottom, free warp is wrapped with a heavy weft and the top with a finer weft. In the center, two warp ends are covered with a figure-eight weft, heavy at the bottom and finer at the top. The shape on the right is outlined by a figure-eight in finer weft.*

creates a wider outline and is much more secure, but may be too wide for the shape design. Outlining may also be done with soumak, but this creates an additional dimension which alters the shape appearance by a change in light reflection and absorption.

A shape may also be outlined by a thin weft that is the same as the ground color surrounding the shape. This is a type of negative space which may be as effective as if another outline color had been added.

Hills and valleys

Hills and valleys is a term sometimes used to describe shapes which undulate and appear in front of and behind each other. A shape that looks as though it is between two hills must be started while the hill shapes are being built up. This type of design may also appear between buildings and similar shapes in which depth and distance suggest a third dimension. (See the Color Reproduction of "Apple Trees".)

They need not always be horizontally aligned but may be vertical or diagonal. In each case, the shape that is being partially or totally covered by the front one must be anticipated with changes in color, shade, tint, shape or texture. These smaller areas usually join with and become part of the shapes that are behind the front ones.

Weaving within a circular frame

There is more leeway in changing weft direction on a circular frame than on the characteristic rectangle. Because the warp climbs the sides of the circle, weft may be entered from almost any place within the circle without too much regard for what has or has not already been woven. The areas below overhung shapes will require needling in, but a needle is frequently used to interlace weft in different shaped frames.

Many designs that work well in rectangular shapes appear awkward if forced into circular boundaries. The limiting outer shape must be able to contain the design elements within it, but the direction the weft takes can be much more varied because of the closer proximity of the frame. Warp that has not been interlaced and remains exposed does not result in the same weaker construction within a circular frame as does the same non-interlacement in a rectangular one.

Superimposed circular frames offer the weaver an opportunity to play more freely with warps that

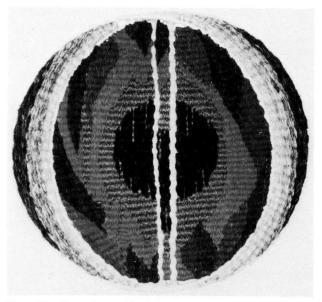

Fig. 13. *Superimposed Circular Frames. Two frames overlap, widening the shape.*

move in different directions, both woven and exposed. Similarly wefts may move in different directions within their own circle or use the warp of more than one circle in common, thus attaching one to another. See soumak, chaining, braiding and twining for further inner as well as outlining techniques which may add interest to a circular design.

Twilling

A one/three, two/two or three/one twill can be woven on a vertical loom as well as on a horizontal

Fig. 14. *Twilling. The lowest band is a 1/3 twill (over one and under three). The second band is a 2/2 twill (over two and under two) moving to the right. The third band is the same as the second but changes its direction to the left. The top band is a 3/1 twill (over three and under one)*

one. The resulting diagonal movement may be used as a ground for shapes superimposed on it or woven into it. Supplementary warp, brocading or a plain weave woven with a highly textured or bulky weft may then be used to make the shape stand out and away from the background.

If the warp and weft are in an equal 50/50 ratio, a 45° angle will result. Under normal conditions this relationship is rarely present in tapestry weaving. A weft faced tapestry has more weft than warp. If it is being woven on a horizontal loom, the threading and treadling can be changed to control the degree of the incline, although these would have to be changed again each time there is a slope alteration. On a vertical loom such changes are made instantly, the angles changing at will.

An angle is flattened by entering the weft more laterally in the next pick. An angle is sharpened by decreasing the rising weft in a pick, i.e., covering the same warp end in repeated picks. A wedge-shaped diagonal rise uses both of these principles at the same time. This slope control is particularly effective when it moves back and forth between two colors in a meet and separate slit.

Eccentric wefts

Wefts that change direction from the horizontal, right-angle relationship to the warp are known as eccentric wefts. Although warps may also be deflected from their usual vertical alignment, the nature of tapestry weaving usually conceals this deviation. Supplementary warps, which can move in all directions, are discussed under that heading.

Non-horizontal wefts may result from pushing wefts together or apart, creating an opening to insert a shape like a wedge or lozenge. Non-horizontal wefts deliberately entered at an angle are called wedge weaves, discussed below, and are among the more flexible techniques which break up the rectangularity between warp and weft.

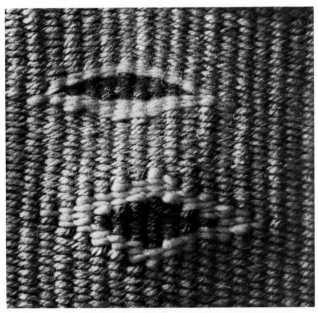

Fig. 15. *A Lozenge. In the lower shape all the wefts are parallel. In the upper shape the body wefts have been pushed apart to insert the lozenge wefts.*

Eccentric wefts vary according to:
Size of the warp and weft.
Spacing of the warp.
Tension of the warp.
Density of the weft.
Arrangement of the weft.
Eccentric wefts may be woven in a kind of openwork weave or they may vary from the closed weft by changing color or texture. A short back and forth weave to fill in a concave shape is another type of eccentric weave. A cup shape may result when the thin part of a thick and thin weft falls on top of another

for several picks. If the surrounding weft remains horizontal, the addition of a few shorter picks to fill in the empty space will hardly be perceptible. If the filled-in space is heavily packed in, it will form a visible wedge and the surrounding weft will curve slightly to accommodate it. If the eccentric weft is carried to excess, the flat surface of the interlacement will start curving and small pockets will form.

Wedge weaves

Wedge weaves deliberately woven at an angle trace back to 1880 when the Navajos used this technique in blankets. Its main advantage for tapestries lies in having to weave fewer p.p.i., thus requiring less time to cover the same space. Two other aspects are the straight line that results between two adjacent shape colors rather than a step-wise slit diagonal, and the change in light reflection that results from the diagonal weft. In this respect it may be likened to lazy lines which offer a change within a shape without altering the color.

Wedge weave is one form of eccentric weave in which the weft moves in a diagonal direction instead

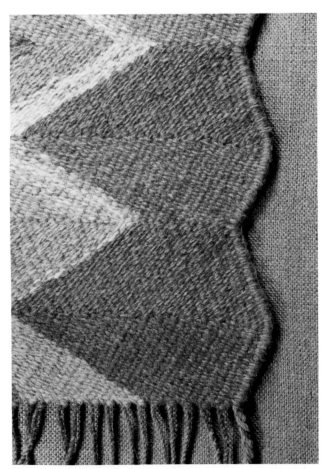

Fig. 16. *Wedge Weave. One corner of a 54" x 46" wedge weave rug of goat hair and English and Norwegian wools woven by Martha Stanley.*

of the usual horizontal and the selvages appear serrated as a result of the warp and selvages being pulled out of their normal alignment. Having been secured by wrapping a few times around a warp end, the weft may be entered at any point and then proceed at an angle over subsequent warp ends. The weft may also be started at a selvage, in which case one side of the wedge will be straight while the other increases its angle as each new warp is covered. Although plain weave is the traditional one used in this technique, there is no reason why other weaves cannot be used and mixed. Directions and angles may be changed at any time as well. The somewhat weaker construction, especially at the point where it meets other weaves, is less important for tapestries than it is for blankets and rugs.

If large areas of diagonal wefts are part of the design, the warp will become distorted. This displaced warp may be acceptable for certain designs but may interfere with the overall plan of a tapestry design. On small wedge woven areas the warp may be controlled by the plain weave that surrounds it by keeping it under more tension than usual. If the wedge is being built up to the left, the bulge will appear on the right. If it is being built up on the right, the bulge will appear on the left. This may not be as apparent when the warp is being held under strong tension but will be more evident when the tension is removed. The steeper the angle of the weft, the further each weft must travel over each warp end, the weaker the construction will be and the greater the selvage bulge.

Gauze weaves

Gauze weaves are identified by warp ends which are moved from their parallel alignment by a weft which twists and untwists them. They are sometimes mistakenly called leno, which is another type of warp-deflected weave. The direction taken by the moving warp end results in a mesh-like effect, precluding a closely woven structure.

The moving or doup warp end crosses the stable or ground end between picks. Two picks are usually considered necessary to complete one weave unit, but in a broader application any number of picks may be used. Where warp ends are free at one end they may theoretically progress from one selvage to the other and back or be deflected for short distances. This is particularly effective if the travelling ends are of a different texture or color or thickness. To obtain the full effect of gauze weave movement, the design should be preplanned so that it is an honest inclusion.

As long as one end is free, the moving warp may change the direction of its twist, may remain un-

twisted, or may become a weft for a time before returning to its original role. Warp locked in by weft is the chief characteristic of the gauze system. When a loose tapestry construction requires reinforcing, the advantage of the locking effect of the twisting warp is obvious.

Spaces between twisting warps can be varied or plain. Other weaves may be introduced at any time, and warps do not have to twist and return in alternating picks. The number of picks before additional twisting can vary and return picks can be eliminated.

To a great extent, the flexibility of the fiber used will control the type and amount of twist. A soft yarn will permit the weft to be beaten in much closer and the twist to take up less space than a hard, stiff cord. The characteristic open structure lends itself to both large and small shapes. Warp tension will also, of course, affect the size and type of locking. A looser warp will permit much more twisting and movement than a tighter one. When a warp doup starts encircling other warps it enters the category of soumak construction.

Twisted wefts

If more than one weft is entered into a pick, the weaver must decide whether the group will be allowed to twist or be kept aligned, in keeping with the desired effect. Holding the wefts aligned is time consuming and in many cases unnecessary, although, if a wide variety of disparate colors are used, allowing them to twist around each other freely may result in

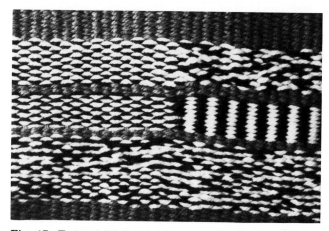

Fig. 17. *Twisted Wefts. In the lowest band the dark and light wefts were left to twist around each other at random. In the center band (left) the dark weft is entered above the light weft in the same pick. On the right, dark and light wefts are alternated, each in their own pick, resulting in vertical ribs. The top band (left) reverses the order of the one below it, first dark then light, in the same pick. The dark and light in both bands look like mosaics in a three-dimensional design. On the right, the two wefts are twisted tightly before being beaten in, resulting in an agitated appearance.*

an unwanted striation or a ropey look. Keeping them unturned makes them look smoother and flatter.

There is an entire area of working with two colors, or shades or tints of one color in the same pick that has not been sufficiently explored in tapestry design. When two colors are entered in a pick-and-pick order, each in its own shed, vertical ribs of each color result. If the same two colors are entered in the same shed, without twisting around each other, each in its own line, both colors will show equally. When the same two colors are wound together in a loose ply and entered into the same shed, a streaked effect results. These different aspects offer an additional technique, which, alone or combined with others, can be effective in emphasizing certain parts of a design which otherwise might not be noticed. If the two colors (dark and light as examples) are entered in alternation, i.e., light followed by dark in one pick and dark followed by light in the next, a horizontal line results. If they are wound together they appear marbled.

When two different color wefts are entered into the same shed, if the dark color is always first and the light color always second above the dark one, a horizontal spotted effect results. If the dark and light colors exchange positions in each pick, a horizontal band results. Bands and spots may be alternated by exchanging the dark and light order of the wefts within each pick.

Vertical and diagonal lines and various geometric and free form shapes may be woven by exchanging wefts. These will of necessity be less defined than those in which the wefts are alone in each pick, but this is an excellent technique for a hazy, blurred impression using fine, hairy wefts.

Correcting errors

Errors that are found within a few picks should be corrected even if it means unweaving to the place of the mistake. If a considerable amount of weaving has taken place before the error is spotted, it is sometimes difficult to unweave to that point. If a warp end has not been covered, a false warp may be added on a vertical loom, just as it is done when a warp end is broken on a horizontal loom and the tails incorporated into adjoining ribs on the back to keep them secure. A weft float on the face can be cut. Both ends are then pulled out for a few inches and a new short weft woven in to cover the now-exposed warp ends.

If the selvage has been pulled in because not enough play was left in the weft, the remedy depends on the amount of weaving progress that has taken place. If a short distance has been woven, it is best to remove the picks until the correct width is reestablished. If too many inches have been woven, it is sometimes possible to cut the weft in different places and add false, looser ones while pulling out the selvages, a questionable solution at best. Such corrections are more easily made when the weft is bulky enough to hide the repair and there are fewer p.p.i.

The opposite occurs sometimes when the selvages belly out. This may be the result of many different wefts meeting and separating in the same shed, especially if some are bulkier than others. The arcs can be shortened so that less weft is put into the pick or, if the yarn has more than one ply, it can be unplied and only one of them used, to reduce the bulk. It is also sometimes possible to pull up the weft on the back for several picks, cut the loop that results and treat the tails like all the others. If the loops are not large enough to secure in that way they may be pulled down with a hook into an adjoining rib.

No matter how complicated the idea or design, a structural balance must be maintained between the warp and weft and the outside dimensions. When released from tension, the tapestry must hang squarely, if the original plan was rectangular. If it sags in one part or pulls up in another, the stability was not sustained. Constant measuring and checking for the predetermined width will quickly indicate where a departure from it is starting.

If the imbalance is not too great, the tapestry may be stretched over a foundation such as plywood, and squared up. The edges may have to be wrapped around the foundation to cover their irregularity and a few inches may be lost. This may be a better solution, however, than rejecting a large piece that has taken a considerable amount of time to complete. Selvage irregularities may also be covered by framing the work with canvas stretchers or rug frames.

If there is a negative space in the design in which the warp was not covered or the warp was deflected leaving an empty space, that shape may be cut out of the foundation plywood with a saber saw so that the open space remains.

As some shapes are completed and new ones started, lint from their weft may drop down onto the already-woven area. This lint will tend to bed down wherever it falls, discoloring and graying the colors. Thin plastic, pinned to the tapestry below the working area, will protect it from such discoloration. This protection is particularly important when opposing colored fibers are being used which shred easily and are difficult to dislodge. Transparent plastic is preferable to tissue paper as it does not tear as easily and the work may be seen through it. It will then not have to be removed when the weaver wishes to see the entire work at any time.

XII
NON-WEAVING TAPESTRY TECHNIQUES

Part 1: Basic Non-weaving Techniques; *Soumak; Chaining; Twining; Braiding and Macrame; Additional Surface Decoration.* Part 2: Additional Non-weaving Techniques; *Armature; Netting; Sprang; Deflected Warps; Supplementary Warp and Weft; Warp; Weft; Brocading.*

Part 1: Basic Non-weaving Techniques

The skills discussed in this chapter are non-weaving techniques as contrasted to weaving techniques which interlace.

Soumak

Soumak techniques stem from the Middle Ages. They consume more weft because the warp ends are covered both front and back in each pass. Soumak completely encircles single or groups of warp ends. When used in addition to ground weave, it takes on a supplementary or double weave aspect. Like other wrapping, the weft passes in front or behind a number of warp ends and returns to complete the circle. Four and two are the traditional number of forward and return weft movements.

Fig. 1. *Soumak. A hard, black weft moves forward over four warp ends and returns under two.*

The floats are always inclined, their rise depending on the number of warp ends being wrapped and the bulkiness of the wrapping weft. The incline points downward when the soumak is wound from left to right and upward when wound from right to left. Two consecutive rows looped in opposite directions look like chevrons. If the soumak is wound in only one

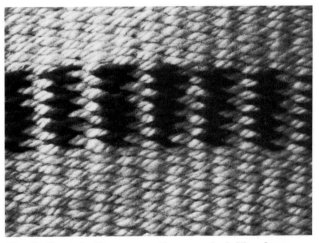

Fig. 2. *Soumak. Two consecutive rows look like chevrons.*

direction, the return pick is made in plain weave in the next pick in the body color. The next soumak row repeats the direction of the first one. It is also possible to float the weft back to the starting side of the soumak behind the warp and repeat the same direction, or discontinue the weft and start again.

When a row of soumak is followed by a pick of plain weave, a stronger structural balance is maintained. Many rows of uninterrupted soumak cause the selvages to curl towards the back. If a thicker, more circular bas-relief surface is desired without the interruption of a plain weave pick, several warp ends of the selvage may be woven in plain weave and the soumak added as a third element to cover it. Soumak may also be used as a third element similar to hit-and-miss or pile.

The thickness of the weft used for soumak will determine how much more dimensional it will be than a plain weave. In consecutive soumak rows, the weft must be wrapped around the selvage ends more than once before it changes direction, or there will be an unequal number of wraps as compared to the rest of the body of soumak.

The raised soumak ridge gives a strong definition to a shape when it acts as an outline. It creates shadows, and colors next to the ridge appear darker or lighter, depending on the light source.

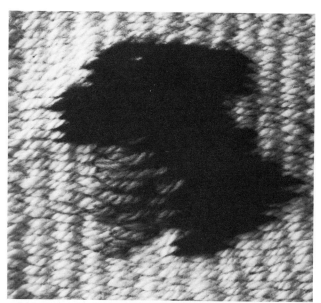

Fig. 3. *Soumak. The soumak on the left gives definition to the shape.*

Hit-and-miss soumak is another way to add a third dimension. The number of wrapped warp ends vary so that in no two consecutive rows do the wraps occur in the same place. Care must be taken that all the warp ends are involved after four or five soumak rows, or the unused warp end will be looser than its neighbors for lack of incorporation over an area of a few inches.

Fig. 4. *Greek Soumak. The dark weft shows as it moves between groups of wrapped warp ends.*

Soumak may be wrapped more than once around one or more warp ends in a row. The diagonal that results after several wraps have been made and the weft returns to start on the next unit may become a design element on the face or be hidden behind the wraps. When weft is wrapped around one warp end three or more times it is called Greek Soumak.

In a modified soumak the weft passes over two or three warp ends and around three or four warp ends. Each row moves one end laterally in one or the other direction.

In a locking soumak the weft crosses in front of the warp ends and floats over a larger number of warps in front than in back: 4/2, 3/2, 6/3, 9/3. In a non-locking soumak, the longer float occurs behind the warp ends.

Soumak can change direction at any time in any area and does not have to move from selvage to selvage; it is therefore an excellent device for outlining and emphasizing shapes. In Busongo soumak

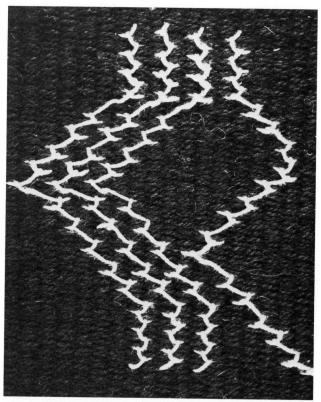

Fig. 5. *Busongo Soumak. The pattern weft passes through the previous loop before it starts the next one.*

the weft is passed through the loop made by the encirclement of the warps. In two-color soumak the colors exchange positions before they encircle the next group of warps. The color that is not circling floats behind the warp. Various color shapes may be designed with this exchange, resulting in an effect obtainable through no other technique. It is also a good method with which to improvise additional designs on the surface.

In Gauze Soumak the weft moves forward over two ends, back behind one and then in front of one. Many gauze weaves and wraps look entirely different when beaten in instead of left open. This one offers a particularly effective textural surface.

Chaining

Chaining serves several purposes for the tapestry weaver. Its best known function is as a warp stabilizer for the top and bottom on a loom that does not have built-in warp separators. Chaining is a basic crochet stitch somewhat similar in appearance, although not in construction, to braiding.

Chaining as a third element is usually used as decoration. In this form, it is independent of the ground construction and may move in any direction, change direction, act as an outline or as a third dimensional shape. It may interlace with the warp or sit on top of it and be held down with invisible stitching from behind the warp. Chain weft may be looped around as many warp ends as the design suggests. The more warp ends that are looped, the longer the float or chain.

In the simplest chain, the weft is anchored to a warp end or to a previously woven weft and then passed behind the warp in a long float. Using the fingers or a hook, a loop is pulled up to the face, and a second loop is pulled up through the first one.

Fig. 6. *Chaining. In this example, chaining takes place behind the warp, showing on the face only where it catches a warp end.*

More than one warp end may be encircled with each loop. The loops may be pulled tight or left loose. To lock the chain, the free end of the weft is pulled through the last loop.

Another way of chaining keeps the weft on the face. The first loop is passed under one or more warp ends, brought to the face and the second loop is passed up through it.

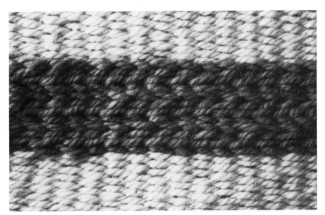

Fig. 7. *Chaining. The opposite of the above where the chain appears on the face.*

Chaining is one way of producing a pile which is bulkier than the usual one weft loop. After securing the weft to a warp end, it may be chained freely without any attachment, making a chained loop. It may then be used as a single weft for interlacement,

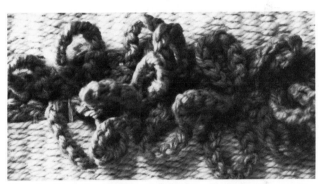

Fig. 8. *Chaining. Different lengths of chained loops are thrown to the face in a Soumak technique. The chain gives the loops body which single wefts lack.*

for other chain loops or spread into broader chained loops by separating the exit and insertion of the chain. Rows of chain in which the loops vary in length and spread may overlap each other and pro-

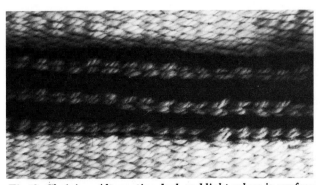

Fig. 9. *Chaining. Alternating dark and light colors in surface chaining gives a bolder definition to a band than plain weave striping.*

vide additional surface interest. Chains may be rechained, adding bulk and body.

Designs which contain chaining also work the selvages in plain weave to keep them from curling. Chaining with a bulky weft will cover several picks of plain weave on either side. Chaining with a thinner weft may be used as a more subtle outlining accent between colors and shapes. It is successful as a division in lazy lines both in the same color and in a slight variation as a thin shadow of the shape color.

Different colored wefts carried behind the warp may be brought to the face and chained for shading, contrasting effects and textural dimensions.

Twining

Although it is structurally more complex than simple interlacing, weft twining is perhaps better known as a basket or rug technique and is among the least explored in tapestry design. It does not require a shed and the warp may remain unsecured at one end. As there is no shed, there are no picks and we speak of twining rows as in soumak.

Weft twining covers the warp but does not encircle it. The wefts enclose or clasp the warps but they do not interlace with them. In a plain weft twine, two wefts twist around each other, enclosing warps between twists. When weft twining is packed closely it resembles a plain weave. Although it is more time consuming than weaving, as each half of the twine must be picked up and dropped for every warp end or unit, each twined row covers the same amount of warp as two rows of plain weave.

The traditional direction of twining is in a horizontal, selvage to selvage movement. In tapestry design this tradition may be ignored and wefts may twist in any direction and as many times as desired before they enclose one or more warp ends. When they do not enclose warp ends they look as though they had been plied. As tapestries do not have the containment requirement of baskets, warps may be left unenclosed in different places. Thus a hit-and-miss enclosure or a shaped enclosure in different rows is possible.

An S or Z twist of the weft must be considered if the twining is to be packed closely, but will be of little consequence if the twined rows are spaced out. A closely packed weft twine is a very strong construction and care must be taken if weaker fiber organizations are woven in close proximity.

The order of the two twining wefts must be maintained once a sequence has been started unless a deliberate break is required. A weft twine float does not enclose each warp end but skips over several before enclosing one again. Such twined floats may be combined with plain twined wefts. The former

need not always move horizontally but can move diagonally as well as reverse direction at any time. If it crosses over other wefts, twined or plain, it will appear as a third, raised weft relief.

In a weft twine each weft makes a half-turn around the other, so that each alternates in front of and behind every other warp end. This plain two-weft twine is half of a full two-weft twine where each weft makes a full turn around the other before enclosing a warp end. The same weft will, therefore,

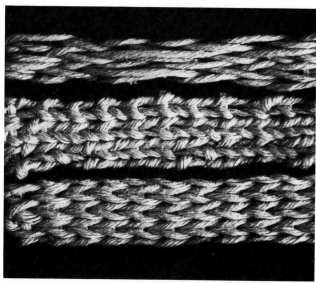

Fig. 10. *Twining. A plain, two-weft or half-twist twine is illustrated in the bottom band. The center band is a full, two-weft twine, each weft making a full turn around the other before enclosing a warp end. The upper band is a hit-and-miss twine.*

always appear in front of one warp and the other will pass behind it. The surface appearance will depend on the rigidity or softness of the two wefts being twined. Obviously, using different wefts, one hard and another soft, will result in a totally different appearance.

Fig. 11. *Twining. A half-twist twine of soft weft resembles a braid.*

Using more than one color in weft twining will create a different effect, depending on the twist, twine and color relationship. Two shades of the same color can create shadows while complementary colors will add movement and contrast. Two colors may twine with each other and then leave to entwine with other colored wefts. Both colors need not pass around the outside warp end selvage. If the edge needs to remain in one color, that color may wrap the warp end once before it returns in the next row, the second color turning back one warp end short of the selvage.

If two colors are used in a full twist, vertical colored ribs are created. Their tight connection is sometimes a better solution for long vertical color shapes than regular tapestry slits which must subsequently be sewn together.

In three-color twining, each weft passes over and under two warp ends. The first weft passes behind the first warp and thereafter moves over and under two. The second weft passes over the first warp end and also moves over and under two warps. The third weft passes over the first two warp ends and then continues similarly to the others. In this way the weft entries are staggered and twisted.

Looped twining combines twining and pile in which one weft comes from behind a warp end and is pulled forward into a loop or looped around a gauge to assure that all the loops will be of equal length.

Twining can serve an overall purpose as in twined raised areas, as an outline for shapes, as a spacing element to hold warp ends in alignment similar to chaining, or for larger sculptural constructions which require more body than some other weaves provide. More than two wefts may be twined to create a stiffer structure, with the different wefts passing in front of and behind different warp ends and twisting as needed. Such constructions tend to be rigid and cable-like and may be used as support for weaker areas or shapes or outlines. The finger technique required for twining, needing neither heddle nor shuttle, lends itself easily to combinations with other techniques. Twining and similar outlining methods may be used to enclose shapes that have warps in adjacent areas that are not interlaced. Tightly twined outlines prevent the woven shapes from moving into the unwoven ones.

Twining is a simple way to decrease or increase the width of a warp. The warp ends are held under less tension so that there is maneuverable space for

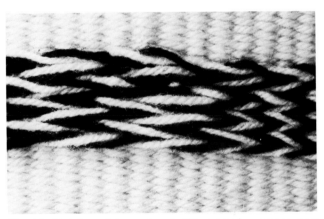

Fig. 12. *Twining. A two-color, half-twist twine passes over and under two warp ends as it moves to the right.*

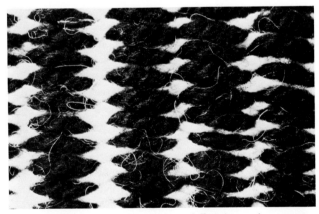

Fig. 13. *Twining. A two-color, full-twist twine creates vertical ribs.*

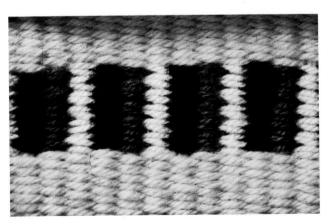

Fig. 14. *Twining. A three-color, full-twist twine.*

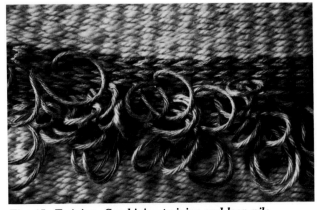

Fig. 15. *Twining. Combining twining and loop pile.*

them to move from their original alignment. The nail arrangement, whereby the warp loops may be moved to other positions or dropped, is helpful here. Rubber bands added to each warp loop by a larks head and looped around a nail increase the length of each warp. For example, two bouts containing eight warp ends each are weft twined in a figure eight for a designated distance. They are then split into four bouts of four warp ends each and twined for a given distance. These in turn are divided into two ends and finally to one end separating each twine. A full two-weft twine will push the warp ends further apart than a plain two-weft twine. Instead of increasing in width, the work may start at its full width and decrease or increase in the same way; nor need the contraction or expansion occur equally on both sides. One side may move at one rate while the other moves faster or slower or not at all.

If two warp ends are enclosed by two twining wefts in one row, they may be separated in the next row. This concept is sometimes called "split-pair twining". When beaten in, the structure loses its rib-like appearance and looks like a twill with its direction depending on the twining direction. When the rows are not beaten in and kept apart, the warp is forced into an open, zigzag deviation. Warp twining in tapestry design is more closely related to supplementary warp and is discussed under that heading.

In *Split-ply Twining*, Virginia Harvey pursues the twining technique further, that of pulling one yarn through the ply of another to produce a diagonal weave. It is similar to the wedge weave in its diagonal appearance, both being among the few weaves that take on oblique directions. By itself and in combination with others, split-ply twining suggests another avenue of investigation for the tapestry designer.

For an extensive discussion on further possibilities of twining with one, two or more colors, see *The Techniques of Rug Weaving* by Peter Collingwood.

Braiding and Macramé

Braiding or oblique interlacing is a single element finger-manipulated technique in which three or more strands are interlaced in a diagonal direction. One end of each strand must be free to be moved, and may interlace or intertwine with other, already existing techniques in other places.

We are most familiar with the three-strand braid. The number of strands and alternating order of interlacement identifies braiding as a technique which may be used in tapestry design. Depending on its inner order, type of fiber and manner of incorporation, braiding may be used beyond its ethnic or utilitarian implications.

Inter-knotting or macramé is also a single-element construction. Its recent overuse should not eliminate it for tapestry design, either within its construction or as supplementary warp and/or weft knotting. Weavers have been inclined to limit the use of macramé to fringe, but its use could easily extend to knotted surfaces whose effectiveness is increased with bulky textures. Such yarns hide the macramé look which might be objectionable, while using the structurally strong knots.

In inter-knotting it is not necessary that all strands be knotted in each interaction. Some strands may act as a support around which others are knotted. They are then active or inactive according to function. The basic half knot, square knot and clove hitch may move in any direction, be repeated as required or combined with other single-element techniques.

Additional surface decoration

If the tapestry is to be a permanent installation, there is a justifiably strong feeling against the use of surface decoration such as feathers, beads, sequins or small mirrors. When they are part of a primitive ritual or have a religious significance, there is a legitimate, spiritual and often beautiful reason for their use. When they are added for lack of another solution, there is little excuse for their inclusion.

Perhaps this prejudice stems from the tradition that tapestries should be strongly constructed so that they may continue as an art object beyond the life of the weaver and consumer. Fragile branches, mosses, and flower pods are very short-lived.

A hand-crafted ceramic bead, pierced in two directions so that it may be secured in both the warp and weft, may work well as an eye of an animal whereas sequins seem out of place in a contemporary piece of work. For a ceramic bead to be added on a vertical loom, the warp loop is removed from the nail and returned after the bead has been threaded on. On a horizontal loom the bead can be added with a supplementary warp.

"Findings", materials other than fiber, must have a valid reason for their addition other than that they were interesting pieces and caught our attention. Odd shaped pieces of metal, wood, stones or glass may be incorporated into the design if they relate to and contribute to the idea of the whole.

If the found piece to be added is one whose appearance or surface may change, then it must be prepared and protected beforehand. If it is metal it may rust and the rust spread to the yarns around it and discolor them. Such materials should be sprayed with a rust resistant substance. Untreated wood should also be treated to preserve its surface.

Found pieces must be prepared in such a way that their attachment is permanent and does not weigh down the surface to which it is to adhere. Holes can be bored so that both warp and weft will hold the piece in its correct position.

Fig. 16. *Findings. A round, metal disk found in a junkyard makes an ideal center for the circulat shape that surrounds it. A weft has run through each of the outside circle of holes to hold the piece in place.*

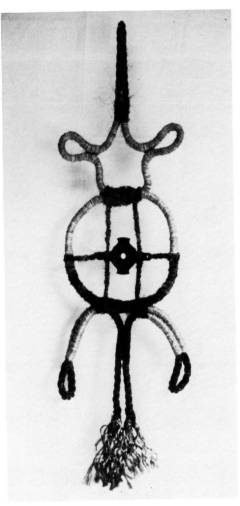

Fig. 17. *Findings. The entanglement (see chapter on entanglements) was built around the center, metal piece found in a flea market.*

Part 2: Additional Non-weaving Techniques

Armature

The use of armature is acceptable when it is required to support a previously thought-through concept. When the support is a starting point for a piece of work, e.g., "I have a large piece of driftwood and want to hang a tapestry from it," the end result is frequently disappointing. It is also unsatisfactory when a prop is added to hold something up which was meant to be self-supporting.

Armatures may be visible or may support a tapestry or woven construction without being seen. They may be of wood, metal, plastic, wire or any material that can be incorporated or that will support and hold. If armatures are visible, however, they must be an intrinsic part of the work. An antique, decorated piece of wood turned on a wood-lathe will not harmonize with a contemporary, geometrical work.

Plywood supports and frames are a form of armature. Partial frames and supports may work well without engendering a feeling of total enclosure. Three dimensional work may be displayed on a floor, on a pedestal, may use some form of armature to defy gravity, or may hang freely and respond to air currents.

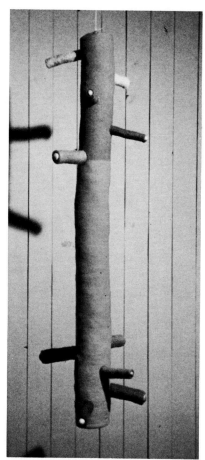

Fig. 1. *Armature. Wire support for the stuffed, double-woven projections are buried in the stuffing and attached to the wooden support in the body. Each finger is tipped with a small, stained, wooden ball.*

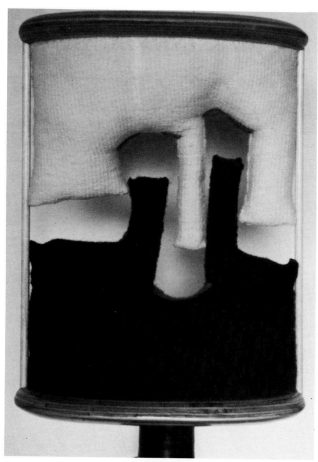

Fig. 2. *Armature. The upper and lower, double-woven, stuffed shapes are supported by birch ovals which are held apart by thin rods.*

Netting

Knotless or knotted netting is one of the earliest known techniques, used more for utilitarian fishing nets, hammocks and bags, rather than in its contemporary use as part or whole of a tapestry. It appears as a loosely linked or looped single element construction. Although we usually think of mesh as a fixed dimension repeat, the mesh spacing and openings may be varied from small to very large.

The contrast between open and closed mesh may be exploited along with other weaving techniques which may also be used open or closed. The main function of netting, that of containment, is not necessarily relevant to a tapestry design.

Knotless netting stretches in all directions and its inclusion must be controlled. It would not be acceptable to have a netted shape stretch if its original appearance was meant to lie flat. However, its containment suitability may be used to advantage in a work that requires pockets to hold objects that should remain partly visible. They create a third dimension and at the same time keep the object shape.

The degree of knotted netting stretchability depends on the type of yarn and type of knots used. The simplest net spirals a strand loosely around a support. The second row uses the loops of the first row as a support and spirals through each loop in the reverse direction. When the strand has made one loop, loops back on itself and passes through the last formed loop before moving on to a new loop, another form of netting results. The front to back order should be consistent throughout any new row, but is reversed in alternate rows to keep the net from shrinking.

For further exploration of this technique see *Beyond Weaving* by Marcia Chamberlain and Candace Crockett.

Sprang

Sprang is among the oldest single element techniques known. Its major feature is the mirror-like appearance of the upper and lower halves of the warp. Tradition requires that the warp be divided by a horizontal line separating the two parts. For tapestry purposes this separation may occur in areas other than the exact center. The reverse duplication could act as a deterrent in a tapestry design that calls for one part to be worked in one technique and another differently. On a vertical loom on which warp loops may easily be disengaged and returned, this should not be a drawback.

Sprang is a form of deflected warp and like other single element structures, may interlace, interlock or intertwine; but in all cases the warp ends which start out parallel to the selvage take on and retain diagonal directions.

The design will dictate whether to use a single, double or triple twist. All twists may be S or Z, be interchanged and may be made with the fingers or shed sticks. For thread manipulation which does not follow a repeated order from selvage to selvage, finger twisting may be easier but a rod or cord must be introduced to hold the twists until the next row has been altered. These securing materials are withdrawn after they have served their purpose, but may remain if their direction, color or texture adds to the total design.

Sprang can be used to add yet another approach to tapestry design if its principles are retained but its customary uses disregarded.

Although traditionally only one way of working threads is used in any one project, there is no reason why a tapestry concept cannot use more than one. Interlinking will produce a construction that stretches. Interlacing and intertwining surfaces can be controlled to remain flat by tension and type of yarn used.

Weaving interlacement starts with aligned warp ends secured at both ends, which is also a major requirement for sprang although longer warp must be included because of the twisting take-up. Having interlinked or intertwined as far as desired in the areas needed, the warp ends change places. A horizontal, stabilizing weft may be entered at any point and the remainder of the work continued in another technique. The duplicating interaction that took place from the bottom up as each row of sprang was added at the top, may be "unspranged" by freeing the bottom warp loops. They may then be realigned for weaving or grouped for wrapping or for other techniques.

The reverse also works well. In sprang, the upper part of the tapestry may be woven and the lower part continued without weft. Again, as the bottom of the warp starts duplicating the upper part, the warp loops can be pulled free and reestablished in their original relationship or changed to new ones.

Both weaving and sprang may be started or stopped at any place and may exchange places, keeping in mind that the reversal principle need not be a permanent factor. Just as intertwining, interlooping, interlacing and interlinking may be introduced as a negative or positive space, so too, sprang may be used in different areas surrounded by other techniques.

Slits will occur when the regular sprang order is interrupted or omitted or warp ends are grouped or regrouped. If the resulting slit opening is large enough, it may be used as a design device by being filled with interlacement or wrapping on supplementary warps with supplementary wefts.

Rows of sprang may be pushed together rather than left as an open mesh. The oblique slant will be retained and may contrast well with the same or another color with close or open weaving.

Striped warp ends may undulate or zigzag up and down or travel diagonally. In *Techniques of Sprang*, Peter Collingwood offers many variations while remaining within the limits of a one element arrangement.

Deflected Warps

Deflected warps are those moved out of their regular course. Such deflections do not usually follow a repeated pattern in tapestry as they do in fabrics. Tapestry warp deflection results from a change made by the weaver, rather than being momentarily pushed aside by a threaded pattern. They are deliberately diverted or turned aside and may or may not be returned. In this context, deflected warps are not precluded from crossing others or taking on any of the previously discussed roles such as becoming weft or a supplement. Weft may, and frequently does, deflect but is used in this way more often than warp.

To deflect warps on horizontal looms, the general practice has been to use a reed with a top bar that can be removed when the warp ends need to be moved. Tapestries that taper or decrease and then return to their original width or spread wider have been woven in this way.

Warp movement was discussed in weft twining, as resulting from pair-splitting, but this is a different aspect of that technique. Warp ends or warp groups that move laterally or diagonally and return are usually the result of threading and treadling sequences. The nail system on a frame loom allows warp loops to be individually deflected as called for by the design without repetition or regard to other warp or weft construction. Deflected warps should not be confused with supplementary warps, discussed in the following section.

Supplementary warp and weft

In some classification systems, weaves with additional warp or weft are considered an intermediary form of weave midway between simple and double weave. The warp may be double, may share a single weft, or the weft may be double with a single warp in common. Other classifications consider them a form of compound weave structure that incorporates elements supplementary to the weave. I prefer the latter concept, labeling ground warp or ground weft as the foundation interlacement or body to which supplementary warps and/or wefts are added.

If the supplementary elements do not show, they can be assumed to serve as reinforcement rather than decoration. If they appear only on the back, the structure is called warp- or weft-backed, in accordance with its function. Supplementary decorative elements change the face of the work, whereas supplementary reinforcing elements change the structure.

Supplementary warp may travel by itself in front of the ground warp, it may be interwoven with the ground warp, or travel behind or be divided evenly or unevenly. In this use it is not necessary for the additional warp or weft to be warped or woven simultaneously with the basic single structure; it may be added later.

Supplementary warps or wefts may be used as a backing to reinforce the ground weave or as a purely decorative element. The uses for supplementary elements divide into:
1. Their purpose — whether for weight, pattern or additional strength.
2. Their structure and distribution.
3. Their direction — vertical (warp), horizontal (weft), or diagonal (deflected warp and/or weft).
4. Their construction.

Horizontal looms with second warp beams and separate braking systems increase the opportunity to use supplementary warps. (See illustration #18 in Chapter XIV.) Pile left in loops or cut, and tucks, as well as bulky and unusual yarns are more readily regulated with a double beam. Lacking a second beam, supplementary warps may be hung from a back beam by chaining and weighting or by being fed from a warp beam from another loom.

The supplementary warp need not be the same as the ground warp. It can be finer or heavier, a different color or texture, threaded and sleyed to a different number of e.p.i., as well as a different pattern.

The same is true for a supplementary warp on a vertical loom which is usually top-warped. Supplementary warps may be diverted from their usual vertical, to diagonal and horizontal directions. In the latter instance these warp ends need not take the place of wefts but may be added to them or incorporated into the work for varying lengths. They may be grouped or spaced, remain on the face or pass through and disappear permanently, or reappear as needed.

A strong warp is better for supplementary use because of the additional pressing, beating in or pushing up that is necessary to achieve the various effects and color density. If both ends of the warp are attached to the loom, a consistent tension is established and maintained and the warp direction remains constant. When warps are diverted, their tension changes. Such changes can be made by engaging each warp loop with an additional warp length or a rubber band to extend it so that it can be attached to another place on the loom.

Supplementary warps may be tied down at both ends or at either end. The latter leaves individual or grouped ends free to be worked in any way, wrapped, chained, braided or woven. If both warp ends are not attached, they may be worked in the hands and then attached wherever required. It is important that the entry and exit places of supplementary warp be firmly anchored so that subsequent work or movement on the tapestry will not loosen or dislodge them. Additional length for supplementary warps may also be added on a vertical loom by extending the warp loops along the nail line projections attached to the loom sides, ceiling, floor or other looms.

Supplementary warp loops, released at one end, may be maneuvered in many ways. They may be twisted into a single unit, wrapped as a single unit or divided, branched, chained, twined or braided. They may also be left to hang loose at any point, returned to their proper alignment or made to disappear behind the tapestry.

Another use for a supplementary warp is in a selvage which has been pulled in beyond the desired width. Several additional warp ends may be added on each side behind the already existing interwoven ends. Additional weft can then interlace with them until such a time as the original width is reestablished. The added warp is then cut at either end and secured behind the ground warp. Additional weft may be treated as part of the design or as a shadow of the adjoining shape. If the line created by this addition is not in keeping with the original design it can be camouflaged by soumak or similar cover.

Weft

Adding supplementary weft to a plain weave is the easiest way to vary the basic structure as it may be added to the ground weave at any point without changing the threading, sleying or warping. It may also augment any weave pattern in any weave technique, although if it is to be an addition to the design, the ground weave is usually kept in a plain weave for contrast. Combinations such as a supplementary weft in a right diagonal loop against a left diagonal twill ground weave could, however, be very effective.

Extra weft patterning may be added in limited

areas or as a part of an overall design. The former would probably be discontinuous, i.e., woven back and forth within a design shape. The latter would probably be continuous from selvage to selvage. If the supplementary warp is continuous, it can be made to appear disconnected by floating it between pattern areas behind the work or by entering into the same pick as the ground, especially if it is a different color or texture.

Supplementary wefts of heavy rope-like material may be difficult to enter after the warp and weft have been beaten together. If an end is tapered to a sharp tip and a diluted glue added and allowed to dry, it will hold its point sufficiently to pierce the tapestry and be drawn through. Depending on the yarn and the density of the surface it is penetrating, the tip may also be wrapped with masking or cellophane tape. If the surface is very dense, a small hole may be made with the point of a fid and the weft pushed through.

Shaped stuffing such as sponge rubber may be held in place with supplementary warp and weft. The number of warp ends covering the stuffing need not be the same as the ground weave, especially if the weft that will cover is not the same as the body. The sponge rubber or other material can be stained or dyed to closely approximate the covering fiber so that there will be little chance of a different color showing through from underneath.

Fig. 3. *Supplementary Warp. Shaped sponge rubber is held in place with supplementary warp. Weft is woven-in in an expanded plain weave.*

Since supplementary warp is an additional warp, it may be added in any direction, giving additional movement to the third dimension.

Supplementary weft, covering a third dimension shape, need not be in plain weave. One weft may be chained, two wefts may be twined and three wefts may be braided.

Brocading

Brocading techniques have traditionally been used and are still used in many part of the world as an embellishment incorporated into weaving. Following are a few supplementary brocading embellishments that could be used in contemporary tapestry design.

Embroidery is a surface decoration on an already existing ground and may be used when there is a need for additional emphasis, coverage or a subtle third dimension. Shapes may be outlined with brocade to call attention to them or to increase the effect of their borders. Shapes may be partially embroidered or totally covered with another color if the original woven one is found to be unsatisfactory. Parts of shapes or areas may be raised by adding one or more solid layers of embroidery with a more bulky yarn.

Most embellishments, additions or corrections are added in a simple, running, outline or satin stitch. Whether brocade or embroidery is added while the warp is under tension or after it is removed from the loom, the tension of the additional weft must be controlled. Additional weft is likely to pucker if the overlay is pulled up too tightly.

There has been a reluctance to add to a tapestry after it is considered completed. If the design or colors look as though they would be improved by being changed or added to, there is no logical reason why such changes or additions should not be made. It is a mark of increasing sensitivity to design and color when, after a work is completed, we can, upon reexamination, see where changes will improve it.

Painters feel free to turn a canvas to the wall when they are dissatisfied with its progress, and sometimes later add or subtract by painting over. There is no reason that weavers are not entitled to the same rethinking.

When it is necessary for a brocade float to extend too far, it may be held down in several places by a false stitch of the same color. This acts as a short warp with no inherent strength, whose only purpose is to secure the long float.

Brocade usually has floats on the back while embroidery usually has knots or loose ends.

Inlay may be in short sections or in a continuous weft. If it is entered in short lengths, the part of the warp that has not been covered by the inlay and cannot be left empty must be accounted for in some other way. If the weft is continuous it may be passed to the back when it is not needed in the design on the face. Long back floats may be left or cut later. Longer floats are better cut, as they have a tendency to pucker the woven areas they cover. Short float lengths rarely affect the construction and are sometimes better left uncut. If they are cut too short, the tails may tend to pull out. If the inlay is entered into the same shed as the weft over more than a small area, the double weft will build up and require compensating weft in adjoining areas to keep the weft line straight and horizontal.

Inlays, overlays and other embellishments may be started, stopped or exchanged at any point. Long floats are impractical in textile yardage but their use in tapestries is unlimited, as they can be held down to manageable lengths.

The weft that binds the inlay may be entered in the same shed and pass under the figured shape or may act as a ground that "meets and separates" with the figure. Ground weft may also be woven by itself in the picks on either side of the figure weft. If the brocade inlay passes over many warp ends for more than a few picks, there is a tendency for the unwoven warp (those underneath) to close in and distort the design, making the return to the plain weave more difficult. If the design weft, echoing the ground weft in a plain weave, is a fine yarn, a subtle tracery effect is achieved. If it is a heavier yarn, it covers the ground weft and appears as its own shape. The design weft may be left to loop through a pre-viously looped row, or it can be cut.

Because of the nature of plain weave ground, each brocade row cannot be held in a straight line as it turns back. If the weft reenters in each shed, it will have to start and end one warp end to the right or left because of the plain weave over and under one warp end construction. Some tapestries are woven of such weft material that this slight staggering does not affect the overall outline of the brocade shape. This saw-toothed edge may even improve the design.

Returning brocade weft can start on the face or on the back. If it turns back in every other shed, the rise over the skipped pick will be longer but the same warp ends will consistently fall over and under the brocade weft. Skipping a pick makes it possible to reenter directly in line with where the weft emerged and does not distort the shape if the picks are very close.

More than one brocade weft can be entered and there can be an interplay of several different colors, textures and shapes. Several wefts may also be entered as one unit and then separate in places, branching out in different sheds.

XIII
WRAPPING

Rope; Starting and Finishing; Tapering; Multiple Cores; Weft Manipulation; Crotch Wrapping; Shaping by Wrapping; Pile; Loop Yarn Estimating; Two or More Warp Beams; Color on Supplementary Warp; Light; Knots.

Weft wrapping in tapestry construction is not intended to serve a utilitarian purpose such as fastening, covering for protection or strengthening. Rather it is used as yet another skill in the technical vocabulary.

Wrapping requires two elements. The fiber being wrapped is treated as warp and the wrapping element as weft. Unlike soumak, the emphasis here is on a wrapping weft that does not have to progress more forward than backward. The same warp core is constantly and progressively being circumscribed. By its nature, the wrapping weft must move at an angle or else the encircling material will be forced to build up on itself.

Wrapping is finger controlled with the weft butterfly or bobbin held in the hand. The nautical wrapping tool called a "serving mallet" is usually too big to be used in small tapestry areas, although it might be useful in large projects, as the mallet holding the weft must pass around the warp core. "Worming" is also a marine term used for encircling the warp with a finer weft in the same direction of the lay or warp ply. It fits into the hollows of the plies and smooths them out between the heavier strands. If a smooth core is used there is no need to "worm". If a plied rope is to be left unwrapped in certain places, worming may be used as a decorative element.

There is an intermediate step called "parcelling" which results in a firmer surface for wrapping after worming. Strips of cloth 2″ or 3″ wide are bound around the core in overlapping circles. As they are usually covered with the top wrap, color is immaterial. If a part of the core is to be dyed and visible, the color must completely penetrate or else the inner undyed fibers will show when the rope is bent. Glues and other weather resisting materials with which

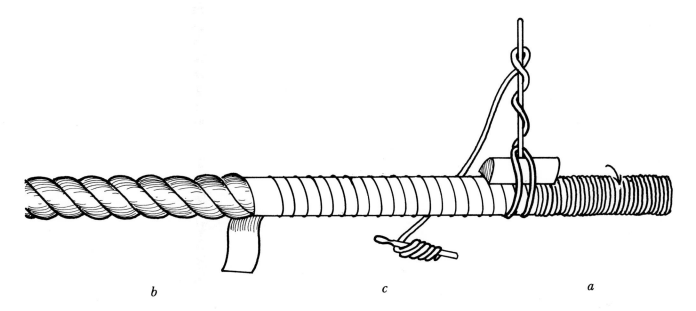

b   *c*   *a*

Fig. 1. a) *A serving mallet. Although used for preparing rope, an adaptation of this tool could be very useful for wrapping larger projects.* b) *Worming. This technique prepares the rope by filling the follows for smoother wrapping.*

c) *Parcelling. A technique that overlaps wide strips of canvas-like fabric to prepare an even smoother surface for wrapping. A seaman's jingle says: Worm and parcel with the lay / Turn and serve the other way.*

plied ropes are generally impregnated resist ordinary dye baths. Such materials must be removed before the rope will accept color throughout its body. Weft materials are similar to those used in weaving and their colors are no problem.

Rope

Rope is one of the easiest fibers to use for a core, but the differing qualities must be considered when choosing one to be wrapped. Nylon rope is slippery and no matter how closely it is wrapped, the weft tends to slip. The rope should not feel soft and should not have "whiskers" that will protrude between wraps. Humidity will change the shape that has ben wrapped as the rope shrinks or softens. Rope made of Manila hemp will maintain its strength and shape longer than many others. Whether the rope is made of three or more strands is not important except that a four strand rope is smoother and a little more flexible.

Depending on the size of the core, the weft slant and direction may be varied or changed at any time. The larger the core diameter, the easier it is to control the weft angle. There is no rule for the size of the butterfly or bobbin or the length of weft strands if they are left unwound. Their bulk or length is determined by the area within which the wrapping is to take place and the size of the wrap.

When rope is twisted in one direction and plied in another, the resulting tension between the two increases in strength. Similarly, wrapping in opposition to the ply increases the strength of the whole unit and does not eliminate the flexibility of the core material. Overspun or very tightly plied weft which would ordinarily be difficult to use as wrapping material may be unplied by using the swivel method illustrated in Chapter X.

The wrapping weft is usually, although not necessarily, thinner and more pliable than the core that is being covered. The tighter the wrap, the less flexible the core will become.

Starting and finishing

Wrapping is an easy covering technique. The simplest way to start a wrap is to align a 2″ to 3″ weft tail with the core, with the end of the tail away from the end where the wrapping will start. The first few wraps pass over the tail and secure it. All weft wrapping tails should be tapered so that their temporary existence and later disappearance is minimized. As the wrap approaches within a few inches of where it will end, the next weft should be anticipated. The new weft is aligned with the core and wrapped with it. The last 2″ or 3″ of the first weft is then laid alongside the core and the second weft picks up the wrapping where the first weft left off.

If the end of a weft has not been anticipated, it is not always necessary to unwrap to secure the starting place of the next one. The new strand can be pulled under the place that has already been wrapped by slipping a blunt needle or a crochet hook between the core and the wrapped coils and the new end pulled under. It may then be clipped clean very close to the wrapping so that it will not show.

Another way to secure an end is by laying in a loop of another strong, thin material parallel to the core with the loop toward the starting end of the

Fig. 3. *Wrapping. Anticipate the end of the wrapping weft by including the next one before the first one has run out.*

Fig. 2. *Wrapping. A weft tail is aligned with the core and wrapped toward the tapered end.*

Fig. 4. *Wrapping. Slipping a crochet hook between the core and the wrapped weft is another way to start a new weft.*

Fig. 5. *Wrapping. Another method is to lay a loop of strong, thin fiber parallel to the core with the loop toward the starting end of the wrap. After an additional inch or more of wrapping over the loop, the tail of the new weft is inserted and pulled through.*

Fig. 6. *Wrapping Additional Branches. Additions to the core should also be tapered or the weft will slip off.*

wrap. The tail of the weft is passed through the loop and after sufficient passes have been made over the loop to secure it, it is pulled out and discarded, leaving the new end securely in place. If an end is left exposed after 2″ or 3″ of wrapping it may be clipped close to the core. Securing with a loop is particularly useful at the final wrap, or a hook or needle can be wrapped along with the core and the final loop pulled through with it. The material used both for the weft and core will dictate which securing method to use. Obviously, a loop of heavy rope will not allow a close wrap, and will, when removed, leave too large a space, which will in turn loosen the wrapping material.

A wrapped work is usually more than two dimensional and will be seen from the sides as well as the front. It is important, therefore, that all ends be carefully and invisibly secured.

Generally, wrapping is used for linear designs but there is no reason why it cannot be a design element itself as well as hold selvages for small weaving areas.

Tapering

To taper ends of the weft or core that are to be covered, the ply is untwisted and torn or cut in a long narrowing end. This is particularly necessary for bulkier wefts that are being added where a bulge would show if a sharply cut stub is left. A hard end also tends to creep out of the wrap more easily than a tapered one.

In designs in which branching shapes leave and/or return to a starting main trunk, tapered cores must be added one at a time or the weft will not cover them. The staggered additions will diminish the small bulge as each new core is incorporated. Sometimes the ends of the core and the wrapping material are so thick or bulky that tapering is not

sufficient to thin them out. They can be unplied for a short distance and each ply then individually thinned out and tapered at different places.

Multiple cores

If the design calls for more than one core alongside another, they may be wrapped together or bound in figure eights. If several cores come together they may be treated as a bout and wrapped as one. This produces a thick unit which may not be in keeping with the design. The cores may be held alongside each other in a flat configuration which will require the weft to relate to them as warp ends

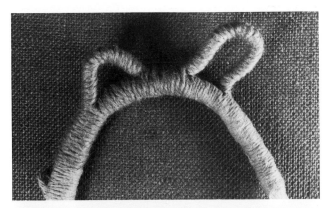

Fig. 7a & 7b. *Wrapping More Than One Core. Two cores are wrapped in a figure-eight.*

and interlace with them. The third and most difficult alternative is to taper each core as it approaches the combined group. Each of these solutions results in a different shape; therefore the desired shape will dictate the technique.

Weft manipulation

As each wrap is made, it must be held firmly in place until the next one is added so that it does not loosen. As the wrapping proceeds, each one must be pushed toward the already wrapped area to insure total coverage. If a new core that will continue in both directions is to be added, the weft which will be used to cover the new projections should be added at the same time. The previous wrapping weft which will cover the core will then also cover and secure the new weft which will be ready for the new cores after it, too, has been secured. The new weft is started from its center, making both ends available for the projection, leaving no unnecessary ends under the old weft. If one of the new cores and wefts is to move in an upward direction, they can be held out of the way by hanging them on a nail from the higher bar until needed.

It is not always possible to start at the bottom of a shape and wrap upward. The design or the progress of the work may require that the wrapping start at the top and proceed downward or at the side and proceed laterally. However, whenever possible, it is much easier to start at the bottom and wrap upward. The downward pushing motion is more comfortable and the pull of gravity assists in keeping the encircling weft in place.

Unlike in weaving, there is no shed to hold the last wrap in place. If the work must be left before the whole wrap is completed it may be temporarily tied with a half knot so that it will not unwrap.

Larger bobbins or butterflies will not penetrate small areas, so the source from which the wrapping strands are pulled may sometimes need to be changed. For instance, the wrapped weft may start out as a butterfly but when a small crowded area is reached, it may become unwieldy. A long strand is then pulled out and the wrapping continues. Having passed the "cramped" area, the strand can be reorganized back into a butterfly by starting close to the wrapping so that the weft continues to be pulled from inside the butterfly as before. A rubber band or notch will keep a bobbin or rug shuttle from unwinding when hanging out of use.

There are critical areas in wrapping, such as right angles and crotches. If the weft is thin and strong, wrapping tightly and closely will be sufficient. If the weft is heavy and many plied, the corner will build up quickly and will not be clearly defined. The weft ply can be separated and one ply cut and aligned with the warp. The remaining ply, now thinner, will wrap more easily. When the corner is passed, the full ply wrap may be continued.

Crotch wrapping

Several inches before a division in a core, a new weft should be prepared and wrapped along with it. When the crotch is reached, the new weft, no matter whether a different color or texture, will be ready for use. If the separation is not anticipated it will be much more difficult to cover completely with a tight wrap in the corner.

Sometimes the design calls for a change of direction of the wrapping or another technique such as plain weave to break up the rounding effect of the round core. This may be done when two cores are being wrapped or a second core is being added to an already existing one. The space between them may be maintained by a small wooden block or sticks, temporarily tied into position to hold the two cores

Fig. 8. *An Unfinished Wrap. A half-knot holds the weft tail in place until it is again required.*

Fig. 9. *Holding Shapes Apart. Two cores are kept apart with a spreader until they have been wrapped and secured into their permanent position.*

aligned and apart until the open area has been filled in, or the cores may be tied off under tension. (See the next chapter on "Entanglements".) The wrapping between the cores then acts as a warp that may be interlaced or wrapped with a vertical weft.

If a color is to be replaced or changed for a short distance, it is simpler to leave that weft to travel alongside the core under the wrapping, so as to be ready when needed again.

Shaping by wrapping

Wrapping, used as a separate technique in its own right, also combines well with other techniques. Pile loops may be wrapped with the same color and material or with different ones. The wrap can extend the length of the loop or over a small part of it. Long loop floats can be extended and wrapped in front of the tapestry, adding another dimension.

There are many places where wrapping can be interspersed with plain weave. Plain weave can be broken up with spaced wrapping that is shaped geometrically and evenly over the warp ends or in a free form organization. Warps or wefts can be wrapped or an additional outlining weft can be laid along the shape contours and included in the wrap. Depending on the diameter of this additional weft, a ridge may form. If more than one ridge is wrapped, it can parallel the first one, create other shapes as it moves away from and back towards the first one and it can be a larger or smaller ridge or change size along its route.

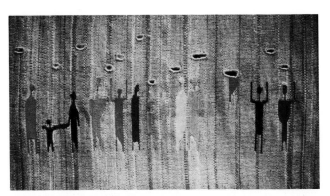

Fig. 10. *Raised Ridges. The figures in this tapestry,* One Escaped, *were woven horizontally. The edges of the escape holes were wrapped.*

Wrapping can cover an entire shape as a third dimension and provide a round, mounded effect as opposed to the cutoff look of a short pile or the undulation of long uncut loops. Such shapes may remain isolated or be tied together with attached or free-floating wrapped floats.

Ladder-like shapes may be partially integrated into the body of the work with other parts hanging free. The verticals can be wrapped together with other warp ends while the horizontal rungs are wrapped as opened-out loops that hang in front of the face of the tapestry. The rungs may also move in other than horizontal directions or cross and wrap around each other.

Shapes can appear to spring in thin wrappings from an already woven weft, joining with each other and becoming thicker as they come together. If two such groupings approach each other from different directions, they can join in a common trunk shape. Wrapping makes possible an endless interplay of branching and joining, within the tapestry or in front of it, in diversified diameters and different directions.

Additional wrapping may be added to already wrapped cores in continuous or discontinuous colors or textures. Chaining and twining can act as cores for wrapping as well as warp ends, either as part of the work or supplementary to it. Parts of the chain or twine can be wrapped, leaving other parts to retain their own characters. Their roles may be reversed so that chain or braid become the wrapping material around another core.

Fig. 11. *Wrapping Cores. Core diameters may vary within one project.*

The cores for a figure eight wrap need not be equal in diameter. One can be single and thin while the other can be doubled or tripled, resulting in two different sized ridges that are interlaced.

The wrapping material can be multiple-plied as it wraps and unplied to become interlacing material for other weaves in other locations.

Having wrapped and completed a project, the weaver should inspect it for protruding tails and unsecured wrappings. It should then be permitted to hang for a few weeks to be certain that all shapes are holding their original formations and have not started to sag. One of the more gratifying features of wrapping is that shapes that have changed their contours, or shapes over which we have changed our minds, can be rewrapped.

Pile

Pile construction is a form of wrapping in which supplementary warp or weft project out from the surface in loops. A ground weave is required to secure the loops and keep them from pulling out. In its simplest form, a weft is entered into the same shed as a ground weft and loops are drawn up as needed. In a more advanced form, the loops are made by a supplementary warp. The loops may vary in length, spacing, color and organization. They may remain as loops or be cut. Pile loops can form an overall pattern in which the ground is totally covered or they may be used in separate distinctive shapes.

The distinguishing feature of pile is the number of loops projecting out from the body of the work. The raised weft is supported by the closely packed ground weft, which may or may not show depending on the spacing of the pile. Pile may be shaped in horizontal weft bars or in vertical warp stripes. The height of the pile may vary from shape to shape or within a shape. Pile may be uncut and left in loops, cut, or be a mixture of both.

In some piles the cutting takes place on the loom after a number of picks have been woven in; in others, the loops are cut after the work has been removed from the loom. In the first instance, the cutting is more accurate and exact because the tension is still maintained. When the loops are cut after the tension is released, the cutting is less exact and the appearance is different. When pile is packed in very closely, each loop, cut or uncut, supports its neighbors and all stand up together.

When the pile is more widely spaced, it falls over and lies in different directions on the ground or hangs down vertically if hung on the wall. In tapestries where tight coverage is not required, very short, individually cut wefts are quite practical.

If the design requires that the loops all be the same length, they are looped around a rod or sword, its diameter determining the length of the loop. The loop holders should be left in place until several picks of ground weave have been beaten in to firm up the structure.

When the design calls for a pile shape above a smooth, plain woven shape, the loops, cut or not, will fall downward and cover part of the shape below them. Any designing in this area is lost by being covered. If the shapes are reversed the top or knot part of the first row of pile will make a dividing line between the two.

In tapestries the ground is sometimes as important as the pile and the choice of ground or loop is made on the basis of design and color rather than on weight or texture. The pile fibers may be fine or bulky, smooth and highly lustered or loosely spun and light absorbing.

Loop yarn estimating

It is difficult to estimate exactly how much warp or weft will be required for a pile surface. A rough calculation for pile warp requires measuring the entire length of each loop, adding the length of the warp that is floated behind the ground warp between pile rows and adding the warp taken up by the interlacing to secure it. Loom waste for the beginning and end should also be included.

For weft looping, the length of the entire loop is multiplied by the number of loops per inch times the width of the warp times the number of inches the pile shape covers. There is no correct or incorrect number of loops per inch in tapestry construction. The total desired effect is the guide as to whether looping will be thickly packed or widely spaced.

On a horizontal loom each supplementary pile warp requires at least one harness. Additional harnesses may be used for as many additional color or texture warp loops as are needed. However, if the loops per inch are to be very closely packed, two or more harnesses will separate the loops and make them more manageable. There will be no easily discernible difference in the final appearance. Two or more harnesses are required for the ground weave weft binder, depending on the ground weave pattern.

If all the rods are the same diameter, all the loops will be the same length. Rods may be graded in diameter so that starting with the largest one and progressing to the smallest one, each loop row is shorter. These could be followed by an area of a contrasting flat surface. Different size pile may also be used for radially symmetrical designing within shapes. A differentiation between the height of the pile which may vary within a shape or between shapes is called pile-on-pile.

Two or more warp beams

When pile is a large part of a tapestry being woven on a horizontal loom, a second beam is necessary for the pile warp. The take-up of the supplementary warp may be ten or more times greater than the ground warp. Although pile weaving is a technique used by a few specialized tapestry weavers, the principle of this weave should be understood by all so that it may be adapted for other uses as well.

The pile warp is usually wound on the upper beam and held separate until both warps reach the heddle eyes. A second back beam above the one that serves for the ground warp will hold the supplementary warp vertical until it passes under it and becomes horizontal, parallel to the ground warp. The harnesses through which the pile warp is threaded should be those closest to the beater. The e.p.i. of the ground warp are usually three to four

Fig. 12. *Second Warp Beam. The upper, second, warp beam has a separate, overhead breaking system.*

times more than the pile. A few inches of both warps are woven together as a header, to establish their tension. A separate braking system for the second warp beam offers increased individual tension control, which is of great importance, as well as an opportunity for different and unusual effects.

The pile warp harness is raised and a metal or wooden rod, the size of the length of the loop, is inserted. If the loop is to be cut, the rod must have a groove cut in its edge which is on top when it is placed in the shed. The rod remains in place, entirely above the ground warp level until the next several weft picks have been added, firming the pile warp into place. The shed with the pile warp is again opened and another rod entered, followed by a few more picks of ground weft. After five or more rods are in place and if the loop is to be cut, a fine, sharp knife is run along the groove. If the loop is to be left uncut, the first rod is withdrawn. Rods are usually pulled out from the same side at which they were inserted. As each rod is cut out or withdrawn, it is reinserted into the next shed that requires a rod, so that at any given time, five or more rods are working in horizontal rows. There is no rule for the number of picks between loop rows. The design and the firm securing of the loops will determine the correct amount.

On a vertical loom, supplementary pile warp may be added by passing it between the nails and over the top horizontal bar, the chains being held down with weights behind the ground warp.

Color on supplementary warp

Colors in one supplementary warp may be mixed or warped in stripes, or they may be separated into different supplementary beams or chains. Separation adds a design and shape control that is not possible from a single beam source. Color or texture separation is much easier in the weft but is more time consuming.

Although there is a softness and depth of color in cut pile, uncut loops appear brighter. This difference is clearly seen when the same dyed yarn is used in both pile versions alongside of each other. Thus the use of one yarn may be extended to serve more than one purpose. Warp and weft can be dyed as in ikat so that certain colors will appear in certain loops. A diversity of shapes and shading is thus attainable not ordinarily possible with customary yarn dyeing. Since it is difficult to gauge the exact length of each loop color and the amount taken up by its interlacement between loops, a certain indefinite misty appearance results which can be very effective.

With regular dyed yarns, different colored loops may be entered to shape and color a design by floating the weft behind the face until it is needed again.

Light

All pile fabrics have two color qualities in common. The color is deeper at the base where crowding together creates shadows, and highlighted at their free ends. Pile loops or ends vary in the direction in which they fall. Although they fall downward in a general vertical line at their source, the ends or loops may vary considerably in their final disposition. Holding the tapestry horizontal, parallel to the floor, and shaking it, will change the pile fall, particularly if it is extra long. Therefore the light reflection will vary. The rippling of the wind through a field of mature wheat is an example of this play of light.

The raised fibers reflect part of the light while the rest of the light penetrates and is absorbed in different degrees. The light that penetrates, filters through the fibers and is reflected back and forth as it is bounced around before it emerges again. The intensity of the fiber color is multiplied by these reflections so that many gradations from light near the surface to dark in the depths of the pile are seen at once. When pile is folded, tucked, or crushed, these values and intensities are increased in proportion to the depth of the fold or tuck. As the round weft strands are bent, the light is turned back at different angles.

Rya is a Scandinavian pile in which the major pile form is a Turkish or Ghiordes knot. Like the loops discussed above, it requires a ground weave and may be left as a loop or cut. Rya is traditionally a weft loop construction with individual short lengths which wrap around two warp ends. The horizontal part of each knot, which is visible, touches its neighbors on each side.

Knots

Ghiordes and Sehna knots are not really knots in that their ends do not cross and, unless tightly beaten in, may easily be pulled out. The Ghiordes knot is a form of warp wrapping which results in two parallel rows rather than in a slanted stroke. It requires at least two warp ends or warp units for each knot and is usually unequal in size, i.e., the upper loop has the same tension as the ground weave (which holds it down) and the lower part of the loop is left to hang free. The involvement of the two warp ends results in two weft ends which hang as pile.

or with a separate weft or be caught by the ground pick weft.

The thickness of the knot usually equals two picks of the weft in plain weave if they are of the same material, so two picks are usually entered between the knots. This rule of thumb may be ignored for various effects where either the knots or ground assume design importance.

The Sehna or Persian knot is similar to the Ghiordes knot, but one of the ends returns in the space between the warp end it encircled and the adjoining warp end, rather than both ends exiting in

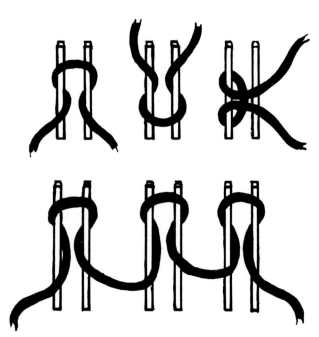

Fig. 13. *Ghiordes or Turkish Knot. The lower row uses a continuous weft. The upper row (left) has a cut weft, the center knot is in the reverse direction and the one on the right is turned sideways with both loops around the same warp end.*

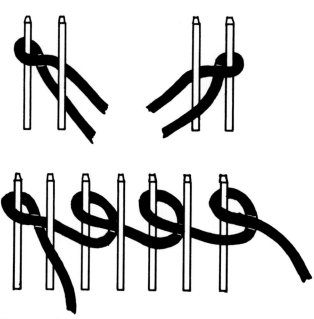

Fig. 14. *Sehna or Persian Knot. The lower row uses a continuous weft. The upper row (left) is a right-hand Sehna and the one on the right is a left-hand Sehna.*

To avoid vertical slots and make a solid knotted area, the second row of knots is entered between the two warp ends that were previously not enclosed. These are like larks heads which encircle two warp ends and cause the pile to fall downward. Ghiordes knots are traditionally not cut but are looped around a gauge to keep them equal in size.

Whether the warp ends in even or odd numbers at the selvage, alternating rows will leave the outside selvage without interlacement. Even though there is no wear on these as there is on a rug, the construction is still weaker at that point. A knot tied at the selvage extends out beyond the selvage line, disturbing its straight edge. The weaver must decide whether to use the unevenness or whether the knots are to cease several warp ends short of the edge. The unknotted ends can then interlace with the pile weft

the same place. This results in one weft tail appearing between each warp end. Here, too, the second row of knots is staggered to fall between those warps which were not encircled previously. The resulting distribution is therefore smoother than in the Ghiordes knot.

The Sehna knot actually encircles only one warp and, as in twining, clasps the second. A left hand Sehna encircles the end to the left and tends to fall to the right. A right hand Sehna encircles the warp on the right and usually falls to the left. On the whole, the Sehna is weaker than the Ghiordes knot but the direction of its pile is more controllable.

Both of these knots may alternate so that the light reflection will fall alternately to the right or left or directly in front. The Sehna knot is preferable where more knots per inch are required, as the distribution of one weft end between two warp ends takes up less space than two weft ends between every two warp ends.

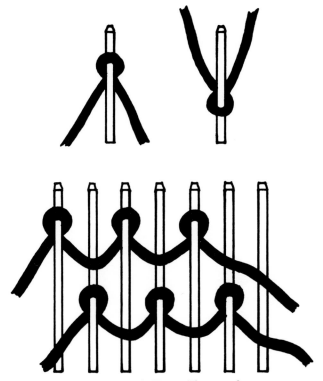

Fig. 15. *Single or Spanish Knot. The two lower rows use continuous wefts, with the second row engaging alternate warp ends. The upper row (left) has a cut weft and on the right the knot is reversed.*

In a Single knot the weft uses one warp end. It should be pulled up tightly and depends totally on its neighboring plain weave picks for its security. Single warp or Spanish knots are usually wrapped around alternate ends with the second row wrapping the ends which were skipped in the first row. This knot also results in one weft end between each warp end. This knot offers more opportunity for fine detailing or outlining and mixes easily with other knots or weaves.

On a vertical loom, where a guide for loop widths is not too easily maintained on an already woven surface, the fingers or hand width can be used for measurement.

Other knots offer interesting variations and possibilities beyond those mentioned above but usually serve specific purposes unrelated to tapestry design. Most knots may be entered from any direction, but all must be beaten in with a ground weave or secured in some other way. The knots must be kept in place and prevented from one end being longer than the other or from pulling out entirely.

In areas between piles, the weft may be passed behind the face to the next position in the same pick where the design requires it. The float remaining on the back must, however, be kept loose so that it does not pull the warp ends together with which it knots.

XIV
ENTANGLEMENTS

Purpose; Advantages; Beginning the Construction; Uses; Shaping.

Purpose

My concept of "entanglements" resulted from a search for a way to help students design and color more quickly. In tapestry designing as in other media that require such planning, there is considerable time to contemplate the work as it progresses slowly. As a result, there is a tendency to over intellectualize each possible change in shape and color. Students were found to stare at their partially finished work for long periods of time. After such long contemplation, the results were often labored and stilted. Planning and starting a new project was sometimes threatening and paralyzing. Planning for and assessing the next step is constructive and necessary, but long contemplation sometimes blocks progress. Walking away from the project and ignoring it for a period of time frequently results in better solutions than trying to wrest them forcibly.

To break the student from this time consuming, delaying and sometimes futile exercise, I tried to find a way that would lead to a quicker rendering and interplay of design and color, coming as close to action painting as possible and still staying within the fiber medium.

Wrapped and woven entanglements are easily and quickly constructed because of the large empty or negative spaces they contain. They require rigid vertical looms with four sturdy perimeters. The supports and pull of gravity aid in design construction not possible on a horizontal loom where the gravity pull extends over the total surface equally. Nor do we use the usual warp end arrangement on a vertical loom. The core or warp rope, or other material, 3/8" to 1" in diameter, is shaped and tied at various places for temporary support and tension. While shaping and arranging is proceeding, it must always be remembered that the final result will hang free and have to support itself. The structure should not sag and change the design proportions and relationships with the passing of time. Most new rope has enough rigidity to retain its shape after wrapping and tying. Old or dyed rope has lost this stiffness and will become limp more quickly.

Entanglements are a useful expression, not only

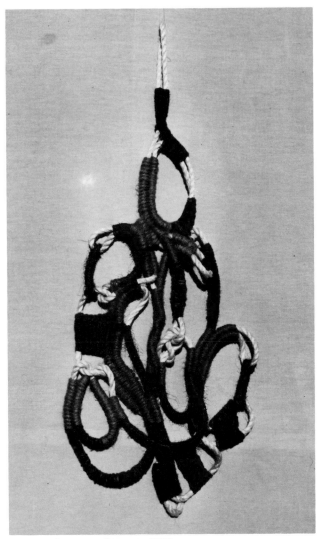

Fig. 1. *An entanglement. #188.*

for rope manipulations in different shapes and directions, but also in that most design elements and fundamentals are quickly used and intermixed. It is practically impossible to experience a single design element by itself. Even the simplest dot on a white ground involves emphasis, tension, position, etc. Entanglements help us spot underlying principles more readily. Our understanding occurs in the quick employment of these design basics.

For the purpose of these constructions, we should reject symbolic interpretation. Such attributes will inevitably suggest themselves later, but should not be permitted to interfere with the original concept, that of a quick and intuitive realization in fiber.

Because this is a comparatively new approach for tapestry designers, and because of its easy changeability, there may be some doubt as to its applicability. I suggest that this method of breaking away from the usual design approaches will not only prove worthwhile but will become an avenue for unblocking old barriers. The major factor in this approach is flexibility, the ability to flow with the work as it proceeds.

Advantages

Entanglements have a linear quality that is even further defined by wrapping. Soft curves and flow-ing linear effects will elicit a relaxed, comfortable response. If most of the directions and angles are sharp and jagged, excitement and tension will be suggested. This is similar to such responses discussed in the section on lines, but they are more readily seen and recognized in an entanglement context.

Color, too, takes on another dimension. It is contained within the wrapping material and is part of the flow as the rope shape moves. If a color is used to connect two cores with a weaving technique, it looks like the more familiar two dimensional weaving. The contrast between the two heightens their interaction. When a wrapped shape appears in front of a woven one and then penetrates it, its color behaves in different ways. Colors may tie a piece together by travelling through it in different techniques. A one-color linear wrapped shape takes on different light aspects as its configuration changes direction.

Beginning the construction

The first decision to be made is how the piece will hang because, in most instances, that is an integral part of the construction. It might start with a large or small loop tied to the top bar or hung from an invisible filament attached to a nail. From there on it is a matter of manipulating the rope, quickly tying off the shapes temporarily until they have been wrapped and permanently secured.

Fig. 2. *An Entanglement. #194*

Fig. 3. *Tying off. Five feet of rope have been shaped and tied.*

The rope is hung, looped, tied back on itself, doubled, interlocked or left hanging. The beginning and end of the core is tapered, fringed, cut, tied into some shape or tied together. As each shape is formed, it is placed under tension by being tied in at least two directions. Since the ties are temporary, the shapes may be changed at any time, before the wrapping starts or during the progress of the work.

Ties are made to the sides of the frame or to other parts of already tied off shapes. They are held with temporary half bows which are easily removed before that part of the shape is to be wrapped. It is sometimes necessary to replace ties until other parts have been wrapped and tensioned. As the wrapping of each individual part of the entanglements is completed, its tie supports should be removed as a check to see if the individual sections will support themselves.

Although almost any weft yarns may be used, it is better to choose stronger and more tightly twisted wefts for critical areas crucial to the design. Wrapping can start at any place in the construction or can start at several places at once, and almost any combination of yarns, colors and textures may be incorporated.

Uses

Wrapping and other non-weaving techniques should be used as carefully as weaving techniques, but

Fig. 4. *Tying off. Five more feet are added. All ends are tapered, wormed and secured.*

Fig. 5. *The completed Entanglement.*

it is the quick plunge that we are after rather than a carefully thought-out effort. At first, entanglements were planned solely as learning exercises, but soon they became interesting constructions in themselves and have since been conceived and used as such.

Not only may design and color fundamentals be developed with this approach, but other techniques and devices previously discussed may be integrated, such as different types of supports and findings. Odd shaped pieces of driftwood and large ceramic beads or unusual metal pieces from other sources seem to be more appropriate to these constructions than to traditional flat surfaced tapestries.

Although these constructions usually hang on a wall, a three dimensional quality is inherent in them. At first, the multitude of shapes may appear chaotic; but as the shaping and wrapping continues, a sense of order appears and unnecessary shapes are eliminated.

Shaping

Like the muscles of the body, all shapes have a point of origin and insertion that affects the shapes to which they are attached. Shapes can take more stress than we would ordinarily expect of them.

They are also capable of reverse pull and are at all times interdependent. Unlike muscles, wrapped rope shapes push as well as pull. This counteraction offers an opportunity to shape some parts in defiance of the usual rules of gravity. Loops may be tied and wrapped in such a way that they will project upward and outward as well as downward. Such directions and shapes add a sense of suspense and marked stimulation different from two-dimensional work.

The first construction should be of larger shapes rather than smaller ones. The interplay of all of the ingredients discussed above may more easily be seen and internalized in structures with larger components.

It must be stressed that the creative flow should not be cut off as the shapes appear, group themselves, subdivide, encircle and penetrate each other and regroup. It is obviously not possible to suggest all of the variations, but the few illustrations should be sufficient to suggest some of the possibilities.

XV
NINE WEAVERS — NINE APPROACHES

An Experiment; Criterion; Different Approaches; Individual Comments; Titling.

Every human being is capable of some form of expression that is true for that person alone. As imagination, background and experience differ from person to person, so does the resulting expression. As our vocabulary in our chosen field develops, we learn to rely more on our own creativity rather than imitation. We also arrive at standards that help us distinguish the genuine from the contrived or sham.

An experiment

A group of students and apprentices were asked to participate in an exercise to underscore this important principle. Each participant was given a photograph and the following sheet of instructions.

> Enclosed is the 8x10 black and white glossy we talked about. The metal pieces were taken from a beach in Mendocino, California, which has been a dumping ground for metal parts for many years. The wooden shapes are leftovers of loom parts from Gene's shop floor. The fabric is part of an old handwoven piece left outdoors to weather for a short time.

Criterion

You may weave in any color and use any technique you wish, but since the reproduction will be in black and white, remember that some colors like dark reds, dark blues and purples photograph black. You will, of course, keep the tapestry, but I will make a black and white film for reproduction. Size is your decision but again remember that minute details are lost when reproduced. You may use the whole or any part or parts or combination of parts.

The whole point of this exercise is the reaction to the same stimulus by a group of weavers with different experiences, all of whom have worked with me for varying lengths of time. Those participating in this project are looking at it as a challenge. Thanks for joining us and have a good weaving time.

Each weaver was also asked to write a paragraph or two expressing their reaction to the photograph, giving reasons for their choices.

The photograph of the collage was taken on a particularly dull, grey day, although there were some patches of filtered sunlight through the redwood trees. The composition was photographed in black and white with emphasis on the shapes and their relationships to each other in an evenly distributed, subdued light. Choices would be entirely those of the weavers, uninfluenced by highlight or color.

The metal shapes had been exposed to salt water, rain, and sand for many years and had devel-

Fig. 1. *Black and white photograph of the collage given to each participant.*

oped subtle shades of orange through oxidation but the weavers did not see the original collage and could only respond to the reproduction.

Many shapes and textures were included so that each weaver could choose those which appealed to her most, leaving the others in reduced importance or ignoring them entirely. No other rules or regulations were placed on the work. The weavers used their own background, experience, weaving materials and current weaving interest, working in their own studios so that no one knew or saw what the others were doing. Until the tapestries were brought in to be photographed, I did not see them or comment on them.

In preparing the collage, symbolism was avoided as far as possible, leaving the weavers free to use whatever approach they desired. The outstanding design elements were related wooden angles and unrelated metal circles.

Different approaches

Starting with similar subject and framework, different weavers treated design, space, shapes, values, and images in totally different ways. The same fiber in the hands of another weaver, starting from the same stimulus, would result in as many different images as fiber artists who undertook such a project.

Some weavers drew preliminary sketches and chose one as a take-off point. Others started with several sketches and then combined the parts they liked best into one final cartoon. Some were moved by an accidental combination of shapes and textures, improvising freely as the work progressed. Following her cartoon carefully, one weaver found she had woven herself into a corner. Searching for a way out, she arrived at new solutions which became the foundations for future tapestries. Most of the participants did not know each other and their time with me ranged from several months to over several years.

Individual comments

Given the 8x10 glossy, I was faced with my age old problem of simplification. Many unacceptable drawings later the photograph was refiled. Only then was it possible to come to terms with a simplified design. First and foremost the pattern of the mechanical parts, as well as the strong diagonal thrust of the central wooden piece, had to be dealt with. Finally, wastebasket filling and frustration mounting, I remembered that Laya mentioned having sprinkled sand over the arrangement. This gave me the clue to reexamine the design possibilities. Sure enough, it created a very agreeable counter movement to the troublesome central wooden piece. At last the design was tied together. Now I could start to weave.

Jacqueline Baldwin
Santa Cruz, California

Fig. 2.
Jacqueline Baldwin
Santa Cruz, California
Title: Aftermath
Size: 39" x 25"
Materials: rug yarns, berber and Mexican handspun

This piece came into existence as a result of my interest in aerial photography. The collage reminded me of one I had seen of an area in Florida, so I chose this motif since it coincided with the current direction of my work.

I disregarded a more literal interpretation of the photo because of the infeasibility of weaving so many circles in such a small area.

Trudi Eldridge
Felton, California

Fig. 3.
Trudi Eldridge
Felton, California
Title: Aerial Landscape #2
Size: 35" x 27"
Material: Wool and silk weft, camel hair warp and PVC
 armature.

After having received the black and white photograph, the area that drew my attention most was the large circular wheel in one corner and the rectangular shaped board next to it. Having decided what interested me most I drew numerous 2"x3" thumbnail sketches of different areas of the photograph. I found that each sketch had some portion of the circle and knew it must be in my tapestry, as well as the rectangular shape next to it.

Although the photograph was in black and white, the choice of color was very important to my tapestry. I consciously chose colors that correlated with what I expected the true colors might have been. For example, rusts and reds for the wheel and browns and tans for the wood.

During the actual weaving process I found the circle-like shape most difficult, but it was a learning process for me.

Cynthia Handel
Livermore, California

Fig. 4.
Cynthia Handel
Livermore, California
Title: Untitled
Size: 26" x 19"
Materials: Synthetics and wool

My approach to the photograph was to find within it an area which interested me. After cutting out this shape, I made a few sketches. The result was long and narrow, so I added side panels to widen the tapestry. My interest was in working with different materials in different size relationships of interlacement, and the feeling which that part of the photograph evoked in me.

Jude Lamare
Sacramento, California

When first presented with the photograph, two ideas came to mind. One was to deal with the circular elements and to do an abstract piece, the other was to use the shape of one of the metal pieces for the shape of the weaving. I chose to weave a piece more in keeping with my work in landscapes and use a metal shape. I chose the arch shape and found that it made a window-like format for the landscape I designed.

Lynn Murray
Aptos, California

Fig. 5.
Jude Lamare
Sacramento, California
Title: Untitled
Size: 37½" x 22"
Materials: wool, linen, cotton, rayon and tree rope

Fig. 6.
Lynn Murray
Aptos, California
Title: Untitled
Size: 60" x 36"
Material: all wool

The challenge here was to simplify the given elements in Laya's collage. My plan turned out to be (after much deliberation and many rough sketches) to select the key features and, in a primitive fashion, to create a weaving as if painting with the fibers. Thinking of a flat canvas, I tried to keep the piece solid and rectangular in shape. The treatment of the warp ends at the top and bottom reflects the use of a frame for the "painting".

Jean Peterson
Aptos, California

First I picked up the images which attracted me, and made a rough cartoon. In consideration of balance, I decided which materials and technique I should take. It was based on three colors and I used wool in the center.

Etsuko Seki
Kawaguchi-shi, Japan

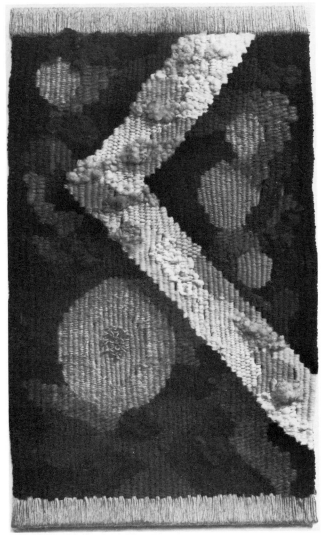

Fig. 7.
 Jean Peterson
 Aptos, California
 Title: Laya's Collage
 Size: 27" x 18"
 Materials: linen warp, wool, cotton, jute and unspun
  fleece weft.

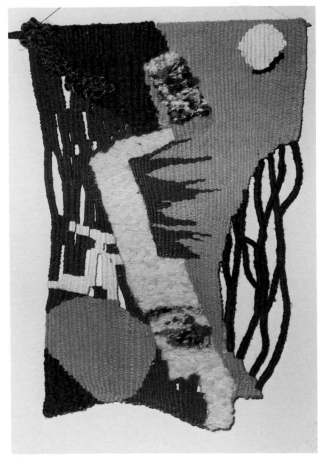

Fig. 8.
 Etsuko Seki
 Kawaguchi-shi, Japan
 Title: untitled
 Size: 85cm × 63cm
 Materials: hemp, cotton, wool

I was first intrigued by the light and shadows in the photograph of junk. I chose the large metal bar and the large wheel because their juxtaposition suggested a thrusting movement. The light and shadows provided the third dimension of space in which the wheel became the earth floating with the junk metal bar. I used a diagonal twill weave for the bar to emphasize movement. I used my own junk metal ring to suggest that the blue-green earth is in a gun sight. Another circular piece was included to suggest a distant planet and to enhance the sense of the vast dimension of space.

Incidentally this tapestry was completed some months before the world's concern over falling debris from the space satellite Sky Lab.

Barbara Vogl
Soquel, California

When I first saw the photo with it juxtaposition of wood, metal, and fabric, I was inspired to try to incorporate the three materials into my tapestry. Not owning a tapestry loom, I began a search for a frame which led me to use a window frame from the school my father had attended. Wanting to somehow capture the feeling of the Texas ranch country where the school was located, I made an effort to limit myself to earth tones and yarns that would not distract from the weathered frame. The horizontal bar that divided the frame, my decision to include metal pieces and the challenge of executing diagonal lines helped me to decide what portions of the photo to use as the basis for the tapestry design.

Nancy Winkenbach
Boulder Creek, California

Fig. 9.
Barbara Vogl
Soquel, California
Title: Space Debris
Size: 60" x 35"
Materials: jute warp, wool, acrylic, goat hair weft and discarded metal ring

Fig. 10
Nancy Winkenbach
Boulder Creek, California
Title: untitled
Size: 40½" x 33"
Materials: wool and findings

Titling

Naming or giving a title to a tapestry has always been a matter of personal choice. Completed work should be identified in some way, whether by referential title, a number, or totally unrelated words. In an effort to escape the confinement of labels, some artists deliberately choose an enigmatic or obscure reference, forcing the viewer's participation for a meaning.

The same problem has always existed for the music composer, as well. Sonata is a musical form and has nothing to do with the feeling that the music evokes. Opus is an arbitrary numbering system not always related to the date of the composition's completion.

Recognizing the public desire for a label, some artists turn to an automatic contrivance such as opening a book or dictionary and blindly pointing to a word. When a series of the same subject or design is presented, the same title may be used, simply calling the first of the group, Landscape I, the second, Landscape II, and so on. There is also the practice of using an ordinary title translated into another language or making up a word which sounds esoteric but is meaningless to anyone but the artist. Since each person sees something different in the same work, titling becomes more a matter of record keeping than adding significance to a woven work.

If the weaver feels that the work warrants being shown or offered for sale, he or she must be courageous enough to take the responsibility for the tapestry by signing it. Whether this is done on the face or on the back is also a matter of personal taste as is the question of signing with initials or a full name. An alternative is to initial the face in the right hand corner so that it does not interfere with the composition and attach a tag to the back with the weaver's full name, title of the work and the date of completion.

Some individuals are born with the ability to impart life to inanimate materials, others plod along and rarely reach that goal. Most of us fall somewhere in-between and profit from clearly stated principles, suggestions, disciplines and some ground rules to expedite our work. The illustrations in this book are of color and design principles, weaving techniques and some ground rules to expedite the work.

Major emphasis was placed on bringing together well known as well as lesser known methods for translating ideas into tapestries. Some of the solutions included are those observed over the years in the work of other tapestry weavers or gleaned from old and new texts. Others are some that I found and developed during the years of tapestry weaving and teaching.

Bibliography

Weaving—General

Emery, Irene. *The Primary Structures of Fabrics*. Washington, D.C.: The Textile Museum, 1966.

Hochberg, Bette. "When Moths Fly Out of Your Closet." *Interweave* IV:3, 1979.

Platus, Libby, "Flameproofing Fibers." *Shuttle Spindle & Dyepot XIII: 2*, 1977.

Thorpe, Azalea Stuart and Jack Lenore Larsen. *Elements of Weaving*. Doubleday & Company, Inc., 1967.

Weaving—Tapestry

Bennett, Anna G. *Five Centuries of Tapestry*. Fine Arts Museum of San Francisco, 1976.

Blumenau, Lili. *Creative Designs in Wall Hangings*. Crown Publishers, 1967.

Brostoff, Laya. "An Approach to Tapestries." *Interweave* VI:2, 1979.

Constantine, Mildred and Jack Lenore Larsen. *Beyond Craft: The Art Fabric*. New York: Van Nostrand Reinhold, 1972.

Kaufman, Ruth. *The New American Tapestry*. New York: Reinhold Book Corporation, 1968.

Moorman, Theo. *Weaving as an Art Form*. Van Nostrand Reinhold, 1975.

Weaving—Techniques

Albers, Anni. *On Weaving*. Middleton, Connecticut, 1965.

Beutlich, Tadaek. *Woven Tapestry*. New York: Watson-Guptill Publications, 1967.

Collingwood, Peter. *The Techniques of Rug Weaving*. New York: Watson-Guptill Publications, 1968.

Cyrus, Ulla. *Manual of Swedish Handweaving*. Boston, Massachusetts: Charles T. Branford Company, 1956.

D'Harcourt, Raoul. *Textiles of Ancient Peru and Their Techniques*. University of Washington Press, 1962.

Gregg, Dorothy. "In the Gobelin Tradition." *Shuttle Spindle & Dyepot* X:1, 1978.

Halsey, Mike and Lore Youngblood. *Foundations of Weaving*. New York: Watson-Guptill Publications, 1975.

Held, Shirley. *Weaving*. New York: Holt, Rinehart & Winston, 1973.

Mattera, Joanne. "Exploring Wedge Weave." *Interweave* III:2, 1978.

-----. *Navajo Techniques*. New York: Watson-Guptill Publications, 1975.

Marein, Shirley. *Creative Rugs and Wall Hangings*. New York: Viking Press, 1975.

Sevensima, W.S. *Tapestries*. Universe Books, 1965.

Todd, Osma. "Deflected Warps and Wefts." *Creative Crafts Folio #31*.

Tapestry—Additional Techniques

Allard, Mary. *Rug Making—Techniques and Design*. Chilton Book Co., 1963.

Andes, Eugene. *Far Beyond the Fringe*. New York: Van Nostrand Reinhold, 1973.

Ashley, Clifford W. *The Ashley Book of Knots*. Garden City, New York: Doubleday and Company, Inc., 1953.

Baizerman, Suzanne and Karen Searle. *Latin American Brocades*. St. Paul, Minnesota: Dos Tejedoras, 1976.

Chamberlin, Marcia and Candace Crockett. *Beyond Weaving*. New York: Watson-Guptill Publications, 1974.

Dendel, Esther Warner. *The Basic Book of Fingerweaving*. New York: Simon and Schuster, 1974.

Gibson, Charles E. *Handbook of Knots and Splices*. New York: Emerson Books, Inc., 1968.

Harvey, Virginia I. *Split-Ply Twining*. Monograph Series Issue I. Santa Ana, California: HTH Publishers, 1976.

MacFarlan, Allen and Paulette. *Knotcraft*. New York: Association Press, 1968.

Skowronski, Hella and Mary Reddy. *Sprang*. Van Nostrand Reinhold, 1974.

Art—General

Battock, Gregory. *Minimal Art, A Critical Anthology*. New York: E.P. Dutton & Co., Inc., 1968.

Barzun, Jacques. *The Use and Abuse of Art*. Bollinger Series XXXV:2, Princeton University Press, 1973.

Kagan, Andrew. "Three Fundamental Concepts of Form." *Arts Magazine* Nov. 1977.

Raynal, Maurice. *Modern Painting*. Skira, 1956.

Rickey, George. *Constructivism*. New York: George Braziller, 1967.

Art—Design

Anderson, Donald M. *Elements of Design*. New York: Holt, Rinehart and Winston, 1961.

Bates, Kenneth F. *Basic Design*. World Publishing Co., 1960.

Belvin, Marjorie Eliott. *Design Through Discovery*. New York: Holt, Rinehart and Winston, 1970.

Collier, Graham. *Form, Space and Vision*. Englewood Cliffs, New Jersey: Prentice-Hall, Inc., 1965.

de Sausmarez, Maurice. *Basic Design: The Dynamics of Visual Form*. New York: Van Nostrand Reinhold, 1971.

Faulkner, Ray and Gerald H. Ziefeld. *Art Today*. New York: Holt, Rinehart and Winston, 1963.

Garrett, Lillian. *Visual Design*. New York: Van Nostrand Reinhold, 1967.

Graves, Maitland. *The Art of Color and Design*. 2nd ed. McGraw-Hill Book Company, Inc., 1951.

Hartung, Rolf. *Creative Textile Design*. Reinhold Publishing Co., 1964.

Kepes, Gyorgy. *The New Landscape*. Chicago, Illinois: Paul Theobald and Co., 1961.

Knobler, Nathan. *The Visual Dialogue*. New York: Holt, Rinehart and Winston, 1966.

Kranz, Stewart and Robert Fisher. *The Design Continuum*. New York: Reinhold Publishing Corp., 1966.

McKim, Robert H. *Experiences in Visual Thinking*. Monterey, California: Brooks/Cole Publishing Co., 1972.

Moholy-Nagy, Laslo. *The New Vision and Abstract of an Artist*. New York: George Wittenborn, Inc., 1947.

Proctor, Richard M. *The Principles of Pattern*. New York: Van Nostrand Reinhold, 1969.

Rand, Paul. *Thoughts on Design*. New York: George Wittenborn, Inc., 1947.

Rhodes, Mary. *Needlepoint*. London: Octopus Books Ltd., 1974.

Ross, Denman W. *A Theory of Pure Design*. Boston/New York: Houghton, Mifflin and Co., 1907.

Saxon, Erik. "Planar Straight Line and the Primary Plane." *Artforum* April 1979, New York.

Scott, Robert Gilliam. *Design Fundamentals*. New York: McGraw-Hill Book Company, 1951.

Seiberling, Frank. *Looking Into Art*. New York: Henry Holt & Co., 1959.

Art—Color

Albers, Josef. *Interaction of Color*. New Haven. Connecticut: Yale University Press, 1963.

Birren, Faber. *Principles of Color*. New York: Van Nostrand Reinhold, 1969.

Bustanoby, J.H. *Principles of Color and Color Mixing*. McGraw-Hill Book Company, 1947.

Graves, Maitland. *Color Fundamentals*. New York: McGraw-Hill Book Company, 1952.

Itten, Johannes. *Elements of Color*. New York: Van Nostrand Reinhold, 1970.

-----. *The Art of Color*. Reinhold Publishing Co., 1961.

Justema, William and Doris. *Color Course*. New York: Van Nostrand Reinhold, 1971.

Kuppers, Harold. *Color*. London: Van Nostrand Reinhold, 1972.

Marx, Ellen. *The Contrast of Colors*. New York: Van Nostrand Reinhold, 1973.

Sloan, Patricia. *Color: Basic Principles and New Directions*. New York: Van Nostrand Reinhold, 1971.

Taylor, F.A. *Color Technology*. London: Oxford University Press, 1962.

Art—Visual Perception

Arnheim, Rudolph. *Art and Visual Perception*. Berkeley/Los Angeles, California: University of California Press, 1954.

Baldinger, Wallace S. *The Visual Arts*. Holt, Rinehart and Winston, 1960.

Gregory, R.L. and E.H.J. Gombrich. *Illusions in Nature and Art*. New York: Scribners, 1973.

Kanizsa, Gaetano. "Subjective Contours." *Scientific American* April 1976.

Luckiesh, Mathew. *Visual Illusions*. New York: Dover Publications, Inc., 1965.

Taylor, Joshua C. *Learning to Look*. Chicago, Illinois: University of Chicago Press, 1957.

Index